CHELSEA FO

Chelsea Footprints

A THIRTIES CHRONICLE

ANGELA HUGHES

QUARTET

First published in 2008 by
Quartet Books Limited
A member of the Namara Group
27 Goodge Street, London W1T 2LD

A catalogue record for this book
is available from the British Library

ISBN   978 0 7043 7136 1

Typeset by Antony Gray
Printed and bound in Great Britain by
T J International Ltd, Padstow, Cornwall

Contents

To
Natalie and Robert, Christian,
Yves and Emma,
Richard, Antonia, Jacques,
Jean-Baptiste and Charlie

Author's Note

At the corner of Old Church Street, Chelsea, is a square house with a studio at the top where the ceramist-novelist William De Morgan and his wife, the painter Evelyn, spent their last years. Once a place of ill-repute (there were several in that street in the 1880s) it survived the twentieth century, but only just. It escaped demolition in the thirties, the Blitz in the forties and more recently the threat of a loft conversion. My father, the Irish musician Herbert Hughes, made it his home in 1922 and turned it into a well-known meeting place for writers, artists and musicians.

I lived there as a child. Today the façade and De Morgan's blue plaque are half hidden behind the lime tree I knew as a sapling. By pure chance some years ago I was shown over the house. I described this strange visit on a closely-written postcard to Mavis Gallant. She answered, 'Write about your London.' I did and this book is the result.

A. C. H.

PART ONE

The London Magnet

1

Chelsea 1915

Moving into her studio, Evelyn De Morgan set her easel on a platform for better light. In a little room on the floor below, her husband William, ceramist turned prolific novelist, was struggling to produce two more volumes as the war got into its stride.

He had begun to escape from his writing table. It was after he had worked for years in ceramics that his first novel had at last brought him financial security, and in its wake, riding on his easy fluency, he had produced six more. The war came and with it the relentless news of the loss of friends and sons of friends which so disturbed him that he put down his pen. The old compulsion had gone.

More often now he was seen along the Embankment, a figure with a pronounced stoop and flutey voice chatting with friends. A chance encounter with a young neighbour at 117 Church Street, the daughter of his former business partner, led to a ritual morning walk up the King's Road – William De Morgan, Anna Pearce with her baby David, and the shopping bag hitched over the pram handle.[1]

Driven back from novels to his first love, chemistry, De Morgan turned his inventive gifts towards the war effort. He dreamed up extravagant devices for linking submarines with battleships and in the process blew out the Polytechnic windows. The Admiralty was not impressed, still less the college authorities who asked him to leave.

Knowledge had always fired him as he learned from the places and the people: the kilns of Rhages, of Iznik and Pesaro, the Saracen King of Majorca and Maestro Giorgio, the sculptor of Gubbio. Spurred on by his passion for science he searched for a technique lost for three hundred years: the perfect iridescence of lustre. Although London rewarded him with a medal and rich men gave him major commissions, largely through his own lack of flair he made little money.

The adventure had begun in Fitzroy Square with designs for the sacerdotal William Morris. Intrigued by the yellow stain left by silver on glass De Morgan built a kiln in a bedroom fireplace for experiments in glazes, characteristically straining relations with his landlord when he blew the roof off. De Morgan's fortissimos were to become a habit but he had an imagination aroused by failure. It was also ignited by metals and minerals: copper, silver, ruby, turquoise gleamed in his pots and tiles. Springing to life under the glaze were snakes and frogs and fish, birds and flowers, sea monsters for ocean-going liners, volcanoes, palms and Chinese junks, tigers, elephants and, on a whim, the odd mischief of an indignant raven or an intruding asp.

When fear of illness sent the De Morgans to winter in Italy, their friend the architect Halsey Ricardo continued to manage the pottery business as best he could, although harassed by the extra work when his own practice claimed his attention. Designs, tile samples and correspondence shuttled between Fulham and Florence as funds diminished. Nobody was surprised when the ten-year partnership ended; later it was William's thumb which settled the matter, neuritis putting an end to his drawing. The Sand's End factory was sold to the Bluebell Polish Company. 'A far more useful stuff,' was William's comment, accepting change in his usual way. When his lease expired at number 1, The Vale and the landlord reclaimed the property in order to pull the house down, William returned to the site, observed the scene without rancour and remarked with satisfaction on the healthy state of the mulberry trees which had once been his. He had found two houses at 125 and 127 Church Street, and knocked them together with a studio for his wife Evelyn on the top floor. Unwittingly the couple had moved into two former brothels, not that this would have troubled them greatly.[2]

William and Evelyn De Morgan were well-suited: neither was mercenary, they had a matching sense of humour and held each other's work in respect. But for the war and its effects they had every reason to be content; in the event William was to leave the last two novels unfinished.

At Christmas 1916 he had a visit from the diplomat, airman and novelist Maurice Baring and in the little study the two men examined De Morgan's model aeroplanes. When a few days later De Morgan fell dangerously ill it was widely believed that he had caught 'trench fever' from Baring who in fact had never served in the trenches. De Morgan lay for nearly three weeks in a delirium, believing he was a soldier in a French hospital. He died in the Church Street house on 17 January 1917, leaving his widow to complete the two novels. 'Yours was one of the blessed marriages,' Georgiana Burne-Jones wrote to her.

When Evelyn herself died in 1919, some of the tiles remained *in situ*, forgotten by the unworldly pair. The blue carnations on the window-boxes would eventually be removed for safe keeping (they were perilously close to the street), but the fish tiles in William's study were safe if only for a time, the time when I was a child. After that, not finding their way into the safety of a museum, they were left to a fate which curiously would mirror our own.

After Evelyn's death my grandfather made the Church Street house his London home, leaving it three years later to my parents, newly-married in 1922. Evelyn's old studio was soon filled with music stands, instrument cases, sheet music and bottles of wine.

2

Goodbye, Belfast

Out of the blackthorn hedges
I caught a tune
And before it could vanish, seized
It, wrote it down.

IVOR GURNEY

My grandfather Frederick Patrick Hughes was a Belfast mill-owner[1] who married the young Mary Elizabeth McLean from Mull in 1877. They had seven children of whom my father, Herbert, was the second, born 16 March 1882. Of his elder brother Jack I know little beyond his early death, probably of tuberculosis. I failed to ask some key questions while there was still time and, besides, our elders were always keen to avoid painful or disagreeable subjects. My Californian cousin Kathleen generally got nothing for her pains beyond her own father's stock reply designed to put an end to any further questions, 'Oh, I don't know, he was probably in gaol.'

Born a Catholic, my paternal grandfather F. P. H. left home in his teens, angry at his father's fecklessness and at the sight of his mother giving money she could ill afford to the Church. He brought up his own children as Protestants (which didn't prevent two of them from becoming Catholics in later life) but he was non-sectarian: although he signed the anti-Home Rule Solemn League and Covenant of 1912 he believed in advance of his time that mixed-religion schools were the solution to the Ulster problem. (When F. P. H. was taken ill in Rome a young seminarist, later Father Collins, took care of him. They became lifelong friends. Years later Father Collins attended Herbert as he was dying.) While in the street F. P. H. was often mistaken for Parnell, 'the uncrowned king of Ireland', for us children he was a reassuring image of God the Father and would not have looked out of

6

place in the Sistine Chapel. In fact he was a hard-working business-man and an excellent sportsman; he had a talent for drawing and with his whole family gave much time to music. When Edward Elgar came to Belfast to conduct *The Dream of Gerontius* the entire family sang in the Philharmonic Choir.

F. P. H. was also a provider. After the death of his brother John, a widower, he took in the six orphaned children. Then as each boy reached the age of eighteen he was shipped off to the US or Canada to be given a home and employment and to be cared for by a vast family network. (The Irish and the Italians had much in common, and not only in the police force.) Arthur Hughes, my great-great-grandfather, had emigrated to Philadelphia in 1843, even before the Famine.

One evening in December 1912, her Christmas shopping done, my grandmother Mary Elizabeth called at her husband's office on her way home, suffered a massive heart attack and died. The story goes that they took her home and, finding the quietest place in a house fuller than usual as Christmas approached, turned the dining-room into a chapel of rest. In a scene which has a flavour of Marlowe or Webster she lay in state on the table while her distraught husband, refusing to leave her, paced round and round her lifeless body.

Mary Elizabeth was never to know the Great War nor the particular fate of one of her boys, Leslie. Of all the Hughes children he is said to have had the most beautiful singing voice. Living in Toronto he enlisted in the 5th Canadian Mounted Rifles. In the trenches, the family was told later, he was continually begged by his comrades to stay behind and sing to cheer them all up. The day in August 1917 that he saw this as an unfair advantage he went over the top and was instantly killed. Not the smallest trace of him was ever found. With the loss of my mother's brother Vincent this represented two families' contribution to the squandering of life in the Great War. Reporting Leslie's death, the *Toronto Evening Telegram* added, 'Two months ago he sang at the YMCA in France.'

Among the Hughes children musical and especially singing stan-dards were demanding enough for them to tell the youngest boy Stanley without ceremony that he simply wasn't good enough. Witty and puckish, he later became an actor. Freddie won the Children's All-Ireland Singing Championship.

Unlike many Belfast Protestants, the Hughes family had Catholic friends, notably the gifted Campbells at whose house the young gathered to talk, read poetry or sing around the piano – Herbert, his sister Lena, Joseph and John Campbell (respectively poet and 'black-and-white' artist), the poet Padraic Colum and Sam Waddell, brother of the scholar and author Helen Waddell.

Aunt Margaret, his mother's sister, had given Herbert his first piano lessons. Soon he was the pianist in a family of singers and at fourteen the organist in St Peter's Church. He went on to study with Dr Francis Koeller, conductor of the Belfast Philharmonic Society. F. P. H. gave him a place in the family firm but Herbert's business career amounted to no more than a week of goodwill in his father's office after which he escaped to London and the Royal College of Music. There he studied piano with Herbert Sharpe, and organ with Sir Walter Parratt, 'of the brain-power and caustic tongue',[2] who later taught John Ireland and Herbert Howells. He also accompanied the singer pupils of Gustave Garcia. His composition professor was a fellow Ulsterman Charles Wood whom Howells later described as 'the most completely equipped teacher'. Lena, Herbert's closest sibling, visited her brother in his Kensington lodgings and the two went to concerts together, had supper at Appenrodts in the Strand and cooked mixed grills in a lodging-house near Olympia. They once heard Edvard Grieg accompany his own songs.

The composer Charles Villiers Stanford taught at the College. He had a notorious temper and he and H. H. crossed swords over Irish folk music which Stanford dismissed as 'a lot of peasants singing out of tune'. This could be expected given Stanford's temperament and his Dublin Establishment background while H. H. was fiery and idealistic in his youth and remembered by the pianist Ivor Newton as 'ardent, a purist'.[3]

Stanford could be cruel to his students. He threw out the young John Ireland's string quartet as 'dull as dishwater' – a quartet which in Sir Hubert Parry's hands subsequently earned Ireland a composition scholarship. Herbert Howells later recalled the two Charleses,

Wood and Stanford, neighbours in the same RCM corridor but totally different in temperament, 'each richly gifted, each an exile of sorts, the one from Dublin, the other from Armagh, [sharing] a scintillating wit, the one [. . .] sardonic, the other kindly'.[4] Nevertheless I suspect that in my father's case the older man was having a private bit of fun, preferring to ignore quarter-tones and all the rest to tease a hot-headed student.

Long drawn to Irish folk music, Herbert had no ambition to be a concert pianist despite the hopes of his professor Herbert Sharpe. The seed had been sown by the family nurse, Ellen Boylan, with her songs learnt from the 'mountainy men' who came down to the fairs with their fiddles and pipes. These were poor farmers of a gregarian egalitarian society who worked the harsher hill soil and were pariahs to the lowlanders: 'You don't marry up the hill.' From them Ellen learned 'The Ballynure Ballad', 'The Next Market Day', 'I know where I'm goin'' and 'The Lowlands of Holland'. She had arrived at the house from her native Sperrin mountains as a barefoot fourteen-year-old. She was to remain with the family for the rest of her life.

Whilst a student in London Herbert's home was still in Belfast where a minority among the young were fired by the Celtic revival. They tended to cluster around an 'Irish-Irelander' Francis Joseph Bigger. Presbyterian, freemason, solicitor and antiquary, he was a man of means who had turned his house into a small university which attracted much talent: Douglas Hyde, poet and first President of the Irish Republic; Stephen Gwynn, prolific man of letters and future MP at Westminster; Roger Casement, on leave from consular duties in Lisbon; the poets Padraic Colum and Joseph Campbell and Joseph's younger brother John. Bigger encouraged Herbert's research and took a group on a Donegal holiday, Herbert with his notebook, Bigger with his camera. The result was a volume of songs, *Songs of Uladh* (Ulster), published in 1904 at Bigger's expense and dedicated to him. There were verses by Joseph Campbell, woodcuts by John and music collected by Herbert and in which with all the purist ardour of youth he eschewed 'drawing-room' accompaniment.[5] For Joseph the offer to write verses for these collected airs was something of a compensation after his exclusion the same year from George

Russell ('A. E.')'s anthology *New Songs*; for Herbert the enterprise determined the course of his life. In the same year with Mrs Milligan Fox he co-founded the Irish Folk Song Society and began to edit its journal, contributing also to the *Ulster Journal of Archaeology* edited by Bigger. Genealogical research revealed that the family was descended through the male line from Hugh O'Neill, he of the 'flight of the Earls' in 1607, not one of Ireland's happier moments. (O'Neill is said to have died in Rome of melancholy.) Among H. H.'s other forebears on his father's side were two nineteenth-century Establishment figures: the reputedly dour Ulster lawyer Hugh McCalmont, Lord Chancellor and the first Earl Cairns, and John Wilson Croker, Tory MP for Downpatrick, First Secretary to the Admiralty, part-time journalist and friend of Walter Scott and Wellington.

In the course of their exploration Bigger and his young protégé visited the Dunfanaghy workhouse and heard traditional songs remembered by the inmates. The workhouse master Andrew MacIntyre (who would later become the county librarian) introduced them to other singers and fiddlers. This Donegal journey appears in the memoirs of Stephen Gwynn who goes on to describe a Gaelic Feis at Cushendal in the Glens of Antrim the following year where again he was Bigger's guest with the same group. What was easy in Donegal could have been a problem in Antrim, the most Protestant of all the counties, although the Glens themselves were Gaelic and Catholic and remnants of Gaelic speech survived there. That an entertainment of Irish songs and dances in a courtyard should have been well attended surprised the visitors from Belfast. Gwynn spoke diplomatically about good relations; the much younger Herbert muttered darkly that he would rather be 'in a place where a man would have stones clodded at him for his opinions'. 'Belfast all over,' mused Gwynn.[6]

When Hamilton Harty made his own beautiful arrangement of 'My Lagan Love' (the air had been a find of Herbert's), a Belfast music critic took exception to this and said so. Bigger, perhaps over-protective of his young disciple, ill-advisedly urged Herbert to sue for breach of copyright. Of course the case was thrown out, there being no copyright in folk song. Later Herbert and Harty met at a London party and my mother invited 'Hale' to luncheon with some friends. It all passed, she recorded, with great gaiety. The following day Harty sent Herbert a fine photograph of himself at the piano. At the top of the mount he had written 'The Lagan' with below at one end 'From H. H.' and at the other 'To H. H.' The end of an *histoire* which should never have come about. The two remained the warmest of friends.

In his early days Herbert signed his work 'Padraic MacAodh O'Neill', a conceit which led to his being saddled for a while in a certain Dublin circle with the nickname 'Paudeen'. The poet Padraic Colum reported a Dublin woman declaring that Paudeen ought to be wearing a stock, 'and this was a neat way of imaging him for, round-faced, wearing spectacles, and with a smile that seemed to come from relish of some naughty thought . . . Herbert Hughes brought some eighteenth-century portrait to life'.[7] As for Joseph Campbell, he signed his work 'Seosamh McCathmoil' until he heard a woman ask for the poems of 'Seo-sam McCatwail'.

The inauguration in Dublin of the new Abbey Theatre and the triumph of W. B. Yeats and Lady Gregory inflamed the Ulster friends in their passionate involvement. Herbert began to attend meetings of the Dungannon Clubs, founded in Belfast in 1905 by Denis McCullough and Bulmer Hobson but soon with branches in Dublin, Glasgow and London. This was a small, separatist, but not secret organisation which advocated independence and was against the Boer War. It was also puritanical and anti-alcohol. This was not a combination to attract the convivial Herbert so there must have been a considerable bending of rules when he founded the London branch, Dungannon Club No 4, with the help of his friends from a literary club at the Napier Tavern in High Holborn. These were Robert Lynd and the Morrow brothers, George, Eddie and Norman, and the painter Paul Henry. The new Dungannon Club met at Norman Morrow's house, 324 King's Road, Chelsea. It was reported that Hobson's Belfast branch of the Dungannon Clubs, inaugurated in 1905, had some difficulty getting people to come to meetings until a magic lantern was introduced and slides shown from cartoons by Jack Morrow.

To return to Dublin, H. H.'s name as a musician was being put about and Yeats considered engaging him to write music for intervals at the Abbey Theatre.

'I have plans for improving our new poets myself,' wrote W. B. Y. in his Olympian mode to the poet and novelist Katharine Tynan in September 1906. 'I want to get them to write songs to be sung between the acts. Herbert Hughes will set them and we have a fine singer in Sara Allgood.'[8] In March 1905 in a letter to Lady Gregory he had mentioned a coming meeting with 'Hughes the Irish musician Synge is always speaking of'.[9] Yeats is known to have liked Herbert personally if not his republican leanings, for W. B. Y. had little taste for radical politics: although he himself had been a Fenian in the 1890s, Ireland's re-birth was to come about through literature, not propaganda.[10] However he was quick to see that Herbert Hughes's contacts might be useful to his theatre, the questionable associations notwithstanding. 'If Synge comes over [to London],' he wrote to Lady Gregory, 'and if he and Robert [Gregory] think Hughes a competent man, it might be a great advantage to leave our music wholly to him. He would take pride in it and as he cares for very little except folk songs would make it as Irish as possible.'[11] But there was an obstacle in the shape of the Abbey's *mécène*, the English tea-merchant heiress Annie Horniman, who had a deep mistrust of Irish nationalism. Furthermore she disliked H. H. and his music and she was too important to be crossed over the choice of a musician. H. H. had already written some music for the Abbey Theatre – for W. B. Y.'s *On Báile's Strand*, for example, in 1904 – but the new project came to nothing. At this time he was thinking of accepting the paid secretaryship of the Irish Literary Society to escape from the hack work with which he was earning his living.

The Presbyterian values of hard work, honesty and sobriety had channelled the growing Ulster middle class into the professions or towards the making of money, 'one eye firmly fixed on God, the other as firmly fixed on Mammon'.[12] It was a non-literary culture: creative writing and works of imagination, shining individuality or a taste for the theatre were largely suspect and discouraged. Short of both incentive and patronage many artists left Ulster, among them the writers George Russell ('A. E.'), Robert Lynd and Joseph Campbell, the painters John Lavery and Paul Henry and the musicians Charles Wood and Hamilton Harty. Herbert Hughes joined this diaspora and never returned to live in (to quote E. M. Forster) 'that great city with its ponderous purposes'.

Herbert found work as organist-choirmaster at Monken Hadleigh and conductor of the Hertfordshire Philharmonic but London soon beckoned. In the interval of a Promenade concert in London's Queen's Hall he fell into a passionate discussion with a stranger who said to him as they parted, 'Put all that in writing and give it to me in the morning.' The stranger was A. R. Orage (1872–1934), editor of *The New Age*, which he quickly invited Herbert to join as its music critic. So began a thirty-year career in London journalism.

A Yorkshireman with a mother of Irish descent, Orage was one of the outstanding intellectual figures in London. The author of several works on Nietzsche, he was preoccupied with socialism and mysticism, a mixture very much of the time. With George Bernard Shaw's backing he and another Fabian, Holbrook Jackson, had bought the ailing paper *The Age* and, changing its name to *The New Age* with a masthead by Eric Gill, were turning it into the liveliest weekly in the country. Orage was indifferent to his collaborators' beliefs and politics so long as they knew how to write, and the twenty-five-year-old Herbert now found himself in the company of Shaw, Arnold Bennett, H. G. Wells, Hilaire Belloc and G. K. Chesterton. With *The New Age* the quality held up but the finances were always a problem. Orage struggled on until 1922 and then left for Gurdjeff and Ouspensky's settlement in Fontainebleau and lecture tours in the USA. Shaw called him 'a desperado of genius'. Oscar Wilde's friend the art critic Robbie Ross used to make a point of pronouncing Orage's name in the French fashion, saying, 'How could a socialist be better named?'[13]

Herbert's first wife, the brainy Lillian Meacham, described elsewhere as 'bony and nervy' and the very model of the Fabian New Woman, was intellectually adventurous and sexually liberated.[14] She found a place in memoirs first through her affair with a fellow Fabian Eric Gill (with whom she visited Chartres and read Nietzsche in the evenings) and later in books by her son, my half-brother the composer and author Patrick ('Spike') Hughes.[15] Unsurprisingly, the misalliance with my father ended badly and the pain of the unravelling was exacerbated by the First World War and Herbert's absence from the scene. Details from both sides eventually came to me in later life and fall beyond the span of this memoir. Enough to say that a long rift was created by a string of misapprehensions, procrastinations and sins of omission, the barnacles which cling to wrecked marriages. Happily this rift was eventually closed and it amused and pleased me to see in how much besides musicianship the son resembled the father: the fastidiousness, the professionalism, the impatience, sensitivity, warmth and wit.

Patrick was born in London in 1908 and spent much of his childhood travelling in Europe with his mother, later studying music in Vienna with Egon Wellesz. Turning to jazz he became a very successful player ('Britain's Best Bassist', trumpeted *Variety* magazine). He led a band in New York, wrote a ballet called *High Yellow* and played jazz with, among many others, the eminent violinist Joseph Szigeti, to whom he dedicated a piece, *Arabesque*. He was a notable journalist and could write equally about Mozart, Verdi, gardening, coarse fishing or bad language. He translated Italian opera singably, a very difficult operation. His handwriting was beautiful, his letters very funny and his records have now become collectables. My own opinion is that in music he could have done anything. He once played me a record of his pastiche of a Beethoven scherzo with full orchestra, a wonderfully witty piece of work but which reminded me sadly of how he had never taken himself seriously enough. We sat one morning in the garden at Ringmer where he had found happiness with his third wife, Charmian ('Chim'). At the time I was reading a book peppered with Greek words and Patrick was helping me look them all up. He was enjoying himself like a child, and like a child he looked disappointed when we were interrupted as Chim called us to the lunch table.

In the First World War Herbert's defective eyesight disqualified him from action but he volunteered, completed his officer-training at Trinity College Dublin and joined the Artists' Rifles, the kind of move which was anathema in Dungannon Club circles, but by now he had long been a Londoner. The Artists' Rifles, which included the painters John Lavery and John and Paul Nash, drilled in the quadrangle of Burlington House, 'rather a scrubby lot of painters, sculptors, actors, musicians, hairdressers, scene-shifters, etc. of all ages'.[16]

Towards the end of the war, H. H. was in the Sudan under General, later Field Marshal, Allenby. In his kitbag he had put a first (limited) edition of Nietzsche's *The Dawn of Day* in translation, but not with any new religion in mind: characteristically it served as a guest book for jolly gatherings of army friends.[17] One last entry in this worn volume stands out after scores of soldiers' names with their regiments – Suzanne McKernan and the date 3 May 1919. As a playful reminder this guest added the years back to 1913.

One afternoon that year the young actress Suzanne McKernan had visited the Belfast painter Norman Morrow in his Chelsea studio. She remarked on the surprising tidiness of the place: even the pictures were straight. 'That was Herbert Hughes who came this morning,' Morrow explained. Half a century later Suzanne remembered how that name had jingled in her head for the rest of that afternoon. At the studio party in the evening Herbert looked across the room at Suzanne and said to his host, 'There's the girl I want to marry.'

It was easier said than done. There would be the long separations of the war, but also rewards when peace returned: travel books and volumes of poetry celebrate the bliss of escapes to France before Suzanne and Herbert were finally united.

3

Au Revoir, Dublin

As a child Suzanne dreamed of being pale and shy when instead she had inherited vitality, blooming health and a friendly nature. The only girl in a family of five, she was bonny rather than beautiful and had the look of a Manet: she had greeny-blue eyes, a rounded figure and corn-coloured hair which, growing to her waist, turned later to auburn. When as a drama student she sat for the painter Ambrose McEvoy he noticed her 'little continental hands'.[1] Into old age she had an animal enjoyment of the sea and sun so that it seemed almost fitting that she should leave this world on the shortest day of the year.

Born in 1847, her mother Maria Dowling had lost both her parents as a result of the Famine and the widespread disease which followed, but some combative element in the Dowlings ensured her survival into her eighty-eighth year as well as the robust health she passed on to her daughter. Thwarted in her ambition to be an actress because the profession was considered disreputable, Maria consoled herself by writing verse. Her husband James is a shadowy figure like an unfinished portrait, by all accounts a strange man given when angry to locking himself up in the bedroom with the Bible and the complete works of Shakespeare. It was always clear that Suzanne was closer to her mother. It must have been easier.

Opposite the McKernans' house at Fairview in 1900 lived a slender undergraduate from University College with pale eyes and unpressed clothes who had just earned himself twelve guineas for an article on an Ibsen play and, what was more remarkable, congratulations from the playwright himself, transmitted through his English translator, William Archer. The message reached the young James Joyce in Richmond Avenue at an idle moment after a dancing class (he had early ambitions as a dancer) in the company of his small neighbour, Suzanne.[2] The arrival of the postman that day marked a turning-

16

point: from now on he would consider himself a European and begin intensive studies of languages and literature, reading prodigiously. That was the plan which indeed he carried out. In the immediate future the twelve guineas, minus a pound for his mother, would go on a trip to London with his impecunious father John Stanislaus whose perpetual skirmishes with Dublin grocers and landlords Jim continued to observe with an cold filial eye while awaiting the opportunity to embark on his own.

It was at the McKernans' house that the Joyce children took refuge one evening when John Stanislaus, having come home in a terrible mood after a day's drinking, attacked his wife, bawling, his hands around her throat, 'Now by God it is time to finish it!' Luckily Jim knocked his father to the floor in time. The police were sent for and the shame of this was to hang over the family, especially John Stanislaus who henceforth limited his abuse to verbal assaults.

Three years after the Ibsen letter, when the McKernans had moved to Shelbourne Avenue, Jim rented the large first-floor room in their house. Here he installed a piano in order to practise for the tenor competition at the Feis Ceol (or Fish Coil as it was often called). The rising young tenor John McCormack was encouraging, his own career having begun in this way. But in this case like father, like son: Jim failed to pay the rent. For a while the McKernans who were fond of him made allowances for the delays. But these became longer and longer and in the end they lost patience, closed the house and went off on holiday.

When the time came, vicariously realising her own ambitions, Maria McKernan accompanied her daughter to London to study at the not yet royal Academy of Dramatic Art, setting Suzanne on a path which would take her into the Irish Players, an offshoot of Dublin's Abbey Theatre Company. In Vicarage Gate they shared lodgings with the painter and Slade student Jo Jones, the future painter of Spanish gypsies, who was to become a lifelong friend. Later, when Herbert came into her life, Suzanne was quickly adopted by the whole Hughes tribe. During Herbert's wartime absence she visited the Belfast house and small inscribed volumes of plays and poetry survive as mementos of reunions with his sisters Lena and Dorothy.

On his retirement F. P. H., my grandfather, took De Morgan's old house. Bohemian Chelsea was not the obvious choice for an Ulster Victorian mill-owner, but Herbert had already put down roots there and his father had a habit of escaping the mould of his class. At 125 Church Street F. P. H. provided a base for his younger children while they were students, and at 127 he gave a home to Suzanne and her mother. So at one of the bloodiest periods of Irish history, when the Anglo-Irish War was to be followed by the even more vicious Civil War, the combined Chelsea household included on the one hand a Belfast Protestant anxious to see the completion of his son's divorce while protecting two Dublin Catholics (one of whom his future daughter-in-law); and on the other a devout Catholic, Maria McKernan, who contrary to most of her Church still nursed in her heart a deep admiration for the disgraced Parnell.[3] When 'Mamma' McKernan was away Herbert missed their 'gossipy breakfasts in the kitchen before the others had rubbed the sleep out of their eyes'.[4]

The situation was less uncommon, however, than one might suppose, at least according to W. B. Yeats. In the USA he had observed how among Irishmen abroad 'common Irishness' had a habit of dissolving religious prejudice.[5] Common Irishness and, in the case of the Hughes family, a common hunger for music and the theatre. Although the issues were different there was something Chekhovian in the group, with Ellen, the family nurse, at the samovar in the garden. (See illustration.)

In August 1920, together with Vera Collum who was writing a book on Carnac, Susie and Herbert went to Sarzeau in the Morbihan. The fare from Waterloo to St-Malo was £2 3s. 1d. The little Breton train resembled a glorified tram, and Suzanne was surprised everywhere at the amount of luggage women were prepared to carry. Susie had begun to keep a journal, with occasional entries by Herbert. His contributions dwindled as work increased but Susie kept up the habit, most days, for many years.

At the Sarzeau hotel one evening there was a dance.

Madame-with-the-two-boys-and-black-hair hammering the piano like the devil. They danced a quadrille in the most courtly and proper fashion, led off by Madame-Pink-Jersey's beautiful daughter and the dancing master who is now a saddler. Afterwards they dragged Herbert to the piano and he played the whole evening. It seems so convivial – Joséphine, Renée, Mme Pink-Jersey's maid and all the guests hopping about together. [SHJ, 11 August 1920]

Bathing at Raliguen they saw Monsieur l'Abbé in his white voluminous drawers and vest sitting happily in the sun with the dark ladies from Nantes. Before dinner he told them he came from Orléans and made jokes about his great girth which made him look like a balloon in the water. 'Pity he is going away,' Suzanne commented. She was enchanted at the costumes seen at High Mass 'their beautiful caps and black silk *mouchoirs*, their sleeves loose with huge velvet cuffs and their aprons of all colours – purple silk or blue, terracotta or magenta'. Women in ordinary smart clothes looked tawdry beside them, she thought.

Collum (as they always called her) tactfully took herself off on her work, leaving Susie and Herbert to their own devices and dreams, smoking in the shelter of dolmens, reading their books in caves and living the future in the present. The state of women's rights surprised Suzanne 'in a country so keen on liberty' as France. 'Dîner seule avec un monsieur? Non, non, non, on ne peut pas,' was one opinion.

'Monsieur', the patron, acted as chauffeur and offered to show how he fished for frogs, an unpleasant experience. He had to stop when he was bitten by a leech. They watched harvesters threshing with flails and singing as they worked. Suzanne tried to use a flail but decided it was as difficult as a good golf swing. She and Herbert walked all over the wild countryside while the discreet Collum worked on her photographs.

The fourth holiday companion was 'a poor mangy bitch' at the hotel, Finette, whom Suzanne treated with an ointment of sulphur and lard while a crowd collected to watch. As her coat grew, Finette gambolled in the heather.

My first job was to bathe Finette. I found soapy water in the stable. Collum helped me. Poor beast she was angelic. I took her to the heathery field where Hughes was sitting and he and I read until déjeuner. Afterwards we were whirled off to Madame Jouen's orchard to see the children's play. The trees were loaded with rosy apples. The relations all jabbered hard during the entire performance and kept telling the children to speak up, to come closer and so on.   [SHJ, undated September 1920]

Watching a wedding procession arriving at Sarzeau mairie, Suzanne asked Herbert to find out who was paying for the refreshments for so many people. 'A treasurer is appointed,' she learned. 'Everyone pays in something and they visit all the cafés and dance around the town until the money is all spent.'

On the last night of the holiday all the guests stayed up to wish the three goodbye and Suzanne was given a Breton cake to eat in the train. Renée the chambermaid, in tears, brought Finette to the station.

In Paris on their way home, having walked from their Montparnasse hotel to the Place de l'Opéra, Herbert and Suzanne took in *Phi-Phi* at the Bouffes-Parisiens, a historical play at the Français and blood and gore at the Grand Guignol, including a man with his hands cut off. Suzanne was wide-eyed at the perfection of the make-up: 'One could literally see the blood drip.' They finished the evening dancing at the Moulin de la Galette and Bal Tabarin, Suzanne commenting afterwards that the Parisian chorus compared badly with London musical comedy: 'These girls move about anyhow. None seemed overburdened with talent. But where in London,' she conceded, looking back at the Grand Guignol, 'could you see two thrillers and three little comedies in one evening?'

She was less attracted to the grandeur of Notre Dame than to the beauty of the Sainte Chapelle, 'hiding as if from harm in the midst of the Palais de Justice . . . The colour leaves one breathless.'

Back in Church Street, Joe Kerrigan of the Irish Players came to say goodbye before going to the States. 'Well now for work,' she ended her diary. 'The play is over for another year.'

She might have written, 'And now for the plays.'

The Abbey Theatre Company had been chafing under the management of St John Ervine, the Belfast playwright having in a very short time ruffled a great number of feathers. He had ridiculed the Dublin critics in a play and stated in a lecture that the Irish were not only sick but lunatic. During the Easter Rising of 1916 he regretted that the English gunboat *Helga* had not blasted the Abbey to pieces. (To be fair, in the last instance he probably had notions of the compensation badly needed to provide a more suitable building.) Why was he there at all, one might ask. The answer must be that the management was willing to put on his plays, for Ervine was out of sympathy with the actors who were largely republican, and when he imposed twice-daily rehearsals throughout tours they revolted. He retaliated by giving them one week's notice; greatly embarrassed, Yeats and Lady Gregory concurred. A formidable section of the company then broke away – Arthur Sinclair, Sydney Malone, Joe O'Rourke, Cathleen Drago, Eithne Magee. They were soon joined by my mother, the young Suzanne McKernan. To Yeats and Lady Gregory's relief, Ervine resigned the same year. In July 1921 the Irish Players came to the Court Theatre in Sloane Square.

The Court had a brilliant past under Harley Granville-Barker and later J. E .Vedrenne who had put on eleven of Shaw's plays, six of them first productions. In September 1918 the theatre came under the management of J. B. Fagan.

James Bernard Fagan had come to the stage after flirting successively with Holy Orders, the Bar and the Indian Civil Service. He spent two years with F. R. Benson and another two with Herbert Beerbohm Tree, and then turned from acting to writing plays. In a theatre redecorated with new lighting designed by Fagan himself (and carried out by the local Charles Hammond in Sloane Street – it was a thoroughly Chelsea affair), the Irish Players gave Synge's *The Playboy of the Western World*. Suzanne played a village girl, Susan Brady; the leads were Fred O'Donovan as Christy Mahon, Máire O'Neill (Molly Allgood) as Pegeen Mike and her sister Sara Allgood as the widow Quin.

During a run of *Othello* with Godfrey Tearle and Basil Rathbone, Fagan lent the theatre to the Irish Players for an Abbey Theatre Fund matinée. A poster by Augustus John was auctioned in the interval, Fagan's wife Mary Grey sang French songs and the company gave three one-act plays. In *Riders to the Sea*, Máire O'Neill played Maurya and Suzanne her daughter Nora.

The American tour which followed was spoilt for Susie, not in the theatre but in the digs which she shared with the warring Allgood sisters. Since their thirst for drama was endless they spent their leisure screaming at each other and throwing things across the room. When tired of this they blithely turned to other matters while Susie was the one left shaking.

These extraordinary sisters were born in Dublin and brought up in an orphanage. Sara was the first to join the Abbey and played the lead in Yeats's *Cathleen Ni Houlihan* and in Synge's *Riders to the Sea*. She had triumphs in O'Casey's plays, as Juno in *Juno and the Paycock* and as Bessie Burgess in *The Plough and the Stars*. She appeared in several Hollywood films but died there in poverty. Her sister Molly (her stage name was Máire O'Neill) played Pegeen Mike in the first productions of *The Playboy of the Western World,* and became engaged to its author, Synge. They were never to marry for Synge broke off the engagement after contracting Hodgkin's Disease. Molly's second husband (her first had been Gerald Henson) was G. H. Mair of the *Manchester Guardian*. On his death she married a fellow actor, Arthur Sinclair. It was not a peaceful ménage.

Release for Susie from the boarding-house inferno came when Herbert followed her to the States. Announcing to 'Mamma' McKernan that he was going to sail in a few days, he asked her, 'Would you mind very much if I married Susie? RSVP!'

> I don't yet know when her tour will end, but we are to meet in New York. She will not want to break her contract and may have to stay behind for a few weeks but I am hoping that she will be back in Chelsea before the Spring . . . But apart from seeing Susie my visit to New York is really business, camouflaged. I am to meet John McCormack and Albert Coates the conductor and my publishers' agents and others, so that my holiday will be more than half WORK again.
>
> Do, dearest Mamma, write and give me your blessing before I sail . . .

PS. My address in New York will be c/o The *Daily Telegraph*, 66 Broadway, New York City.[6]

'It's a terrible thing to run off with your daughter, but how could I help it?' he quipped, once blessed in Mamma's reply.[7]

On 1 February 1922 Suzanne and Herbert were married in New Jersey by the Governor, their friend General William Heppenheimer, who liked to call himself their 'foster father'.[8] He lent them a chauffeur-driven car for their honeymoon. In New York they met Prokofiev who said, 'They accuse me of writing whistlable tunes.' The way he pronounced 'whistlable', Susie recalled years later, was impossible to express in print. The conductor Albert Coates, also there, she found 'wild – half Russian, affectionate and convivial, inconsequent and susceptible'.[9] In spite of a very promising start, Suzanne never returned to the stage. It was not an easy decision but she saw it as inevitable. 'Your father wanted me with him always,' she told me. 'He would never accept an invitation which was not for both of us.'

With most of his offspring settled, F. P. H. went off on a world tour which included Japan where he met Prince Tokugawa, the President of the House of Peers. Their relations must have been very cordial to judge by the closely-written postcards F. P. H. received from him for several years. Crossing the States, F. P. H. recorded the gloom which descended upon him on seeing Pittsburgh and his enchantment at the beauty and climate of California. He resolved to move there, and marrying the faithful Ellen, he bought a house at 2027 Canyon Drive, Hollywood, where they both believed they would live to the end of their days.

Coming to London, Suzanne was not immediately at ease with the English. When she first arrived she was sometimes reduced to tears by what she perceived as their outlandish coldness and indifference – the brisk impersonal manner, the sliding eye contact. That these things might be masking discretion or diffidence was something she was to learn in time, when many of these disconcerting people had become her staunchest friends. Only rarely did her Irishness provoke hostility or superciliousness, or the hoary old jokes which were the

Victorians' legacy from *Punch* cartoons, the origin of the 'stage Irish-man', a tradition slow to die. But at one Chelsea party, the sculptor Derwent Wood launched the classic diatribe: the Irish were disorderly, drunken, feckless, priest-ridden . . .

Suzanne raised her voice above the din.

'The Irish have many faults. But one thing an Irishman never does.'

'And what is that?'

'He never insults a guest.'

Her host crossed the room and in front of his silenced friends knelt at Suzanne's feet and planted a kiss on her evening slipper.

4

Ireland in London

(i)

One Sunday afternoon in May 1931 a visitor wearing dark glasses appeared in the studio. He was tall and thin and had a gentle Irish voice. He talked for a while with our father and then, propping up a leather-bound volume, he sat down at the keyboard. (I noticed that it was an awkward book for the piano, the kind that bursts with pride at its contents.) With Helena and myself standing on either side he began to sing French songs. When he had finished he said to our mother, 'Don't let the children sing in German,' and he presented us with this book.[1]

Although he visited us many times when he was in London this is the occasion which crystallises my memories of James Joyce. I have no recollection of even one of the other guests at this tea-party. I had eyes only for the stranger with the dark glasses.[2]

Between Joyce and Herbert, besides their common year of birth (1882), was a steady accumulation of coincidences. As early as 1904 the young Joyce sang H. H.'s setting to Yeats's poem 'Down by the Salley Gardens' at a concert where he shared the platform with another young singer, John McCormack. It earned him two guineas which led Nora Joyce to comment years later that he ought to have stuck to music rather than bother with writing. (He had done better than John McCormack on his first London engagement with John Barbirolli's father Lorenzo: McCormack's fee was a mere guinea.)

As a child Suzanne was present on the day when Ibsen's letter reached the young Joyce. Later, when miserably employed in Rome (a city he hated and where he wrote little), Joyce was planning an ironic short story revolving around Suzanne's brother Joe and to be entitled 'The Last Supper'. A casualty of the struggles to get *Chamber*

Music published, this story never appeared. Twenty-five years later when Joyce was in London recording the closing pages of 'Anna Livia Plurabelle' for C. K. Ogden and the Orthological Institute he spoke of this. Ogden told him he was a friend of Suzanne whom he had met during the Irish Players' season at the Court Theatre. It was finally in Paris that Joyce and my father first met and dined together. Suzanne and Herbert were guests of the musical patron Elizabeth Sprague Coolidge at a chamber music festival in October 1929.

> Left Victoria at 11.30 with Arthur Bliss and his wife. The journey to Paris was over in a twinkling, the conversation was so good. On our arrival at the Danube we found that our room wouldn't be ready until the next day, and they sent us to the St Thomas d'Aquin where we had a startling suite. Called at the Joyces and took them out to dinner. James remembered me quite well. He told me how he rediscovered me through Dear Brutus. He was thinking of the quotation which he had written in a book to Joe [Suzanne's brother] and [had] said so when Ogden mentioned my name. His blindness is pathetic. He and H. H. became friends at once as if they had met before. We talked of Ireland, of music. He teased Herbert about Belfast. We parted at midnight and then went on, H. and I, to the Coupole and met the Blisses and finished up at 2 a.m.
>
> We changed to the Danube where they gave us a good room on the front (but oh the noise of the early morning dustbins!) We went to the Deux Magots for an apéritif, lunched at the hotel and in the afternoon went to the Joyces. We met Lucia and Giorgio. She's a most attractive creature with a slight squint, and Giorgio has a very fine voice. I had a long talk with Mrs Joyce whom I liked immensely. She's dying to come to London to live. Meeting them set me off thinking of family things in Ireland, sad things mostly. We left Sq. Robiac just in time to meet Rollo Myers and Arthur Bliss and his wife at the Dôme. From there we went to dine at the Du Guesclin and then to Myers' apartment where we stayed until midnight. I was almost asleep but I enjoyed it all immensely especially Bliss's stories of the Siena Festival.
>
> We took Mrs Ernest Boyd to the Deux Magots where we had

mandarins and a conversation about Ernest Boyd, J. M. K. [the actor Joe Kerrigan], J. J. and lots of other things. From there to Loch's flat for lunch. He's a nice creature but so solid and British and so is she – untouched by Paris. It's like stepping into Cheyne Court or thereabouts. After lunch we went in search of Chopin's house in the Square d'Orléans. We were awed by the ghostly feeling in the staircase. The square has trees and a fountain not working. It's full of offices and flats. We went from there to a rehearsal at the Salle Gaveau and back to the Danube.

We went to the Majestic and lunched with Lionel Tertis and his wife, [Hans] Kindler and [William] Kroll. Kindler amused us with his stories of D'Annunzio for whom they played at Lake Gardone. He fired off shots for Mrs Coolidge, called her Santa Elisabetta and gave them all jewels made by his own jeweller. He lives in great state. Kroll told us that Kindler sat so near his [Kroll's] fiddle that he couldn't play at all and had to move. After lunch we went to Malipiero's room and met him and his English wife and Henri Prunières.

In the afternoon we went to the Salle Pleyel and saw Chopin's piano and also the new hall. We were much amused by a young man who said stiff shirts were bad acoustically and that they made an echo. The hall is padded and rounded off everywhere to make it perfect. We dined with Blisses and Goossenses and afterwards went to the concert at the Palais Royal where the Joyces awaited us. Excellent concert, Roussel Trio a success, Malipiero not altogether. Went to Fouquet's and had a merry night of it, Hans Kindler telling funny stories.

Mrs Coolidge's lunch at the Majestic [see menu illustration]. They were all there – Roussel, Malipiero, Martinů, Barrère, Bliss, Casella, Leon Goossens, Prunières, Tertis and so on – a pleasant enough affair with no speeches.

Dined with Goossens and Bliss once more and then on to the concert – Bliss, Pizzetti, Ornstein, etc., rather too long. Afterwards we went to Chez Francis with Lucia, James and Nora Joyce, Rollo Myers and the Baronne von Falz Fein. We were tired and thirsty but talked until 2 a.m.

Left Paris 10 o'clock with Fay [Goossens] and the Blisses – bad crossing but we weren't sick. The children's greeting was worth going away for – they screamed with delight and dissolved into giggles and we all kept on giggling for quite ten minutes. The house was shining and Violet as ever serene. Bed early for the first time in over a week. [SHJ, 27–30 October 1929]

Herbert who was a good mimic told Belfast stories in a local accent much egged on by Joyce. In one of these a mayoress of Belfast is showing guests a row of portraits and pointing proudly to her husband's saying, 'Oil painting by hand.' Herbert's mayoress was to surface in *Finnegans Wake*.[3] One of Herbert's early songs, 'I know my love by his way o' walkin'/And I know my love by his way o' talkin' ', was also transformed.[4]

The idea of *The Joyce Book*, a tribute to the writer, sprang from a conversation in Paris between Herbert and the composer Arthur Bliss as they left the Majestic Hotel after the Coolidge luncheon. Joyce had accompanied them to a chamber concert at the Palais Royal where a work by Bliss was performed. The writer, hampered by his blindness, was much in the thoughts of both musicians so that the idea occurred to them simultaneously: the association of chamber music – intimate music – with Joyce's poetry, 'like the association of wind and wave, of light and heat'.[5] The conversation continued at Fouquets where the embryonic notion of four or five settings expanded until it embraced the whole of *Pomes Penyeach*, a project which would soon mobilise a baker's dozen of composers separated by thousands of miles – 'Celt, Anglo-Saxon, Latin, American', a very Joycean mixture. Writers, they said, and a painter should also be involved. The painter was to be Augustus John with a frontispiece sketch.

The book took three years to put together. On the way were acceptances, hesitations and refusals, generally worded with great modesty. H. H. wrote to Yeats recalling past meetings in the company of the actress Florence Farr, 'many years ago when [he] had attic rooms immediately over Mrs Emery's in Holland Road', and how he was greatly honoured one evening when Yeats came upstairs with Synge and Robert Gregory 'to look at the ceiling decorations [he] had improvised with candle smoke!'[6] Yeats declined to write a piece for the book, saying he wished he could join in the tribute for he admired Joyce's 'heroic intensity' but could do nothing without engaging the subconscious. With the composer Darius Milhaud there were misunderstandings. Recruited by Joyce himself to set 'A Flower given to my Daughter' and unaware that all the other contributors had waived their fees and royalties for this tribute, Milhaud was outraged when Herbert explained. A publication was a commercial enterprise and not a work of charity, Milhaud argued. In the end it was Albert Roussel who set the poem.

There were difficulties with Colum's first Preface which nobody approved of, and all the while Herbert was busy researching Irish folk song, preparing a biography of Chopin and carrying out his duties at the *Daily Telegraph*. (He had joined the *DT* in 1911 after leaving the *New Age*, no doubt for a higher salary.)

Suzanne was on holiday with us in Jersey when he wrote:

Yesterday I fiddled about with the music page, with music for review, and eventually hours over Bunting [*The Bunting Collection of Irish Folk Songs*], one little light on the piano. I take Niecks to bed [two-volume *Life of Chopin*], and that mad *transition* (as they call it, without the capital T) in which there is a most interesting analysis of *Ulysses* you *must* read. A surprising essay. Today I had two telephone conversations with Joyce. He submitted, if you please, Colum's Preface to the opinion of 5 different people: his brother, his wife, Miss Weaver (?) and my colleague in the *DT*, Gerald Griffin (an old University chum) and someone else he mentioned. They all agree it is wrong. I feel myself that Colum has struck the wrong note. [Or] not so much the wrong note as an overdone treatment of the right note. I am to dine with [Joyce] tomorrow Friday night. They leave for Paris on Saturday.

[H. H. to S. H., 21 August 1930]

Unsurprisingly there was a piano in the little room at the Euston Hotel where they conferred the next day,

a piano and two friends: one Gerald Griffin (of the *Daily Telegraph*,

Dieu merci!) and the other, [Herbert] Gorman, Joyce's American biographer, a charming young man, quiet-voiced . . . Joyce made me play a bit of my song ['She Weeps over Rahoon'], and 'The Quilt', that lovely thing he sang to us in Paris. Mrs Joyce and Lucia were dining elsewhere so Joyce insisted on going to Gennaro's and there we dined scrumptiously, J. J. ordering everything in perfect Italian, being highly respected therefore by the waiters. We dined and dined and dined, Griffin and Gorman making most of the talk, Joyce very little, but obviously enjoying himself. Taxied back to the hotel. A bottle of champagne. More talk & more talk. Colum's Preface completely turned down. They had each liked it in a way, but thought it more suitable for a magazine article. I told Joyce to keep it himself and hand it to Colum in Paris . . . So we decided (we were really a committee dining!) that Colum should sell this script to anybody he liked and [write] a shorter preface, concentrating on the musical quality of Joyce's prose, or some other aspect of his work. Presently Mrs Joyce and Lucia came into the drawing-room, about 11.30. More drinks, more talk, and then to bed. But the evening was so full of mental excitement that I simply could not go to bed and when I got back to Chelsea about one o'clock I walked from one coffee stall to another, drinking Bovril and listening to weird conversations and it was 2 o'clock before I turned out my light.

[H. H. to S. H., 24 August 1930]

The Prologue was the work of James Stephens. After much soul-searching Padraic Colum wrote a study of Joyce as poet and the Epilogue was provided by Arthur Symons, poet and critic of an earlier generation but one of the first English writers to have recognised Joyce. Augustus John, enthusiastic from the start, contributed the portrait – he had found the Anna Livia recording 'a terrific thing'. He reported afterwards that the writer had been a patient sitter.[7] When the finished work appeared on Joyce's fifty-first birthday he thanked Herbert with a ditty entitled 'Pennipomes Twoguineaseach':

> Sing a song of shillings
> A guinea cannot buy,

Thirteen tiny pomikins
Bobbing in a pie.

The printer's pie was published
And the pomes began to sing
And wasn't Herbert Hughesius
As happy as a king!

Joyce wasn't unhappy himself even if incommoded when 'net proceeds' he had expected (more immediately advantageous than a 'tribute') turned out to be 'netissimo, that is a net nothing', as he wrote to his son. Indeed to Harriet Weaver, Joyce commented, 'Not bad for a book which E. P. [Ezra Pound] told me to put in the family Bible.' To Herbert he wrote, 'You have certainly made a fine thing of it and I feel greatly honoured . . . Well, for a little libriaciattolo, *P. P.* has had two remarkable editions.' He accounted for a 'lake' (of wine?) on this letter by explaining that he was writing on the salon mantelpiece. He sent H. H. of a copy of the first edition of Jean-Jacques Rousseau's opera *Le Devin du village* thanking him for all the trouble he had taken 'over that joyce of a book'.

Herbert first met Harriet Weaver, former editor of *The Egoist* and Joyce's chief benefactor, at Victoria Station where she was the only other friend to see the Joyces off to Paris. She came to the studio one wet October afternoon and 'was difficult to talk to'.

Before she left I noticed that she had been perspiring freely with shyness and nervousness all the time. How we tried to make her talk! I wonder if she is like that with Joyce? We showed her the de luxe edition of *Pomes Penyeach* with Lucia's illustrations.

[SHJ, 21 October 1932]

The first performance of *The Joyce Book* songs took place on H. H.'s fiftieth birthday, St Patrick's Eve 1932, at the London Contemporary Music Centre. As he was guest of honour at an American colony luncheon in Paris Joyce was unable to come, but he wrote from Passy sending H. H. a copy of the review *transition* with the now famous César Abin caricature of himself as a question mark. Invitations had been sent on his request to Harriet Weaver and T. S. Eliot. A studio party followed with a performance of the *Toy Symphony*.[8]

We had 82 guests not including the family [. . .] Hubert Foss
conducted the Toy Symphony, with [Frank] Howes, H. H., Dunton
Green, Calvo and Hugo Wortham playing toys, supplemented by
May Harrison and William Busch, [Antonio] Brosa, [May] Mukle,
Rebecca Clarke and Lauri Kennedy in the orchestra, with Ivor
Newton at the piano. It was as good a performance as last year, but
much funnier. Lauri Kennedy played the fool and asked idiotic
questions, and William Busch's cuckoo raised the roof. Foss's
conducting was great fun. He stood on the 'throne' where all could
see him.

Afterwards Mrs Kiernan [Delia Murphy] sang 'Mrs Mulligan the
Pride of the Coombe', and Dr Coyne sang 'He was a bad rogue, a
wild rogue, a rogue of high degree, and I'll tell you in a minute
what the rogue done to me!' He sang it all in one breath! Such a
feat, no singer could do it. His diction was clear and his brogue
made the song quite perfect. Jack Monsell [the novelist Margaret
Irwin's husband] sang one song with great enthusiasm but no
diction, and another, 'Phil the Fluther's Ball', very well. H. H.
accompanied this. Hugh Campbell sang, Lena sang. We went to
bed at 5 a.m. or so, having kept a running buffet since 10.30, Violet
sending up sausages and bacon and drink from the kitchen.

[SHJ, 16 March 1932]

Joyce had a fanatical admiration for the tenor John Sullivan and
hoping influential friends in London and Paris would help the singer
he brought one of these, the young Dublin barrister Michael Lennon,
to the studio to meet H. H. Joyce saw a parallel between his own
difficulties and Sullivan's. H. H. perceived something of this when,
after Joyce had told him on the telephone of another attack of iritis,
he wrote:

Isn't it odd? A man's career affecting another man's eyes! J. is
wildly Quixotic I'm afraid. My hope is that if his Sullivan plans
mature the young lawyer Lennon will take a good deal off his
shoulders. A man may be so Quixotic in one side of his nature that

his sense of humour – wonderful though it may be – fails him at a
certain crisis . . .   [H. H. to S. H., 9 August 1930]

Introduced as a friend, Lennon appeared witty, intelligent and
charming. 'As amusing as Gogarty,' Herbert wrote to Suzanne, 'and
leaving a far nicer taste in the mouth.' (H. H. to S. H., 8 August 1930)
Susie, however, judged him later as 'a simple sort of creature with
little humour'. [SHJ, 16 January 1931] There is something piquant in
the juxtaposition of these two names, for Lennon was soon to publish
a scurrilous piece on Joyce and his family in the American review
Catholic World and Gogarty to compound the treachery in his own
vicious article. Joyce never recovered from these betrayals, nor did
he return to Dublin. In the studio he talked quietly with Suzanne
about the little shops and local characters they both knew – 'Milburn
Avenue, the Butterlys, Joe, Pat Harding, the Cat and Cage, Rickard's
sweet-shop' – but although grief-stricken after the death of his father
whom he had neglected for years he refused to go back. He wrote to
Herbert, 'I could not go to see him because he lived among savages.'
Lennon's shabby article carries only one small advantage: it
demonstrates, if further proof were needed, what the writer was up
against in his native city. 'There are people,' Joyce told Colum, 'who
would refuse to sit in the same room with me.'

And yet Joyce loved the place. Old friends found the walls of the
Paris flat covered with pictures of Dublin and portraits of Dublin
personalities, pictures which would later be sold by the landlord
during World War II to cover the rent. One visitor was surprised to
find that Joyce had been to a Rugby International match. 'I had to see
the boys in green jerseys,' Joyce explained, and like so many elements
of his life this found its way into *Finnegans Wake*. He questioned
another friend about Dublin and the shops they both knew,
reminiscing as he had done with Susie. Asked why when he made
such play of being a continental all his thoughts seemed to
be about Dublin, he replied, tongue in cheek, that 'like an English
queen' and Calais, with him it would be 'Dublin' found written
on his heart. Asked by a friend why he didn't return to Dublin, he
answered, 'Have I ever left it?'

At the Euston Hotel Herbert found Joyce lying on his bed, fully dressed, with an eiderdown round his shoulders, in agony.

He was very sweet and glad to have someone to talk to. It was a return, in the sightless eye, of iritis. He confessed to me that during that little dinner at Gennaro's the pain was so deadening that he could only forget it when something especially funny or interesting was being said. (And the rest of us had been enjoying ourselves so forgetfully.)

He is obliged to stay now where he is for a few days. I spoke with him for a few minutes on the telephone this morning and he said he had a good night – he is allowed 3 aspirins a day and no more – and the pain is no worse if no better. He has a Harley St man looking at him and James told me that he only wanted the doctor to tell him what he couldn't actually <u>see</u> for himself. He knows more about his own affliction than half the specialists of Europe, I suppose . . . Lucia came in as I was sitting with him yesterday; he asked her, in Italian, to come round and look at his eyes; they spoke for a few minutes, still in Italian, and she quietly disappeared.

If he is better, and well enough to come out, I'll take him to the Promenade [concert] on Tuesday evening to hear a new work of Villa-Lobos. This might distract him for half and hour.

[H. H. to S. H., 10 August 1930]

When J. J. was in good form, as he was during a lunch at the Commercio, he told stories. One was of 'a crook and his lady taking him and Nora to lunch pretending that they were friends of Augustus John. When they vanished one afternoon the hotel people opened their suitcases only to find them full of potatoes!' Another story was of a horse in Paris called Largo 'who unseated his jockey and ran around the course 1½ times'. He added, 'If I knew where he was now, I'd send him a bag of oats!' [SHJ, 17 May 1931]

After one Sunday afternoon's music in the studio the Joyces stayed on. Having yelled a few days earlier about Sullivan, J. J. was now being threatened by Nora 'with all sorts'. As Suzanne noted, although he was dying to begin he didn't – except for screaming, 'Cane!' when

34

they put on a record of Gigli. He began to sing himself and that seemed to soothe him down.

Nora confided her anxieties to Susie, especially the crippling effect on J. J. of even a small quantity of white wine, and it was rarely limited to that. (A companion of Joyce's once told Padraic Colum, 'He gets drunk in the legs, not the head.') 'At times two glasses of wine render him helpless,' Nora explained, apologising for her severity. She had misgivings about accepting invitations of which there were a great many during this London visit. Should they go to the O'Connors'? In the event all went well. There was salmon from the Shannon and champagne. The younger ones sat at a side table with Lucia. Herbert played and Joyce sang – 'Youth and Folly' and other ballads many of them from his father's repertoire. In May 1931, J. J. wrote to Sylvia Beach that there were only two people he had seen in London, 'T. S. E[liot] and Hughes' – not exactly true, but that had been his intention. Indeed Joyce and Herbert and their wives spent a succession of evenings together, at Covent Garden, in restaurants, and often in the company of John Dulanty the IFS High Commissioner. Susie remembered a notorious evening which started at the RAC. The other guests were John Dulanty, his assistant T. J. Kiernan and the Joyces.

It began very gravely with a lot of dignity but gradually it became merry and noisy especially when J. J. got on to the subject of Sullivan. We finished the evening at the HC's office in Piccadilly. Joyce sang and shouted, such top notes! He became quite excited, singing 'Nicka nicka norum when the weather was hot, hah!' The HC (who called himself the Low Commissioner) obliged with 'The Auld Orange Flute'. It was all very funny and very Irish. The HC hired a Daimler and drove us all home. In the car he and Joyce sang 'I'll be your sweetheart, if you will be mine' and there were shouts of 'Vive Sullivan!' from Joyce in spite of all Nora's efforts to restrain him. He had screamed it in the offices and on the stairs, and gone back again with Dulanty. Then Herbert, Nora and I could hear them singing at the tops of their voices. Nora had to go upstairs and bring them down.   [SHJ, 30 May 1931]

In his youth Joyce used to sing his vast repertoire strutting in the vaudeville style with cane and eyeglass. The words which Susie had caught in flight on this occasion were shreds from the refrain of a serenade.[9]

When the following year there was a dinner at Kettner's with the Joyces, their son Giorgio and daughter-in-law, the mood was sombre. Susie put this down to J. J.'s bitterness – his blindness, the banning of his books and his failure to promote Sullivan. A dinner at Scotts with the Lynds was a happier affair, a funny and mad evening which ended up at Church Street. James Joyce sang and Lucia danced.

> H.'s contribution to the evening was to organise a prohibition meeting in the salle de bains to the detriment of all the males concerned. [SHJ, 28 June 1931]

There were many shared evenings at the opera – *La Forza del Destino*, *Turandot*, *Bohème*, *Fedora*. On 17 June they all went to *Tosca*. 'Stabile was too kindly for Scarpia,' Susie thought, 'though he sang well. Pertile was well up to his usual low standard.' '[J. J.] was very piano and good,' Suzanne noted after *Gianni Schicchi*. 'He was alarmed about a blister on his finger so I went with him to Boots.' [SHJ, 17 and 29 June 1931]

'Letter from H. H. full of news,' Suzanne wrote in her journal on holiday in Jersey.

> The *Morning Post* has found out through Somerset House that the Covent Garden Syndicate mortgaged the subsidy to the tune of £16,000. James Joyce has married his wife Nora!!! He would never surprise me. [SHJ, 6 July 1931]

'You will notice in the *DT* today a report of Joyce's marriage,' Herbert had told her:

> The office rang me up about it just as I was dressing for the opera and asked me if I could get into touch with J. I was extremely embarrassed and just as I was going to ring him up he rang me. Immediately I said, 'What's your news?' He chuckled, and I laughed. I said the office had rung me up. He said the papers had

been pestering him all day and he refused to say anything except through his solicitors. As his mood was happy enough I daringly asked him if it was true and he said it was. Then he hitched off to ask me if I could dine chez Lynds at Hampstead, but I explained that I was on duty and I had scarcely finished dressing when a wire came from Sylvia asking me to dine. So that's that.

[H. H. to S. H., 4 July 1931]

Life was soon to become more difficult for both men, Joyce suffering from his eye trouble and in continuing anguish over Lucia's mysterious and threatening illness, Herbert anxiously looking for another job after his departure from the *Daily Telegraph*.

In 1934 Joyce sent H. H. a postcard asking: 'J. J. would like to know why J. J. never receives a word from H. H. Are these old next-door neighbours no longer on writing terms?' Herbert responded by sending a cross. Joyce replied: 'This blessing is valid.' They met again and for the last time in Paris in 1935.

Lucia Joyce came to tea with us at Church Street several times and I remember her dancing round the nursery to our delight. No wonder she 'got on well with the children', as Susie reported, she of the rhythmical name, the light which her father was fighting not to lose. She read to me while my mother bathed Helena, and read to Helena when my turn came. Like many fathers in such cases, Joyce was slow to measure the severity of her illness. Or was he, in his heart of hearts? Soon family life would be disrupted by her violence and friendships skewed by her allegations. A supplementary hell.

Padraic Colum spotted in a letter from Joyce that of all the names mentioned as his life became more sombre the only one with no painful association was Herbert Hughes's – 'a transition between the lively times and the subdued ones . . . Halcyon days and ambrosial nights had, after the sessions with Hughes, no recurrence.'[10]

(ii)

V. S. Pritchett wrote of James Stephens, 'If only one could have preserved a line or two from . . . that nimble little gnome!' for Stephens was a captivating talker with a head full of fantasy. He was generally believed by the Irish circle in London to share Joyce's and Herbert's birthdate, 1882, and much was made of this when in fact it was perhaps wishful thinking: brought up in an orphanage after his father's death, Stephens's birthdate was unknown. But what matter? He was to have taken over the completion of *Finnegans Wake* if Joyce failed to do so. The combination of initials J. J. and S. with its associations with Irish whiskey pleased Joyce. Poet, novelist and short-story writer, Stephens had found success with his philosophical fairy tale 'The Crock of Gold'. For a time he was Registrar of the National Gallery of Ireland under Robert Langton Douglas, but by 1930 both men were living in London where Langton Douglas gave a very Irish dinner.

> Jean Douglas and Ernest Boyd telephoned me and invited me to dine even if H. was engaged – they said he could turn up afterwards. I cooked his dinner and then dressed.
>
> I was just in time at Hill St. It was a splendid little dinner party. I sat between Langton Douglas and James Stephens . . . Douglas has travelled a great deal and knows all kinds of people. He was amusing about the Irish. He'd like to endow a college and send them all back to Ireland to found a seat of learning – Colum, Stephens, Joyce, [George] Moore, [Ernest] Boyd and all the rest. He'd have cloisters and a common dining hall where they could eat or not as they wished, and they could have their wives to live there too. It would be fun to see this in operation. James Joyce, James Stephens, Padraic Colum, Seán O'Casey – there would be some grand differences of opinion to be sure!
>
> Stephens is a fantastic little fellow with funny dark eyes not quite straight, his evening clothes sprinkled with fluff. If he had money, he said, he's give it away, a thousand here, a thousand there, sometimes to a poor man in the street. When I said this mightn't make for happiness he said, 'You can't make anyone

happy: it's inside them or not. If a man wants to get drunk, let him. He's miserable when he isn't drunk.' I wish I could recall all the wonderful things he said so passionately. He talked of the sixth sense which man will develop later, that of being able to penetrate another's mind, to enjoy another man's smoke, or drink, or even his wife. He told me how he used to sit staring at a cat for hours trying to penetrate its mind, or he would sit in front of a flower and think of nothing else.[11]   [SHJ, 27 January 1930]

*   *   *

'Ah you have to persecute people,' Seán O'Casey replied at a St Patrick's Day reception when Suzanne had voiced her misgivings about Hitler. 'Amn't I persecuted every day I get out of my bed?' Herbert was invited to provide music for a new play *Within the Gates*.

'It's a queer play,' Suzanne wrote,

> woven round the people who inhabit Hyde Park, the Marble Arch end – preachers, nurses, soldiers, prostitutes, a gardener, a bishop, down-and-outs . . . The dreamer who is the central figure must be Seán himself.   [SHJ, 15 August 1933][12]

A day with the O'Caseys at Chalfont St Giles left Herbert charmed by the family and optimistic about the work . He had seen *The Silver Tassie* in 1929 with scenery by Augustus John and Suzanne recalled being 'awed by it all and thrilled . . . Good luck to Seán anyway!' [SHJ, 11 October 1929] But the euphoria didn't last into this new production. There seems to have been resentment later over Herbert's need to be paid for his work. 'Some of this had to be shared with the musician Herbert Hughes who had arranged the simple tunes Seán had provided,' Eileen O'Casey wrote balefully of an advance that was badly needed. Herbert had no taste for arguing over money and when a royalty cheque arrived from Macmillan's, publishers of the play, Suzanne commented that this was 'some compensation' – a sad postscript to a collaboration. Seán came to a party in the studio with an eloquent elbow sticking out of a persecuted hole in his jersey.

*   *   *

The Irish High Commissioner John Dulanty was seen by many as little more than a socialite. He was indeed a great party-giver and party-goer but he drew a firm line between carousing and politics. Behind the gregarious and charming exterior was a serious diplomat scrupulously discreet in his work which in the Anglo-Irish climate of the thirties was delicate and demanding. With the release of British and Irish papers he is now shown to have played a far more important role in the difficult Anglo-Irish relations of the 1930s than most people thought. He was the only messenger between the two governments until 1939.

Among his admirers were George Bernard Shaw, Winston Churchill, whose political campaign he had helped in 1908 and who remained a friend right until the 1939 war, and de Valera, who admired his understanding of the British political scene. Vincent Massey, his Canadian opposite number, found him engaging, lovable and witty.

It fell to Dulanty to deliver the 'Note' of March 1932 whereby de Valera abolished the Land Annuities paid by the Free State to Britain. He argued that they were illegal, having been neither published not ratified by the Dáil. The British, still hoping to cancel debts to America and initially outraged, agreed to set up a Commonwealth Tribunal in Ottawa to examine the question, at which Dulanty would be a negotiator. The abolition of the Land Annuities was only one of de Valera's demands; others would follow to support his own credibility at home.

> Called on Bessie Foxe [Dulanty's secretary] at the HC's office and met there a Mr Conlan full of auld chat like most of our race. We discussed de Valera's programme. Bessie adheres to the Treaty and he inclines towards the Fianna Fáil party. Personally I think de Valera would have no platform unless he differed strongly from Cosgrave. The late President [Cosgrave] was a great little man and won the respect of all nations. Bessie says Dulanty is very quiet and depressed these days, and no wonder: everything is held up because of the Note. [SHJ, 6 April 1932]

Bessie [Foxe] is sick about de Valera but Kiernan is obviously in his heart of hearts a supporter of this strange patriot. He says England doesn't really care about the Annuities but they want to get rid of de Valera. The President is arriving today and Kiernan is going to meet him. This tariff will hurt England as well as Ireland.

[SHJ, 15 July 1932]

And it did. Following 'a prolonged bout of shadow-boxing'[13] there was indeed a loss of trade in England and Scotland, exacerbated by world depression and increased unemployment. Only in 1938 with the Finance and Trade Agreements did this trade war ease.

Dulanty has been described as enigmatic; he was certainly prudent, leaving no papers since he preferred to conduct business by direct contact. Occupied with haggling over cattle exports from Ireland and coal imports from Britain, and being an approachable soul, he was often asked for the latest news but with no success. However his convivial nature was well ingrained and it took little to persuade him to prolong an evening, especially when John McCormack was in town. McCormack had an inexhaustible fund of musical gossip and told Susie about Toscanini whom he admired for his simplicity: the great conductor considered himself unworthy to conduct *Parsifal*. According to McCormack, Furtwängler is supposed to have said of Toscanini, 'Not bad for an old man.'

Late nights held no fears for McCormack and he could be merciless.

We felt very tired after a late night. H. tried to work and we went to bed early. John McCormack dragged us by telephone out of our bed at midnight. We dressed and went to the Mayfair and found MacSweeney [McCormack's business manager] and Dulanty there, having had a long evening together. We stayed up all night talking. Poor Dulanty had to go to the Wheat Conference at 10 a.m. John and Mac were trying to prise Irish news out of him but the only answer they could get was 'I'm Jones of the Lancers' or 'Poor Devil-may-care'. Dulanty is no fool. [SHJ, 23 August 1933]

Paul Henry came for the evening, Mac [Dr Kiernan] and Dulanty with three delegates to the Indian Trade Talks. Dulanty brought his luggage (3 bottles of J. J.!). He kept breaking into 'You are My Heart's Delight'. Clery (a delegate) obliged with a dreadful song. Having asked H. to make sympathetic noises on the piano, he proceeded to wander into about 7 different keys for each verse. No sooner had H. got the key than Clery departed from it. Clery told Dulanty that he spoiled all his arguments by extreme verbosity. The HC took it well. His generosity, his humour and his charm must be a great asset to Ireland just now when the Irish are almost in disgrace from the English political point of view. Dulanty has been threatening the Indians that Ireland would now only drink China tea. But if Ireland were deprived of Indian tea of the strongest blend I think there would be a revolution.

[SHJ, 13 April 1934]

*   *   *

Robert Flaherty's celebrated film *Man of Aran* came to London in April 1934, a masterly picture of island life of the harshest kind, one woman and five men searching for soil to grow vegetables, harvesting kelp, fishing in a threatening sea. The islanders came to London, including Pat Mullen. Dulanty gave a brilliant party for him to which he invited T. S. Eliot, Walter de la Mare and J. B. Morton ('Beach-comber'). Suzanne observed the islander receiving his guests, 'a fine man in grey tweeds with a grey woolly pullover up to the neck, shy and a little nervous'. [SHJ, 11 October 1934]

Dulanty's assistant Dr T. J. Kiernan ('Mac') was married to the ballad-singer Delia Murphy ('Murphs') whom I can remember as having an overwhelming, almost penetrating personality and a very arresting husky voice. Mac and Suzanne occasionally disagreed, even or perhaps especially at the end of a party:

We began our Irish festivities [part one of St Patrick's Day] with a party at the Lynds. It went on till 3.30 a.m. The guests included Mary and J. B. Morton, the Priestleys, the Kiernans, Dulanty, Rose Macaulay, the Gollanczes, Lionel Hale, Jack Squire (unbidden and fortified with strong waters), Alan Thomas, etc. Dulanty too was greatly stimulated and literally took the floor. There were literary games, songs, recitations and stories and conversations. We left innocently meaning to go home, but the HC offered us a lift and furthermore hospitality at Piccadilly House. There were more songs and stories until 6 a.m. It was a beautiful morning. We went to Lyons Corner House and had breakfast and read the newspapers. I had a lovely argument with Dr Kiernan on the subject of rivalry among women. He gently reproached me for admiring a lady, assured me that no woman sincerely admired another. In every lovely female she saw a possible rival, and no man, said the learned doctor, would tell his wife where he saw Beauty. This must be continued later . . .

At 8 a.m. we walked into the nursery as Mlle and the children were having breakfast. Mlle burst into tears. She thought we had been run over or something equally frightful, woke at 3 a.m., thought she had heard the telephone, phoned the Lynds, we had left, and as we didn't arrive until 8 a.m. she spent the rest of the time imagining the worst. After soothing her down we had hot baths and went to Mass and then to bed and wiped out the whole day. As I was sleeping at about 10.30 a.m. Jo Jones and Gwen McCormack both rang. I had to be very alert, so that spoiled most of my sleep.

In the evening we went to the Critics' Circle dinner at the Trocadero. [SHJ, 11 March 1933]

When the Kiernans left with their four children for a stay on the Aran Islands they were given a great send-off at Euston. Mac looked exhausted. Murphs looked well but must have been tired with Orla in her arms Colm hanging on and the two larger ones Blon and Nuala doing their best. Colm thought he would make a scene. He lay down on the platform. Herbert gave him his hand and led him gently towards the train. I asked him afterwards how he had persuaded the little boy to get up and he said, 'Oh, I just made my hand soft.' [SHJ, 4 May 1934]

One of the older Kiernan children, Blon or Nuala, told Susie a long story which finished like this:

'And so . . . ' The child paused, the better to pick up the

momentum. 'The little boy went off and fetched a very, very long ladder. Then he started to climb up to Heaven.'

'And . . . ?'

'And it was very high up. After a long time he got to the top . . . '

'And then . . . ?'

'And then God put out His head and said, "Will ye get down out o' that?" '

*   *   *

One look at me, newly-born, and John McCormack said to Herbert, 'Well you can't deny that one!' A few years later Susie wrote after a studio supper party:

> John has had a bad press. Teddy [Schneider, his accompanist] thinks they don't want him in England.[14] But he didn't deserve the slating he got from *The Times*, *Morning Post* and *Observer*. E[rnest] N[ewman] wrote a special article about his Hugo Wolf and that seemed to console him.
>
> Herbert so tired. He really mustn't be allowed to get so fagged out.   [SHJ, 16 November 1930]

McCormack gave few recitals which didn't include some of H. H.'s songs. Edwin ('Teddy') Schneider was his accompanist from 1912 until McCormack retired from the American concert circuit in 1937. Discreet and self-effacing, he had a great influence on the singer and has certainly not received the credit he deserved. Chicago-born but of German extraction and ten years older than McCormack, Schneider coached him in German lieder and his quiet temperament made him on long tours the ideal companion for a singer plagued, like so many great artists, with pre-concert nerves. In 1928 McCormack was created Papal Count (a hereditary title) and as Private Chamberlain to the Pope in a splendid uniform his duty was to usher in visitors to the audiences. Although a hugely successful singer his sense of humour saved him from arrogance. He spent some time in Hollywood singing like an angel in a mediocre film and enjoying life in the little colony of English actors. Later he remarked to Suzanne that he thought his lack of sex appeal was responsible for his failure as a film star. 'The girls who go to the pictures never want to sleep with me,' he sighed. [SHJ, 20 April 1932]

The 1930 Celtic Congress sponsored by the Gaelic League was one of those pleasing initiatives which don't quite come off. Suzanne didn't need much persuading to attend a committee meeting and as always saw the funny side of proceedings.

It was marvellous – Welsh, Cornish, Scottish, Breton and Irish. M. de la Rue, the Breton, said that unless the Congress helped Brittany towards freedom he feared the Bretons would have none of it. He opposed inviting John McCormack to sing, though *en même temps* suggesting Compton Mackenzie as President *au lieu de* Lord Howard de Walden. The Gaelic League want everything in Gaelic where singing is concerned. The Welsh will have none of Augustus John: 'He's not Welsh,' quoth they. One of the two Cornish speakers is on the committee. The Scots are represented by an immaculate young man in a dove-grey double-breasted waist-coat, the Manx by a fervent young woman with a lot of sense called Mona Douglas. The meeting took place in a Welsh chapel in the Charing Cross Road. I promised to write to John [McCormack] and ask him to sing.   [SHJ, 7 May 1930]

But there were other problems.

Kiernan has to mollify the Gaelic League who although they want their songs only in Gaelic will be getting their lectures in English. Their argument is that other Celtic countries might like to discuss the lectures together, whereas music can be enjoyed without knowing what it is about. Isn't that funny? To be really consistent the Gaelic league should insist that all the Celtic countries speak each other's languages: they should at once set about learning Cornish, Breton, Welsh and Highland Scottish to give a good example.   [SHJ, 13 May 1930]

Insufficiently publicised, the matinée at His Majesty's Theatre made no money in spite of a bill which included McCormack, Beatrice Harrison, Plunket Greene and Megan Foster. There were other diversions to follow that day.

45

In the evening we went to the Lord Mayor's reception at the Mansion House. I didn't feel in the least civic: I felt romantic. I adored their furs and chains and ceremonials, their gold plate and their funny Egyptian hall which is not Egyptian. We didn't like the poor little choristers and Miss Dylis Jones or her accompanist – he played all the wrongest notes he could think of! We danced and talked the hours away until midnight. I met Mrs Hugh Kennedy [wife of the Irish Chief Justice], dressed like a village-play Celtic queen in cotton poplin with cardboard crown.[15] It is of her that [the painter] Paul Henry tells this story: she sent out invitations for a garden party in Gaelic which when translated read, 'You are requested to come lusting with us in our cabbage patch.'

[SHJ, 22 July 1930]

Two days later, after the Buckingham Palace garden party where the Kneller Hall band and chorus had sung H. H.'s nursery rhyme part-song 'Dr Foster went to Gloster', they went to Romano's to celebrate with the KC Martin O'Connor.

Mrs Hugh Kennedy and I were on either side of Martin O'Connor and we argued of course. She has very provincial ideas about music, morals and life in general. After I had been holding forth my host said that he had been listening to me with interest and that I was made to fill some high position. Whereupon I accused him of making fun of me. 'No,' he said in his firm Kerry voice, 'I always make a rule of speaking nothing but the truth' (pause) 'outside a court of justice.' I danced with him. He was no syncopator but he held one firmly enough. He said, 'I don't know what's coming over the girls they are sending over from Ireland nowadays. They have no physique.' And at that word he took a tighter hold.

[SHJ, 24 July 1930]

A Saturday call from Teddy Schneider announced that John and Lily McCormack wanted to come to Chelsea the following evening. Herbert invited them to a studio picnic. Suzanne's hair stood on end but she worked all Sunday and it was a jolly party with Hamilton Harty and 'Beachcomber' and his wife, followed by a dozen people after supper. Johnny Morton ('Beachcomber') brought us his new children's book. Helena wanted to sing but it was thought better that we 'trot off to bed'.

> McCormack was mobbed by everyone, and ended up the evening singing quietly at the piano with Herbert. The guests didn't leave until 4 a.m. Katherine and Peter North stayed until the end, and Peter confided that he had been called to the Palace to photograph Princess Marina in her wedding dress. He said it was an ordeal because Prince Nicholas was there fussing, also Molyneux the couturier and Queen Mary. It would be excellent publicity for Peter but he wasn't allowed to mention this. 'The Palace has rung him twice to tell him not to let it get into the Press.'
>
> [SHJ, 24 November 1934]

*   *   *

Born in Co. Mayo, Margaret Bourke Sheridan became Margherita Sheridan for an operatic career which started well. She sang *Andrea Chénier* and *La Wally* at La Scala. She was invited to the US and to Covent Garden. She sang with Gigli and other famous Italian singers but she was short of ambition. Susie had been to see her in Milan in 1925:

> I went to see Peggie in the morning. She has signed a contract to sing Andrea Chénier and La Wally at the Scala this season and she is up in the air, fussing over clothes and things. She doesn't want to go to America at all, wants to stay in Italy which she loves. The various tenors who return tell her how unhappy she'd be, she who conforms to no social life, refuses to go out at night and meet people and so on. Anyway she dreads Chicago. She expects to sing at Covent Garden this season.
>
> Herbert was able to get only one seat for Zandonai's new opera Il Cavaliere [di] Ekebu, so I went with Peggie to the Londra. Though she loves Italy I find her extraordinarily aloof from everything. It makes me wonder if as an artist she won't suffer on that account, for must not an artist have immense sympathy and understanding? I suppose she feels she needs all her strength of mind in this difficult

life so full of intrigue and rivalry. H. was very late getting back from la Scala. He thought the production marvellous in every detail. He met Beaumont, the Italian correspondent of the *Daily Telegraph*.[16]

[SHJ, 7 March 1925]

Two days before a Covent Garden performance of *Otello* with Mariano Stabile and Renato Zanelli, Peggie told Suzanne that she was very frightened since there was to be no orchestral rehearsal. When the day came she was far too nervous to do herself justice. Her apparent lack of purpose allied to a beautiful voice puzzled and exasperated her friends. As I remember her, she was fair-haired with blue eyes and a highly-coloured complexion, possibly enhanced by my father's hospitality. Although she was short and round La Sheridan's leave-taking was ceremonious, a rite punctuating a visit to the studio. Helena and I watched her in admiration as she drew her fur coat majestically over her bosom very slowly left and very slowly right with the reverential care of a sacristan putting away liturgical artefacts.

*   *   *

The poet and mystic George Russell ('A. E.') was exasperated with Ireland's conversion from poetic to bourgeois. He called the unfree Free State with its censorship 'a nation run by louts' and moved to England after the death of his wife in 1932. Once he was there although he liked London he thought England was a dead country with very nice people and like many Irishmen he intended to return to Dublin at a later date.[17] Yeats, whose approach to mysticism was different, thought A. E.'s poetry was uneven in its 'vast and vague' Celtic extravagance. A. E.'s rather Blakelike painting influenced by Theosophical theory was designed to express the mystic harmony of the universe but he lacked technique, failing sometimes to manage his paints or his palette. On the other hand he was a riveting speaker (chiefly in monologues), an excellent and hard-hitting writer on practical matters and an outstanding social reformer. His dream was that the elements of his life – the mystic and the social – would merge into some divine whole in the youngish twentieth century for which, at its start, he had great hopes. Or rather he had had: the new century was producing disorder and violence.

The rumpled tweed which looked to James Stephens 'as if it had been put on with a shovel' and A. E.'s untidy russet beard, together with his out-of-world experiences, led to his nickname 'the hairy fairy'.[18] The abstemious mystic whose only luxury was his pipe sat in his editorial office accepting all callers, patiently listening to aspiring writers, lending his books which were rarely returned and decorating the walls with his murals. That he was the nearest thing to a saint was Yeats's wife George's opinion of A. E.; she added crisply to her husband, 'You are a better poet but no saint.'

> A. E. recited some poems. He asked me the difference between ale and beer. He said, 'I read about it in G. K. Chesterton's books,' as if it were some mysterious beverage. Talking of Ireland he said that the people didn't think properly. There was no philosophy in Gaelic literature. They were never conquered by the Romans and that is one reason why they are different, etc. . . .
>
> [SHJ, 17 September 1933]

*   *   *

In the autumn of 1928 H. H. and Sir Richard Terry were called as expert witnesses in the Clandillon case in Dublin. In his journal *The Irish Statesman* A. E. had published a scathing review by the scholar Donal O'Sullivan of a collection of Irish songs. The article had attacked a rash of errors and omissions which badly let down Irish scholarship.[19] The compilers sued O'Sullivan, A. E. and *The Irish Statesman* for libel. The musicians' testimony full of minute technical details was totally incomprehensible to most of those present and the case was eventually dismissed. A. E., however, was faced with enormous costs and the paper was only saved by a subscription raised by friends.

'The Court sat late,' H. H. wrote to Suzanne,

> and the preliminary passages have been dull and routiny. Three-quarters of an hour for lunch which I had tête-à-tête with A. E.. in a small restaurant where we were the only occupants. A. E. is

devoted to Arnold Bax: told me he had known him for several years and had spent a holiday with him in Donegal before he realised he was a musician. [H. H. to S. H., 29 October 1928]

The composer Arnold Bax had originally come to Dublin with his brother Clifford, drawn there by the poetry of W. B. Yeats. Soon they were part of A. E.'s circle. Arnold was an English Celtomaniac who wore a kilt and spoke Gaelic with such regularity that the mild A. E. was driven to reproach him for speaking to people in a language they didn't understand. Since Arnold was doubtful about A. E.'s visions while A. E. (as he wrote to Lady Gregory) couldn't tell one note from another it would be interesting to know what exchange they had in Donegal; to A. E., Clifford Bax recalled, they were all 'shadows and listeners'.[20] Since at the end of the holiday A. E. was still unaware that Arnold was a musician it is quite likely that the latter hadn't got a word in edgeways.

PART TWO

Two Worlds

5

Immersion

Although at certain moments he liked to imagine moving to Italy or the west of Ireland, Herbert would never have put London behind him. As for Susie, the thought of conventional country life filled her with unremitting horror like the prospect of a dull boarding school – what would she do for conversation? She preferred to ignore where town ended and country began.

We had hoped for an early night but Jimmy Field called with his large touring Buick and took us into the country or at least into Richmond, Putney or thereabouts. [SHJ, 21 June 1929]

'I wasted a whole day going to Dymchurch,' she wrote after searching for a holiday house and enduring the 'inefficiency of the Southern Railway',

a ghastly little place on the Romney Marshes. The only thing I loved was the Light Railway from Hythe to Dymchurch. I got home exhausted having been cured of all desire for Kent in July!
[SHJ, 7 March 1930]

Going abroad was another matter. In April 1929, H. H. covered the ISCM Festival (International Society for Contemporary Music) for the *Daily Telegraph* in Geneva and Paris.

H. sent to a rehearsal at the Grand Théâtre. I rambled through the markets. There was a fierce high penetrating wind blowing and the sun shining. Food is dearer in the markets than in England. I read *La Vie amoureuse de Chopin* by Emile Vuillermoz, then lunched with H.
Went to the first orchestral concert, and heard works by Roger Sessions (Brooklyn), Henriette Bormans (Dutch), Marcel Delannoy

(French), Frank Martin (Swiss). Nothing too wild but all original. I liked much of Roger Sessions' Symphony and all of Fou de la dame. Met Dunton Green, Richard Capell, Harriet Cohen. Her kittenish ways are most embarrassing especially when one hasn't seen her for ages. We glimpsed the reception in the Foyer and slipped out and home to bed.   [SHJ, 6 April 1929]

Met H. for a chamber music concert. The quartet (Julius Schloss) I followed for a little while and then was lost. I liked the five Variations (Viktor Ullmann) and the Violin Sonata (Erwin Schulhoff). We lunched at the Café Musée, all quiet. H. wrote his telegrams and I read rude French comics. Afternoon concert at Victoria Hall of Czech choral music. The Jánacek Mass was thrilling.

At the Metropole banquet we sat with Richard Capell, Frank Howes, Norman Peterkin, [Edwin] Evans, Anthony Bernard, etc. Quite a pleasant affair with speeches afterwards by [Ernest] Ansermet, [Edward J.] Dent and a Councillor of State. We finished up by dancing to music which drove poor R. C. [Richard Capell] into the night. We were amused by Dent's references to the 'admirable et adorable Ansermet'.   [SHJ, 7 April 1929]

We lunched at the Café de la Couronne and went to the 2nd chamber concert. H. had writing to do – Fitelberg's String Quartet and Madeleine Grey singing beautiful songs by Delage. Afterwards we finished up in a little café playing dominoes with the others.
                [SHJ, 8 April 1929]

We had the pleasure of meeting Dommen Minor from Repton. He is music mad. His people want him to go into business and he may have to do so. Meanwhile he is spending his own pocket money on this jaunt to hear new music. He is seventeen and the most charming young thing I've ever met – clever, witty and humble withal. After the last concert (*Flos Campi* of Vaughan Williams and Max Butting's Symphony) we all went to the Café Lyrique and the whole crowd was there. I introduced Dommen Minor to all and he was quite excited. He spoke well and made them all laugh by saying that Dr Stocks, the music master at Repton, claims to have introduced Debussy and Ravel to England.   [SHJ, 9 April 1929]

We left Geneva for Montreux where Jo Jones joined us. A perfect afternoon, first boating and then having tea and dancing in the Café des Sports.   [SHJ, Vevey, 10 April 1929]

Spent the morning at Père Lachaise and covered Chopin's grave with forget-me-nots.[1] There were other fresh flowers there, little bunches of violets and pansies. The sun shone, all was still and the birds singing wildly. We paid homage to poor Oscar Wilde. There's a poem on Epstein's monument about outcasts knowing how to mourn.[2] We saw Musset's tomb with an acacia tree over it, and the tombs of Cherubini, Rossini and Balzac. From there we went to the Majestic and lunched with Backhaus and his wife. He played for us afterwards.

From there to the rue de Verneuil to have tea with Mr and Mrs [Jan] Hambourg. They have a charming flat with old furniture and ultra-modern pictures. We found them delightful, Jan very conscious of the limelight, talking well but with an eye to his audience . . . I was surprised that Jan who is so keen on modern pictures has no ear for modern music. We arrived at Rollo Myers' flat in avenue Sully Prud'homme at 7 o'clock and found the Baronne Olga von Falz Fein there, also Wilenski and his wife. We had apéritifs of all sorts and then at the Auberge du Père Louis we had a delicious dinner. Then on to El Prado, a Russian haunt, and ended finally at Le Grand Ecart, a very chic dancing place designed by Jean Cocteau, walls of corrugated brown paper, black floors, tables with glass boxes of flowers, all charming, coloured band. We danced and admired the youth and beauty sparkling with jewels. From there to Les Plantations for bacon and eggs and so to bed.
                                    [SHJ, Paris, 13 April 1929]

Went to the Ritz for an apéritif before going to Loch's apartment. It was like stepping out of Paris into an American liner.

Loch's place is in the rue du Faubourg S. Honoré. He finds the work exacting as he is never free except for holidays once a year.

His wife is in England with their boys aged three and six. We bought English Sunday papers, read them in a café and then promptly abandoned them as they were so heavy.

At Rollo Myers' party we met the Baronne, the Wilenskis and Gordon Craig.[3] We told the latter our stories of his mother [Ellen Terry] and had some interesting conversation.

[SHJ, 15 April 1929]

For the last time we went to the Deux Magots, had lunch at the Danube [Hotel], spent the afternoon shopping in the rue de Rivoli. Wandered round the Porte d'Orléans and on to tea at Baronne von Falz Fein's flat. Gordon Craig, Wilenski and Myers were there. Craig talked of Shaw and said he was a pike. He has 500 letters from Shaw to his mother and asked G. B. S. if he minded publication. Shaw said they should be in the BM. Craig says he'd like to burn them. He says G. B. S. tried for eight years to get his mother to leave the Lyceum to play in his plays. Craig is off to America and hates the thought of lecturing. He said of Miss Baylis that she is one of the twenty people in England who prevent other people from doing things. We were so sad at bidding them farewell. The Baronne's little boy, a fine fellow of 6 years, was dressed in a yellow Russian shirt. She showed us pictures of her home and told us an old man was burned who refused to go, much like the old servant in *The Cherry Orchard* (or Cherry Garden as she says it should be). She also told me that the Soviets won't permit 1st and 2nd class in the trains, only Hard and Soft Seats. Dined at S. Cécile, and a last visit to La Coupole. Left Paris at 9 for Dieppe.

[SHJ, 16 April 1929]

Two years later H. H.'s work took them to Germany and Austria.

Monday 7 September 1931

How am I to account for all we did since July 18th?

Anyway it was a bad crossing Jersey–St-Malo and a beastly French boat: dirty greasy-looking crew and an old peasant woman lying on deck violently sick, making woeful and most indelicate noises. I caught a rapide to Paris and was there before Herbert. I took a walk to the Coupole and had tea and read a paper for an hour and then sauntered back to the station and spotted Herbert sitting in a café having an amer picon. I had one too. We had so much to talk about. We dined at the Coupole and went from there to the Gare de l'Est. I was thrilled – my first visit to Germany. We had Czechs in our carriage, two men and a woman, and we conversed somehow, a bit of French, a bit of German. Then one of them got out a phrase book and began to teach me Czech. That passed the time. We got coffee through the window at Kehl [?]. It rained and rained. There were floods everywhere. Arrived Bayreuth about 5.30. The next four days were very full.

H. interviewed Winifred Wagner (Siegfried's widow).

Wagner's daughter-in-law, the English-born Winifred, had lost her husband Siegfried the year before. Overnight, like Wagner's widow Cosima before her, she had become an outsider, but from being in the eyes of the old guard not Teutonic enough she swiftly became *plus royaliste que le roi* as she strode forcefully into her new role. Finesse was alien to her and she dealt with the two conductors Furtwängler and Toscanini with little sensitivity. She was irritated by Furt-wängler's manager Dr Berta Geissmar and referred to her as 'the Jewess'. Infatuated with Hitler (who was not yet in power) she followed the Nazi precepts for wholesome German womanhood and wore little or no make-up or jewellery. 'She talked sense and looked beautiful – ' Suzanne observed,

> not smart at all, but a face full of expression, a lovely woman with no artificial aid of any sort. I doubt if she even uses powder! All around the theatre in the sunshine were little groups of artists and conductors chatting, the whole place seemed to be working up to the climax of the opening on the morrow.

Tuesday 21 July 1931
You wouldn't dream there was a financial crisis in Germany, to look at the cars and the German audience. The townspeople come up the hill and stand by to see the people arriving, many in full evening dress at 4 p.m. The spike-helmeted police keep them toeing

the line. We saw *Tannhäuser* with Melchoir and Maria Müller, and Toscanini conducting. Above all I loved Müller as Elisabeth.

Local retailers who might have expected good business during the Festival complained afterwards that the well-heeled visitors had spent little; they had moreover attracted a good number of thieves to the town. Nevertheless the 1931 Festival had been successful and had boosted the tourist trade.

I can't now remember all the details of these wonderful days at Bayreuth with Toscanini and Furtwängler, the concealed orchestra, the audience full of reverence, the walks and talks in the woods in the hour-long intervals. Those are things I shall never forget. Of course we visited the Eule and stayed up much too late, in fact the night before we left we didn't go to bed at all. At lunch we met Géza de Kresz, the leader of the Hart House Quartet. That night we had supper with him and an international crowd of musicians at the Hotel Post – Carl Flesch among them, also Basil Cameron. At 2 a.m. we descended upon the Eule and stayed there until 6, in company with Bockelmann and others. Friday morning was sunny and as we went out on the Market Street Bockelmann sang. Some of the townspeople protested from their windows. Herbert, Basil Cameron and I went to the station and had black coffee so as to keep awake. At the hotel they were amused at us. The maid was full of smiles and helped us stuff in our belongings, and heaven only knows how we caught that train to Munich. We dozed and dozed and arrived at Salzburg at about tea-time.

We stayed at the Oesterreichischerhof with a room on the Salzach – what a view! We decided that Mozart must have been inspired by this swiftly flowing stream. We heard concerts and operas – it was a short feast – la Scala and Mariano Stabile (as always superb), the Vienna Philharmonic with Dohnányi conducting his own [Hungarian Radio] orchestra, also Mozart's Mass in B flat [K 275] at the Cathedral – it was gay and glorious, although I didn't like the casual behaviour of the congregation. But the orchestra makes such a difference. I wish we had orchestras in our Catholic churches, at least in the cities.

In Munich we saw *Don Giovanni* and *Lohengrin*. Why, oh why can we never have the Don in London? The German audiences are reverential and listening to music with them is an experience in itself. We were very sorry to leave Germany.

Long journey to Paris with trains rather empty owing to the financial crisis. We enjoyed the Colonial Exhibition in a kind of hazy dream. In one Sudanese village we watched two men working a loom and muttering some incantation all the while. We drove around in a small electric car, all helpless.

We stayed the night at St-Malo and wandered around in the rain, amused, tired and longing to see our two wee girls.

Back at La Hurel [Martello tower] we had all meals on the veranda. I took to knitting and made Angela a jumper for school.

The National Government was formed towards the end of August to deal with the financial crisis. It was all very alarming.

Mlle F. has proved herself to be an excellent governess. She went quite daft about bathing and riding a bicycle. She has weaned Violet from cinemas and made her interested in nature.

*   *   *

Susie and Herbert were in Vienna the following year for the ISCM (Contemporary Music) Festival.

An easy journey spoiled a little at first by D. M. who was off on a lion-hunting expedition. She doesn't converse, she talks AT one, airing her views. It's boring and makes one feel nasty when one ought to be at peace with the world. She's a discontented woman, she's conceited and self-centred, she's a bore. Now I've said it all and God forgive me for being unkind. She ran down the ISCM and said it should now finish, there was no further use for it. Why then leave home and family to travel thither?

After the official opening Herbert and Susie joined Eric Gedye and his wife. Central Europe correspondent for the *Daily Telegraph* and the *New York Times*, Gedye was uncomfortably clear-sighted about Hitler's aims. He was to stir up considerable controversy in London and this would eventually cost him his job. He retaliated in 1939 with a best-seller, *Fallen Bastions*.

> He's as sharp as an eagle with fine blue eyes. Not musical and not interested in modern art, but like all journalists full of interest in life itself . . . He has had many adventures in Romania and Bulgaria and thereabouts. When he was on the *Daily Express* the Editor, Beverley Baxter, cursed him for not allowing himself to be bayonetted out of Romania. When threatened he had appealed to the British Minister. 'But you sent me to King Ferdinand's funeral!' he protested to Baxter, who answered, 'What's King Ferdinand's funeral compared with the *Daily Express* correspondent being bayonetted out of Romania? You were a bloody fool!'

At the supper after the first concert we saw all the *enfants terribles* of Central Europe – Alban Berg, Egon Wellesz, Malipiero, Casella. They look tame now that they are middle-aged.

There was an excursion to the Esterházy Palace on 19 June to see the Haydn manuscripts, after which some of the passengers lingered.

> Henri Prunières, Editor of the *Revue musicale,* was behaving in a very French manner, upbraiding the absent ones and cursing the driver and urging him to go on and leave them behind so that we would be on time for the chamber concert at 8 p.m. Prunières was quite right but it was amusing to see him so excited and so cross among all the good-humoured Austrians. He succeeded in making the chauffeur drive on, leaving the culprits behind. For the rest of the journey we were entertained by an old critic Max Unger who suddenly burst forth for no apparent reason on the subject of Wagner's libretti: all, all came from the Persian. He gesticulated, he talked low, he talked loudly, he pointed, he shouted, he screamed. Dunton Green (at whom it was directed) couldn't laugh. He tried now and then to get in a few words but that brought forth more torrents.

The following day Susie and Herbert took two trains to Gänzehäufel where Gedye was waiting for them –

> a perfect place for bathing, a backwater of the Danube with fine

sand, a large tract of land with trees and grass, gymnasiums, games, cafés. Nude sunbathing places are partitioned off for men and women separately.

Gedye was the best of fun. He made H. go down the large chute, and me down the small one promising me I wouldn't wet my hair, which I did. We arrived at Gedye's ravenous, to find his wife and Capt. Kendrick awaiting us. Capt. K. is in charge of British passports [at the British Consulate]. Gedye is proud of a room off the kitchen which he calls the Branch Office of the *Daily Telegraph*.

In 1938 Gedye was expelled from Austria and left with his dachshund Mephisto/Meffi giving a Hitler salute out of the train window. (Gedye decided it is really a clenched fist.) Captain T. J. Kendrick was arrested and detained at the Gestapo HQ, formerly the Hotel Metropol, in the company of Karl von Schuschnigg (the Chancellor) and Baron Louis Rothschild. In the end Kendrick also was expelled.

Tuesday 21 June 1932
We met Moriz Rosenthal outside the Imperial. We listened to the old man saying cynical things about other pianists. If he weren't so witty it would be unbearable.

Found our way to the Grosser Musikvereinsaal – what a concert! Alban Berg, Schönberg and Mahler, and what an audience. Webern was conducting. In the interval we had a chat with an instrumentalist. He said 80% of the audience were Jews – they were followers of Schönberg and Berg. The rest were all for Mahler who was a Jew who turned Catholic. We have our cliques and our coteries in England but they have their politics.

[SHJ, 14–21 June 1932]

On the return journey Susie was bewitched by the Rhineland and wanted to get out and take a boat. At Harwich she was told her books were dutiable but the official relented and let her eleven Goethe volumes through the customs.

In the English train past Dedham Bridge a military-looking fellow passenger was shouting for 'Coopah's marmalade' but had to make do with Golden Shred. There was a terrific welcome at Church Street, 'the children hugging us to death . . . H. and I stayed with [them] in the garden.'

*   *   *

London has an individual masculine charm like a stylish but untidy eccentric. If it lacks the bold and well-ordered plans of some continental capitals its crazy juxtapositions have their own allure and the secret byways and village enclaves will always draw the random explorer as they often did my parents. By today's standards Susie and Herbert did a lot of walking, thinking nothing of the return to Chelsea on foot from Covent Garden: they did this during the General Strike, four days before I was born. (I could well have come into the world during a performance of *Don Giovanni*.) Their life in London resembled a kind of joyous immersion and one of the places they preferred to dive into was the Café Royal which after prolonged transformations reopened in 1928 with a banquet for five hundred people. The old Domino Room had gone (it became the Brasserie) and to Edward Gordon Craig the place had become 'square . . . large and meaningless' while for Susie it had simply lost its magic: she thought it looked 'like a Lyons café'. [SHJ, 30 January 1930] However, if 'decadence' had died with the Domino Room, bohemianism managed to survive a little longer with the Brasserie: even in 1933 paintings were still sold 'under the table' before the world changed and politically correct informality (and denim at all times) became the new bourgeois style.

Pagani's restaurant near the BBC was always busy, as also later was Quaglino's. Kay Vanden Heuvel told Susie about its alleged origin.

> Quaglino was the head waiter at Sovrani's, and when Sovrani went off with Quaglino's wife, in revenge Quaglino left and opened a restaurant opposite, taking the Sovrani clientele with him. Now Sovrani's is closed while Quaglino's is a huge success – good food, moderate prices and individual attention.   [SHJ, 19 July 1932]

On 2 July 1940 the *Arandora Star*, sailing to Canada with 'enemy aliens' aboard, was torpedoed off the Irish coast. Giovanni Sovrani was among the 486 Italians lost. The head chefs of Quaglino's and the Café Royal survived.

Thirty years into the century Chelsea was still the focal point of a huge confraternity of artists, writers, journalists and musicians with some actors and dancers as well. Augustus John continued to stride along the King's Road past Ellen Terry's house, the symbolic Chelsea figure on his way to the Six Bells; the Sitwells were still in Carlyle Square where the young William Walton had first startled a polite audience with *Façade*; the King's Road fauna admired themselves and others during the Saturday morning *passeggiata*. Epstein sat in front of us on the 22 bus, and the critic M. D. Calvocoressi emerged from Bramerton Street with his wife Ethel wearing on her head what looked like a knitted tea-cosy. In the Pearces' garden Reggie Wilenski talked about his latest subject Ruskin who had, he said, written some songs.

> Marie Rambert talked incessantly but very intelligently about her Ballet Club and about Maynard Keynes ignoring both her school and Karsavina when he spoke of the achievements of the Camargo Society.[4]   [SHJ, 19 July 1932]

Not surprising since Keynes's wife was another ballerina, Lydia Lopokova.

H. H.'s address book dated 1934 gives an idea of that concentration of artists.[5] When they moved house it was usually only to another address in SW3. Few people bought a London house: renting was easy. Dorothy Brigg rented a flat simply to escape her refurbishing-fanatic husband and his perpetual hammering.

'Today,' Susie wrote in New Year 1931,

> I saw a horrid accident in the King's Road. A horse and cart loaded with coal fell through the little artists' colour shop next to the Good Intent.[6] A man with the driver was thrown through the window, poor fellow. I hope it wasn't bad. I remember a dog we had in Richmond Lodge, Drumcondra, jumping through the dining-room window, smashing the glass and suffering no cuts at all.
>
> Herbert has seen the Editor and his salary as successor to R. H. L. [Robin Legge, Music Editor] is to be raised to £250 a year. Today I made Violet promise to open a savings bank account and save a little each week. She's a splendid girl and I'd feel more comfortable about her.

Herbert came home to a funny kitchen meal at 7 o'clock. All has been arranged with the Editor. We celebrated with champagne.

[SHJ, 2 January 1931]

Usual Saturday morning saunter in the King's Road. [Luigi] Innes Meo ['Gigi'] called, as usual full of evil forebodings. His conversation is truly original though about the soundness of his theories I have my doubts. He abused me for contemplating sending Angela and Helena to Kensington Square when I ought to send them to Bedales. After the specimens I have seen from Bedales I'm not at all impressed. I just laughed at him.

[SHJ, 10 January 1931]

A letter from Ellen. She says Father [on holiday in Menton] is depressed about the bank failures in Hollywood and his own losses. That he has indigestion and hates [Mediterranean] food. She wishes they were in London and we could all meet.

[SHJ, 12 January 1931]

Trade Show of a new film operetta at the Tivoli, *The Lottery Bride*, a highly improbable Scandinavian story with very good singing. Jeannette MacDonald was the heroine. There were ice fields, a Zeppelin and an air disaster, but she nevertheless raced about the snow in high-heeled shoes.

I met Vera Newman [Mrs Ernest Newman] on the way out. She congratulated me on Herbert's promotion and told me Lord Camrose had telephoned Ernest for his opinion, asking if he considered that H. being himself a composer was a bad thing [for a music editor]. Ernest said on the contrary, it was all for the better.

[SHJ, 15 January 1931]

Michael Lennon from Dublin and [James] McCafferty to lunch. Lennon is a friend of James Joyce. He seems a simple sort of creature with little humour.

H. rushed off to *Tantivy Towers* at the Lyric, the new A. P. Herbert–Thomas Dunhill comic opera. He thought the libretto full of wit and the music lacking in it. A satire on hunting folk.

[SHJ, 16 January 1931]

[After a blow-by-blow account from both sides in a domestic drama – straying husband now unemployed, vindictive wife, betrayed mistress . . .]

It's a strange thing, Mona's [the wife's] love. To me it looks like a wild desire to possess Arthur body and soul and grind him down to her will. Strindberg would be able to analyse it all. To me it is horribly sordid and I pity the unfortunate child being dragged hither and thither in dark, low, dirty, suspicious Bloomsbury. That quarter of London seems to me to be full of evil, and not even definite evil, but weak, sloppy, incompetent evil. Arthur has no balance anyway, and whiskey probably drives him insane. What a chance he has had, at twenty-nine or so to be earning £1,200 a year as assistant editor [at a publisher's], to have had so many good friends and then to have thrown away his chances. How the literary gangs of London will gossip at their parties!

Herbert told me that Mr Andrews [the estate manager] had said we were all – 125 to 141 Church Street – going to get a seven-year renewal of lease with not much increase of rent. Glorious news for us, especially as we may be having another baby. How I love the old house and wouldn't it be sad to go to an ugly dark flat. We were both very happy about these things.

Nurse went out in the afternoon and the children and I went for a walk. A large tea of banana sandwiches & gramophone records & stories & songs & baths & an apple in bed & prayers & good-night.   [SHJ, 20 January 1931]

I went with Dorothy and Guy [Pelham Boulton] to look at a possible flat for them in King's Road over the Chelsea Book Club, £200 a year. They haven't decided yet.   [SHJ, 2–22 January 1931]

*   *   *

In its daily workings our household must have been typical of the time: domestic arrangements were pulled into shape to answer grown-up needs and in that we were joining in the last gasps of the Edwardian era. Professional families had a comparatively easy life: servants being affordable and available, the worst chores could be avoided. There was no need to carry parcels home since everything could always be delivered, and by ten o'clock as my mother insisted. The domestic cogs and wheels appeared to turn smoothly. But what *maîtresse de maison* would ever admit in the days of 'the servant problem' that there were not continual irritations? After the wonderful Nurse Erna who bathed our dollies in real water, there was Nurse Lily with her cat-phobia and unpunctuality, Mademoiselle with her temper and tortuous character and the luscious Mareillen from Cologne, a later arrival who was in love with Hitler and perhaps with a possibly questionable Mr Fox as well. But in the other department, after Violet left for family reasons, the domestic agency sent some interesting candidates for the post of 'cook-general'.

> I interviewed a maid – one Mimosa by name – and nearly took her on when I discovered that she had left her last place on account of a weak chest and had been ordered to live in the country. When I asked her why she didn't obey her doctor's orders she answered that she couldn't leave London as she was having drawing lessons at the Chelsea Polytechnic!
>
> These days I'm having a hectic time looking for a decent 'daily'. Hicks is a decent enough woman, pleasant, a good cook but lazy and extravagant. She complains of 'very coarse veins'. I engaged a woman called Florence, a good kindly little person but with a streaming cold which she said she had had since June last. She coughed all day. I did all the cooking myself when I realised how ill she was. Florence horrified me by leaving her false teeth on the kitchen table in the butter dish. I was sorry for her. She wept on leaving, saying she had taken a fancy to all of us!
>
> [SHJ, 8 December 1932]

Two years later there were more interviews:

> I saw two I thought possible, but no references. Another came in, black beret, black coat, and the most magnificent black shiny leather gauntlet gloves up to the elbow. She was a cook-gen., she said. 'Why are you leaving your place?' 'Because my mistress doesn't like my joining the Fascists' (pronounced Fassists). 'I'm a nurse and I've joined the Nursing Section. Headquarters, not Branch'

(this with great pride). 'Sir Oswald is very nice, so is his mother. She gave a party for us. Oh! You should have seen the girls around Sir Oswald asking him to sign photographs. He must have felt silly' (pause for giggles).

'Oh,' I said, 'you must be an admirer of Mussolini.'

'No' she answered, 'I have never met him.'

'Well,' I said, 'I don't see why you shouldn't be a Fascist if you like, so long as it doesn't interfere with your work.'

'Oh, no,' she said, 'I only go in my spare time. It's nice to have somewhere to go and meet genteel people. I like having genteel people to talk to.'

That was enough for me. I'm sure we wouldn't be genteel enough for her! [SHJ, 12 September 1934]

Two incidents show how common at the time was the gulf between adults and children. Susie watched a smartly dressed woman approach the cinema box office and buy tickets for two boys of about six and eight years old.

She said to the girl, 'It will be all right to leave them. I'll fetch them later.' The box-office girl protested that according to the law children could only be admitted if accompanied. The smart lady said, 'What a bore.' Whereupon a strange woman who looked like a super-annuated street-walker offered to take the boys and the lady handed them over without any qualms of conscience. So much for the law to protect children from unsavoury films! [SHJ, 13 October 1934]

As Susie was walking home across the Park after lunching with Julie Lasdun, a small boy and his nurse were seen talking to a beautiful lady in a gorgeous car.

She was reproaching the little boy for not knowing her. They were walking in front of me in Kensington Gardens and I heard the nurse say, 'I have told you before who she is. She is your mother and don't forget it the next time you meet her!' [SHJ, 10 March 1938]

A Father O'Neill (in my mother's eyes 'a sympathetic, unsanctimonious padre') asked her to do some work for unmarried Catholic mothers while stressing that the work was often very disappointing. This entailed visiting the local St Stephen's Hospital in the Fulham Road (now the Chelsea and Westminster) and dealing with some tragic cases. The golden rule in the medical profession – not to get emotionally involved – would not have come easily to Susie.

We visited the VD ward first and found four. Mrs McG. whose husband is a miner, mother of four, pathetic-looking little person. I felt like bursting into tears, and found it difficult to talk at first. Then Betty K. from Kilkenny, knitting, very gay and smiling, hoping to get back to the still-room of the Dysart hotel, and two others whose names I forget. There were three babies in this ward. We saw Margaret B., a nurse who is expecting a baby, and Margaret C. who was in the day-room. We saw the nursery for infants of inmates of the institution, and the nursery for abandoned children. We saw Edith and Kitty, two infants whose father is out of work and mother just dead – family of eight. I felt depressed. The place is clean and beautifully kept, but all their tragedies kept chasing through my mind. I'll get used to it no doubt.   [SHJ, 21 February 1932]

At St Stephen's I heard about a woman who arrived a few days ago to have a baby. 'Isn't it a pity?' she said. 'I was going to be married today.' 'Oh,' said the sister, 'I wouldn't let a little thing like that stop me!' and the nurses managed to scrape up 4d. and a hat to send the woman off to be married. The doctor would have no hand in it, fearing that the child would be born on the altar steps, but nevertheless they got her off. She returned two days later and had her baby.   [SHJ, 1 March 1932]

Sat on the Catholic Women's League committee for the first time. The types of my sex who interest themselves in rescue work are so strange to look upon that their 'cases' must surely think they belong to a separate species. And I wish they would treat the subject matter in a more professional manner. What is the use of saying 'Tut, tut' and 'How dreadful' at every new disclosure? What would Freud say? Not that that matters, but it is boring. First and foremost, infectious cases of VD should not be allowed to discharge themselves, and secondly proper sex training should be given to children if not by the parents then by competent people like nurses and doctors. I can see myself getting excited at one of these meetings. [SHJ, 9 March 1932]

I met Miss Church at the Chelsea Workhouse or Institute as they call it. Mary F. had gone off with some man, taking her three children with her. It appears that new teeth were provided for her by the LCC and they increased her sex appeal. She had told Miss Church, 'It's not that I'm really bad, but they take advantage of me. I'm so jolly!' [SHJ, 5 April 1932]

At a Sunday Mass in Farm Street two worlds overlapped:

Fr Woodlock preached on the lesson in the play *The Miracle*. I saw [the impresario] C. B. Cochran and his wife and Lady Diana Duff Cooper [who had the role of the Madonna] among the congregation. Fr Woodlock used the legend of the fallen nun and her baby as a stick to beat the modern couples who don't want the responsibility of children. It struck me as incongruous. Fr Woodlock all concerned with the spiritual message of the play, and C. B. intent on the effect of this sermon on his box-office receipts!!

In the afternoon I went to the Hospital. [SHJ, 17 April 1932]

'Lady Diana Duff Cooper looks wonderful as the Madonna,' Susie wrote ten days later after seeing Max Reinhardt's famous play at the Lyceum,

though she has very ugly hands. Baron Freddy [d'Erlanger] objected to the Nun being played by a dancer (Tilly Losch) but I think that if she didn't dance through her part the play as a play would have some very dull moments. Didn't see anything offensive in it. The Procession of the Blessed Sacrament had great dignity. But when the cripple was miraculously cured and was going up to Our Lady's altar to thank the Madonna I heard a north-countryman near us, who clearly didn't know what on earth he had come to see, ask, 'Ee, wot's 'e clahming oop?' [Leonide] Massine was diabolical as the Spielmann.

[SHJ, 27 April 1932]

There was more trouble for the unmarried mothers:

The CWL [Catholic Women's League] has no funds to deal with the unmarried mothers and the VD cases. I urged for more know-ledge. One case was an Irishwoman married to a Chinaman who had sold her to another Chinaman when he was hard up. She had a baby by the second man. Was the baby British and an RC, or Chinese? God help these infants. Another case was a single woman who was expecting a baby. The prospective mother was minus legs. Horrors!

People say that no matter what you do it will be the same but I don't believe that. I know the Catholic Church feels that more knowledge would lead to more promiscuity, but I don't believe that either. Courage is needed to deal with these matters, and faith in humanity.   [SHJ, 20 April 1932]

I spent the morning searching for a foster mother for Patricia Margaret Doyle's baby. I found Mrs Jarvis, 36 Church St, South Lambeth. A character. 'No tea-garden tricks about me,' she said. 'We're plain.'

I took Margaret Doyle and her baby to the foster mother. She was very upset at leaving the little fellow. She was travelling to Liverpool today to stay with her cousin before taking up her work again.   [SHJ, 7–8 July 1932]

*   *   *

In West London you could be largely unaware of the Depression, the worst effects being for the most part hidden away in the East End. But I still recall Battersea where Violet lived, an unforgettable scene of dark streets with half-dressed children and silent clusters of adults around open doorways, as if rendered inert and permanently waiting.

By today's standards working conditions below stairs were uncomfortable. Before detergents appeared hands were chapped, coarse and red from soda crystals. Washing-up water ended like the cotton-headed mop with a viscous surface of grease which clung like a faulty gene to every object within its reach – a revolting situation which put me off any involvement with a sink until circumstances would eventually close off all avenues of escape. Powder shampoo had to be dissolved – 'Friday night's Amami night.' Ice was delivered in great blocks which were put into an imposing affair clad in what looked like mahogany. I remember eggs sojourning in something called waterglass. Cleaning was done with an early Hoover and a wooden Ewbank carpet sweeper. Laundered clothes were tortured through a huge wooden mangle which dominated the scullery and which my mother, in a moment of unusual distraction, suggested should stand on a tripod until it was pointed out by my father that it was the wrong shape. And yet we were quite a modern household.

With recovery from the Depression came a vast number of small objects, cheap books, toys and trinkets within the reach of a child's pocket-money – nothing cost more than 6*d.* at Woolworth's. (At Easter we solemnly presented our mother with a tiny phial of a dubious scent called Californian Poppy.) The housing boom had begun and the adults talked of the mushrooming of red brick in familiar fields at Dedham which so appalled my aunt that she eventually gave up her cottage. Convenient shops and transport were needed as her stepmother Ellen got older and when Lena moved to Sussex and, for a few years, into one of those very suburbs it looked like capitulation. A kind of general sameness had developed, a need for reassurance, the result perhaps of the Great War and the Slump, where people would turn away from the worrying news on the wireless to weeding the garden or tinkering with the car.

The late thirties brought that little explosion of pleasure, prosperity and optimism mirrored in Hollywood comedies, labour-saving gadgets and the foxtrot. Boating on the Serpentine, swimming in the new Wembley Pool, jaunts in the little car, Saturday afternoons in the one-and-nines, and it looked to the great British public as if things would be all right. The unemployed took to the outdoor life, camping and hiking like the *Wandervogel* in Germany. America sent us her dance bands to the fury of Sir Thomas Beecham who called Britain 'the paradise of the low-brow and bonehead'.[7]

I can't remember being class-conscious in today's sense except being aware of a very distinct hierarchy in the domestic world and being taught to be very polite so as not to offend sensibilities. I soon learnt that there was a problem in being Jewish. When my mother was visiting holiday houses in the summer of 1932 one owner took her aside to ask, 'Are you Jewish?' When Susie said no she said, 'I only asked!'

To have used the work 'black' in those days would have been very rude indeed; to say 'coloured' was not, nor was the word 'negro'. Meanwhile among the delicately tilted hats and the bias-cut chiffon with the undulating folds and even among the liberal-minded intelligentsia there was a whiff of very casual racism and antisemitism which would shock today. It was all very light: jokes and allusions had a way of floating in the smoky air of the Café Royal and then being forgotten. They evaporated like dregs in an abandoned wineglass, out of mind almost as soon as uttered.

The last thing people wanted was to awaken memories of the First World War. The possibility of a second was inconceivable but soon the new dangers in Europe became apparent even to the most self-centred of artists in their circumscribed world, all the more so when reported by colleagues or if a newspaper revealed a particularly shocking incident of Fascist brutality. H. H.'s colleague Eustace Wareing, safely assuming that the German censor would miss the irony, sent us a series of extravagant postcards celebrating Hitler.[8] One I still possess shows the Führer standing like a ham actor against the rays of a Nazi sunrise.

Wareing's sister, Mother Aloysia, superior of a Salzburg convent, would leave Austria in 1938 but not before a visit from Nazis who stripped her to the skin in front of her pupils.

The subject of several books, Soviet Russia both intrigued and alarmed many people in the early thirties. Susie had read of Maurice Hindus' experiences in *Red Bread* which dealt principally with the *kolkhoz* or collective farms (a system sometimes mooted for Ireland).

It is pleasant enough to hear of day nurseries and cleanliness, of the decrease in infant mortality, of the poorest of the poor getting enough to eat and drink and being protected against want in their old age. But [the author] doesn't deal at any great length with city life. [. . .] It is a great experiment and we shall hear more about it before we die. The world is changing. I can't feel that the capitalist system will hold. Surely this present crisis proves that it is out of date? On the other hand I don't foresee success for a plan that entirely wipes out everything spiritual as in Russia.

Second thoughts make her add, 'It doesn't wipe out Art which is spiritual. We'll see.' [SHJ, 27 December 1931] The following year she would hear more about Soviet Russia from the conductor Albert Coates on a visit to the studio.

Continental turmoil apart, I often wonder whether my parents sensed that their time was limited. They fitted a daunting number of events into any one day, only sporadically disturbed by the darkening of Europe. Soon, however, this became difficult to ignore as H. H. followed events with increasing misgivings.

In early September 1933 Susie and Herbert dined with Leedle Bax (mother of the writer Clifford and Arnold, the composer).

Arnold was there, Charlie and Violet Lynch and a Mr and Mrs Ormerod. She is on the University Women's Federation Committee helping German refugees to fly from Mr Hitler and his Nazi hordes. She tells me that many of these unhappy people never consider themselves Jews at all and some are Catholic. But to have a Jewish grandmother is enough it seems.

[SHJ, 6 September 1933]

The following day with H. H.'s sister Dorothy and her husband Guy Pelham Boulton the conversation turned to Germany and its 'wonders'.

I mildly said I was sure Hitler was doing a lot, but I couldn't approve of the brutality. This developed into an attack by D. and G. on the French, and Dorothy pleaded that she and Guy had just come back from Germany and the Germans were not warlike.

73

Herbert who had been following German affairs closely in *The Times* quoted *Wehrwissenschaft*, a book which is to be used as a school manual inculcating into schoolchildren from early childhood every aspect of war and brutality and holding it up as the ideal.[9] The French are a very civilised, tolerant and logical people, and I don't want them trodden off the map of Europe.

[SHJ, 7 September 1933]

And Europe fascinated Suzanne: she was not a very fluent speaker of other languages but she could read French, German and Italian, and even in later years made a stab at Russian but didn't get much further than the Cyrillic alphabet. I remember her much later, when she was alone, with stacks of foreign books and dictionaries beside her bed. Languages were almost an obsession. After she saw a Goethe play on a visit to Austria she searched all the bookshops until she found it, and triumphantly brought not one but eleven volumes of Goethe through the customs.

*　　*　　*

'He's a musician. He knows all about that, but NOTHING ELSE.' That was how I saw my father when I was six. He had been grumbling about the tray and asking where the hot water was. 'Daddy never has a plan.' [SHJ, 4 January 1932]

What I took for granted was the care and skill he put into other tasks, the beautiful lettering when celebrating a concert in the party book, drawings such as the perfect ear he drew 'by heart' (without looking at one) when I asked him to show me how to do it. He would have been an artist whatever the discipline.

He was hard-working and prone to exhaustion, not helped by his penchant for late nights and often seen, still at the piano in the early hours, accompanying yet another singer when he was clearly in a trance of fatigue. Sometimes his absent-mindedness had an epic quality. Lost in thought he once forgot to board an underground train and found himself gesticulating at Susie through the window of the neighbouring carriage. One evening he took a tea-tray down into the dark of the kitchen stairs, his foot encountered the cat and he simply let go of the tray. Susie returned to find festoons of strawberry jam on the banisters and reflected that a woman was more likely to break a leg than sacrifice a tea-set. In spite of her careful preparations before we went away he lunched at the Savile Club; the rest of the time he lived on a diet of milk and bananas. An alternative was to welcome some wandering painter, Luigi Meo, George Marston or a fellow musician into the depths of the Victorian kitchen for an improvised supper. 'Sausages and red wine,' he reported to Susie after hours of talk with Philip Heseltine.

One day when our mother was out shopping Helena and I were left in the studio where H. H. was working. We had been allowed to raid an old chest for dressing-up clothes – beautiful 1920s silks, one with a Pierrot design, another with a pattern of balloons – and we moved on to the make-up stage. Our sticky fingers found a Guerlain lipstick brought back from Paris. Small inaccuracies spread quickly in an effort at symmetry and by the time our mother returned our faces were smeared all over with her precious lipstick now past any use.

'Have they been good?' Her voice on the stairs.

'Angelic,' H. H. answered, pulling the last page out of the Remington before he raised his head.

*   *   *

H. H. forgot or ignored a relic of the Great War (as we used to call it).

To Suzanne Hughes at Sennen Cove

Chez Hughes, 10 August 1927

My good intentions towards you yesterday, my darling Susieboo, were frustrated by two things at the last moment: a letter wh. had to be written to Robin [Legge, *Daily Telegraph* Music Editor], and the arrival of an article (v. amusing) from Dame Ethel [Smyth] which had to be prepared for the printer. Otherwise you would have had a long wail from me by your one and only post this morning.

All well here but for a dreadful and uncurable lack of funds. If I had a little courage I'd go and see the bank manager or some money lender.

More pernicious almost is the worrying persistence of the police regarding my blooming old revolver. I cannot find, or do not know where to look for, the certificate for wh. I paid 2/6*d.* three years ago! And now I cannot find the revolver itself!! Mabel has searched all the drawers and likely places, has even taken the books out.

With all the pernickety ruling of British law I can't pay the ordinary 2/6*d.* (payable every three years) until I produce the *original* certificate. On the 30th of June the sergeant i/c at King's Road was unpleasant & I suppose I made it worse by saying we were going away for a month or two. I've had three or four visits before 9.15 during the last week & have nothing to report (not even a revolver to explode!) Where the — is it? A nice sergeant came this a.m. and I told him I'd willingly give them the permission here and now to search the place from top to bottom. *He* had the graciousness (wh. the original sergeant hadn't) to say they might provide me with a duplicate certificate. But even if they did I might be in the position of paying a licence for something I didn't possess! Was there ever anything more absurd or annoying?

I wish Angela were here to point her finger at them!

God love you. I'm afraid I've missed the post again and I've such a lot to say, Herbert.

Before the arrival of antibiotics bronchitis could be very alarming and it was probably the same infection which had struck down both H. H. and Granny Mac at Lena's house in Dedham and myself, aged eight months, in Chelsea. While I caused acute family anxiety, H. H., still recovering but lured to the open road on a sunny day, blithely went for a ten-mile walk.

Acutely self-critical and always nervous before a performance, he was about to appear with Richard Terry as musical expert witnesses in the Clandillon court case in Dublin.[10] He was suffering a serious attack of dressing-room nerves.

Stephen's Green Club, Dublin
5 November 1928

My darling – I have nothing from you today to answer and more myself to write about than I can possibly get into a letter of normal length.

Hugh Law very kindly nominated me for temporary member-ship of this beautiful club where already in the past 24 hours I have met Lord French, Fitzgerald-Kenney (the Minister of Justice), one Gilbert who has something to do with Agriculture, & the head of the Lunatic Asylum!

Yesterday O'Sullivan had a luncheon party at Foxrock which included Cecil Lavery (one of the KCs), Dr Larchet [Abbey Theatre music director], Lord & Lady Longford, Freeman & myself.

Terry was to have been there, but was a little indisposed and excused himself. Afterwards we motored back in three cars to another consultation in Cox's office. At this Senator Brown KC (the former head of the Bar) was present in an unofficial capacity, chipping in with a few words of advice. These consultations are always interesting & amusing, and I am continually impressed by the dialectic skill of these legal gentlemen.

The case for the plaintiffs finished before lunch this morning & Terry was first witness for us. He had a rough time in cross-examination, the leader for the Clandillons bullying & heckling in the approved style. But he came through with flying colours, got several good laughs from judge & jury & did not need to be re-examined in consequence. This ran over the lunch interval & then [Donal] O'Sullivan went in. To the surprise of many people he is wonderful in examination; answered the judge's one or two questions in a way that was a real tour-de-force of memory. He is the kind of nervous, highly-strung subject that seems to excel at a crisis. His cross-examination will, of course, be the test. I dread the ordeal for myself. My turn may come tomorrow & and I am tuning up for it.

Jelly d'Arányi is playing at the RDS [Royal Dublin Society] today, afternoon & evening, & there is a wire from her at the Shelbourne, but I don't know where she's staying.

Hope to have a letter from you in the morning. God bless my wee family. Terry returns to England tonight.

Love ever, Herbert.

To Suzanne Hughes

Shelbourne Hotel, Dublin
Tuesday 6 November 1928

My darling – Here's another day gone – a stage nearer my own début, which must now take place tomorrow morning. Each day I have felt I was being myself tried – examined and cross-examined; living every moment of each witness's embarrassment or triumph. D. J. O'S. has been the whole day in the box and has behaved brilliantly throughout under brutal questioning. One longish passage was taken up with my Songs of Uladh (where there are no 'precise citations') and another with the Irish Country Songs where my prefaces were quoted on points of editing – to my intended discredit. O'S. came through it wonderfully; explained <u>me</u> in a way I could not have improved upon. No doubt the hostile leader will also put <u>me</u> through it tomorrow.

I felt very nervous this morning in anticipation but the reading out of those bits of my own prefaces somehow gave me courage. I hope it won't ooze out during the night.

God love my darlings,

Ever, Herbert.

Everybody was in court today: rank, fashion, scholarship. And I counted well over twenty wigs unconnected with the case.

To Suzanne Hughes

Stephen's Green Club, Dublin
6 November 1928 (later)

Darling mine – Just another line or two while waiting for dinner – tête-à-tête with Hugh Law. This legal adventure is headachey work, and an intellectual and psychological experience none of us can ever forget. After each session one comes away in a highly-strung condition and at the end of the day as physically tired as if one had been playing some strenuous game. The air in court is electric, the struggle between brain and brain, wit & wit, the deflections, the side-trackings, the strategy, is communicated to each of us who is interested (or rather concerned) in it.

One could see today, for example, how the counsel for the other side was perverting O'Sullivan's service in the Navy into an appeal to the gallery. 'We Irish,' he said, 'lift off our hats to the fighting forces of all the world,' and harped on that and twisted it until D. J. was able to say he had never heard 'Rule Britannia' in the Navy – which brought a sympathetic laugh. He dropped the Navy, as the moment for that rhetoric had passed, and took up quotations from my volumes and from certain notes of Joyce. He thought he could score here but D. J. was, as I have said, more than equal to him. In answer to one question D. J. was obliged to say that he had gone to Paris on a Monday. 'One of those joy-rides at the expense of the State?' was the next question of the counsel! and D. J.'s answer, dignified and emphatic, that he had gone on particular duty for the Senate . . . That sort of thing. Dirty and truculent.

Later. The Tovey block belongs to Adila Fachiri. You can send nurse round with it. I imagine it is not urgently required.

Still later (7 Nov.) My ordeal is over and I shall probably leave here tomorrow (Thursday) night. I don't think they'll re-examine me. In any case I'll wire you sometime during the day to let you know.

All my love, Herbert.

I was less nervous in the end than I thought I should be. I had one or two stiff passages with the opposing counsel & was congratulated by A. E. and others after.

*   *   *

The only time I remember my mother being ill during my childhood was the sequel of an outbreak of flu.

> It is almost three weeks since I wrote a line. I'm in bed recovering from 'this epidemic' as the doctors call it. Nurse, Violet and the two children have all had it, and now I am on the mend.
>
> [SHJ, 13 February 1931]

But she wasn't. The last in the family to catch flu she was slow to recover and in early March 1931 she had a miscarriage. The gynaecologist called in emergency, Mr Meyer, 'as nice as it is possible for a human being to be', had worked at the Coombe in Dublin and told Susie how the poor women in the slums tried to give the doctors little bottles of port by way of appreciation.

While we were away in Dedham, Violet became my mother's devoted nurse and I also recall the new governess, Mademoiselle, carrying trays up to the studio. The whole experience left Susie depressed and debilitated and reading more than ever – Maupassant, Pierre Benoit, Lytton Strachey, Jack Squire's *Grub Street Nights' Entertainments* . . . Unlike a sick-room the spacious studio was congenial; 'Herbert spends all his spare time with me.' [SHJ, 21 March 1931] It took Susie many months to recover her normal stamina and she gave up the idea of learning to drive.

The effects of the Depression were spreading to all domains, including music and the theatre. The actor Hugh Sinclair told Susie he could not survive without film work.

Politics occupied most people's minds until the general election on October 28th when the country completely turned around and voted Conservative. The pound being worth 15/- (as we are off the gold standard) makes people think twice about travelling and altogether life is going to be pretty strenuous this winter. Everyone will suffer. There's a call for a tariff wall around Britain which seems to be the most sensible way to alleviate unemployment.

In November H. started a campaign at the suggestion of the Brainwaver [Oscar Pulvermacher, *Daily Telegraph* Assistant Editor] for the protection of British musicians. The discussion is still raging. Foreign artists get large fees for coming here, fees they couldn't get in their own countries. Organisations are therefore impoverished and the artists at home have to suffer in consequence.

[SHJ, 17 November 1931]

*   *   *

With all the journalism and his own work, the odd broadcast or a paper on Irish music for a university, H. H. continued to make music with friends and when the Music Page had been put to bed the music-making started in earnest. He spoke with the keyboard, improvising with relish, often 'in the manner of' which made people laugh. When

John Ireland visited the studio the two men improvised piano duets. It was the same with Arnold Bax at a children's Christmas party, the combined embonpoint at the piano making them look, I thought, like two teddy bears.

The scholar Donal O'Sullivan remembered H. H. at the piano:

> When [Herbert] was in the mood, away he would dash with brilliant improvisations on the theme, often far exceeding what would ever be required by way of accompaniment. The difficulty was to get him to stop and commit what he had played to paper. Once I remember saying to him, 'Now, Herbert, you lifted that from Schubert!' and he replied with a guilty smile like a schoolboy caught stealing jam.[11]

H. H. had started giving his musical parties after the end of the Great War, in Kensington first and finally in Chelsea with a spirited wife as convivial as himself. During the daytime we children heard him at the piano upstairs. At night it became a festival: if the floors had been reversed we might have been living above the shop at the Wigmore Hall. One evening Myra Hess, too shy to perform in front of Backhaus, asked for an orange. She then played a surprising version of Chopin's black note study (in G flat, Op. 25, no. 9) using it in her right hand. The guests all rushed to the piano to watch. Susie was alarmed at the amount of weight on one side of the room and the next day called a surveyor to reassure her that her daughters were not at risk of being crushed in their beds by a grand piano falling through the ceiling.

When H. H. thought it was all too good to be missed he would come downstairs in the middle of the night and ignoring our governess in the next room switch on the nursery lights and sweep us upstairs to listen in our dressing gowns. Around the two of us were the grown-ups enjoying the surrounding brilliance at least as much as their own, many of them artists lured up to the studio like the children of Hamelin by the Pied Piper.

6

Strands

The web of our life is a mingled yarn, good and ill together.
Shakespeare, *All's Well that Ends Well*, 4, 3

From my bed I could hear the staircase come to life as musicians and their cargoes of instruments rolled and tossed their way up to the studio. Stage whispers detonated outside the nursery door but like circus children we were serene awake or asleep as the talk and the music continued long into the night above our heads.

In the daytime I could see the passers-by in the street below. Some I knew by name: Dr Gubbins, Mrs Northover, Mr Jaffe from Elm Park Road, Anna Pearce with her dark hair drawn back from her forehead, Bess Norriss who painted miniatures and the critic Mr Calvocoressi who wore a wide-brimmed hat like a French curé.

On a platform below the great window the sofa was just high enough for my purpose. I was at the core of a body of light, its arms a penumbra stretching along the walls right and left. Here they would sit, half concealed beyond the reach of the lamplight, the people I had heard on the stairs and whose chatter was so quickly silenced by music. High on the wall to my right were trophies, assegais and other weapons which my father, this very peaceful man, had brought back from the Sudan. Below them was a huge oak dresser displaying an incense-burner and brightly coloured ceramics and in front of this the long oak table with the Remington. On the other side of the room was the piano and along the wall behind it black built-in cupboards with drawings on every panel. A leopard skin covered the sofa beneath the big window over the street and durries were scattered about the floor. Two windows flickered in the bronze ceramic stove behind me and around the corner, as if protected by the books and the piano, was a wide paisley-covered divan, my parents' bed. All life could be lived in this room above the trees – my father's work, our children's parties, the music at night, visits from singers with tales of woe. Through the window at the back of the house the evening sun from World's End sent an amber shaft across the keyboard. I was safe at the centre of an untouchable universe.

*   *   *

Marconi believed that all sounds from the past survived if only we knew how to recapture them.[1] This conjures up waves rolling into infinity like the travelling of prehistoric starlight. Less demanding, my memory echoes healthily enough with the sounds of thirties London. In the womb our hearing is the first sense to awaken and, provided we don't lose it on the way, it is often the last to go.

The first thing you heard on Sunday mornings was the muffin man coming up Church Street swinging his handbell, the tray on his head resting on a pad of folded green baize. On weekdays the Co-op horse trotted bossily round the corner into Elm Park Road, mimicked by the little donkey, its cart laden with neat cuts of wood or with a heap of those long red or green cloth sausages with a white fringe at each end designed to keep out draughts. In the King's Road the barrel organ's song was muffled in starts by the huge roar of a passing bus. There were robust smells: coal dust, roasting chestnuts, the damp hessian of a horse's nosebag and everywhere the smoke, sending the sun down like a great red balloon beyond World's End.

In summer voices floated up from neighbouring gardens. Our street was a place of trees and birds; thrown off bricks and mortar in a town enclosure their song has a special resonance. After the lamplighter had passed (like Stevenson's Leerie) and I was open-eyed in bed tracing the pencil of light escaping through the curtains and across the ceiling, a harpist sitting under the street lamp spun a sound from another world. On our winter island of blurred outlines both isolation and comfort came from lights seen through fog.

In the morning, when vaporous nocturnes and London par-ticulars had dissipated, I was bewitched by the colours, shapes and textures to be found in the Montessori class in Kensington Square. At the first interview, while my mother was talking with the specialist teacher Mother Isabel, I unjumbled the musical bells into a scale. It was the first taste of a creative freedom which is part of the Montessori ethos. Initially developed for deprived children in Italy, Maria Montessori's basic principle was the individuality of each child, who with the deliberate use of the five senses and natural materials could progress gently from one stage to the next, free from notions of competition or punishment.

When the term started I spent a fortnight emptying every child-size drawer on to the floor. Hoping to hear of my progress my mother was surprised. 'That's all right,' said Mother Isabel, 'she's satisfying her curiosity.' And having turned out the classroom I became more tractable and revelled in the coloured beads, the mats and cubes of early and painless mathematics, the sandpaper letters our fingers were taught to trace, the metal geometrical shapes to be coloured in, the triangle, drum and tambourine of the percussion band, the white line to dance on, the reading corner secluded behind the upright piano. We were read *Madame Souris* by a French lady on whose exuberant bosom the tip of a gold crucifix designed to suspend from its chain nestled cosily, feet upwards. My eyes fastened on this strange and marvellous continent.

One morning a silent visitor in black sat on the bench against the wall, watching us infants in our multicoloured smocks, cross-legged on the floor, each on her own mat. It was the initiator, Dr Maria Montessori.[2]

A girl in a poppy-coloured smock asked me would I be her best friend. We were five years old. I looked at her. Black hair, dark skin and coffee-coloured eyes: different from me with my reddy-brown hair and freckles. I thought she would do. Yes, I said unsmilingly, so that was that. Her name was Christine. Her Irish ancestors had owned a shipping line and her father was a doctor – one who would later be working day and night through the London Blitz.

Free of the governess for a few hours, I was enchanted with the school and its seasons and rhythms and ceremonials. There was a certain liberality about this English house sprung from a French order. My mother was surprised to learn some years later that the seniors were offered tap-dancing classes. 'It is so good for their tennis,' Mother Anna Magdalena explained.

The convent had a garden of more than four acres tucked away behind the *Sturm und Drang* of Kensington High Street. Beyond the wall were the trains rumbling above ground beside Pontings (the department store), just far enough away not to drown the liturgy and music in the chapel. We had the riches of 'Tantum ergo' and 'Ave Maris Stella', the lusty 'Praise to the Holiest' and the wanderer's 'Hail, Queen of Heaven' remembered by the poet Patrick Kavanagh,[3] splendid hymns now widely sacrificed with the inspirational Latin Mass, the Mass of Byrd, Bach, Mozart and Beethoven . . .

Walking to school with my father meant a great deal of talk, from Church Street past the honey-pots in the window of Bunce's Dairy,[4] up Onslow Gardens with hardly a pause for breath between Gloucester Road and the open door in Kensington Square.

What's a coincidence?

Hens give eggs. Do lions give tea? (I read a great number of advertisements.)

What are nursing mothers? (That one came from the Ovaltine tin.)

For the twentieth time I pulled the glove off the hand mine was in. It was easy with the button always undone. Leaving me with Sister 'Cyppie' at the door, my father set off for the number 9 bus and Fleet Street in his vast tweed coat, his hat at a jaunty angle and a review copy of a book under his arm. He was a Londoner by choice and in the Sudan during the Great War he had missed Fleet Street and its fog and his chats with the compositors.

Friendly musicians moved along the street to allow him to work undisturbed. Violet, our 'cook-general', came from Battersea every day, a figure of unchanging warmth and loyalty whom we all loved. Nurse Lilly, who preceded the governess, was a kind soul if a little slow, always late with everything and prone to hysterics when exposed to cats. The arrival on the stairs of Sambambina and her offspring Tristan and Isolde caused a major crisis but our mother had no patience with such nonsense. Eventually developing health problems, whether due to the cats or not I never knew, Nurse Lilly returned to Switzerland and in her place came Mademoiselle and with her a change of regime.

Mademoiselle was Swiss and in her late forties. She had swarthy

Alpine skin, sound teeth and a steel-grey bun relegated to the nape of her neck. I made a quick comparison and decided on that basis that our mother's rich and abundant auburn hair was gathered into a full-size cake. On weekdays Mademoiselle wore a white overall, the belt neatly slotted through the side in the continental fashion; on summer Sundays and feast-days a stylish print dress and a straw hat where flowers peeked out of a double brim – a fashionable thirties conceit. There was nothing dowdy about her nor did any practical task defeat her. She made dresses and knitted jumpers and would pick up and finish those begun by our mother who soon gave up altogether.

Mademoiselle had spent some years in Rome and spoke Italian as well as French and German. Our mother held that if someone was employed to look after us she might as well also teach us another language, preferably two. Mademoiselle more than answered that need and I recognise that my love for the French language sprang from my early years in her care: in the nursery we never spoke a word of English. In an unforced way we visited museums and art galleries, choosing our favourite pictures and, as I remember, never bored or indifferent. We also saw the Crown Jewels, Traitors' Gate, Hampton Court and the chestnut trees blazing in Bushey Park. Mooning as usual as I watched the river craft, I dropped my glove into the Thames.

We always used the formal 'vous'. Mademoiselle taught us to fold our clothes at night on our chairs, turn our socks half-inside-out for morning speed and smooth our starched cotton dresses before we sat down. At school we curtseyed to Reverend Mother, we curtseyed to our parents' friends, on the beach out of habit we even curtseyed to our friends in our bathing suits.

I have never known what first led me to fear this woman, to lose all spontaneity in her presence and to sink into mutism even with my sister there when confined in the nursery. Perhaps she had alarmed me by nothing more than shouting in a loud and ugly voice, something I was not used to and have always detested; it was her habit when crossed as my mother recorded later. More likely it was the indefinable hostility which emanated from her and was directed only at me. Whatever it was, from that moment the yarn of daily life began to unravel: there were now two strands, or even three if you counted the hours at school. The studio became the unattainable, the fount of all delights between tea and bath-time or when Mademoiselle was out. From the nursery below the music was clearly audible as were our mother's steps on the stairs or the voices of extrovert friends, the artists and visiting Irish whose laughter reached us between the bellrings. In our house there were two worlds: orderly convention on the first floor, light-hearted and comfortable bohemia above.

Mademoiselle must have found me a difficult charge. 'Angela is not the ideal nursery child, I know,' Suzanne recorded in her diary. Assiduous one moment and the next, my ear on the staircase, distracted, breathless, impatient to be off, I would slump ungraciously into my small chair to go on with my French reading. 'Angela is like the Irish weather,' my mother observed. After the celebrations of my First Communion at Kensington Square, I was taken to tea at Hill's in the High Street. 'She is a funny child,' Susie reflected, trying to cope with a difficult six-year-old who didn't want to be dressed and complained that the day was over.

That might go some way to explain Mademoiselle's special hostility but it was only half the story as we discovered some years later. My unease must have been perceptible: Mother Isabel, vigilant and sharp-witted, remarked that something was wrong.

A black velvet hooded coat lined with white. A green pendant touching my chest as I lie in bed. My eyes swivel to follow the bright pendulums in her ears.

Where are you going?

We are going to dine with friends.

Dine. Die. No.

She has gone. I lie very still. I will not shift by one inch the cover she has smoothed.

'Vous n'êtes pas naturelle,' Mademoiselle once complained. Grown-up talk. In the winter my coughing kept her awake and from her room she would angrily call out for me to stop, which of course made it worse. Once during a country walk she gave my leg a swipe with the dog's lead. I was far too nervous of her to have embarked on any wild and inventive naughtiness but perhaps I had said something too accurate for comfort. Perhaps she craved the love I could give only to my mother. In the end I felt it was enough simply that I existed: the elder child, the one she didn't want in her care. (Years later old photographs revealed that the distinction Mademoiselle made between my sister and myself went as far as the two different styles of cotton dresses which she ran up on her machine. At the time it was wasted on me: I wasn't yet vain enough to notice.)

Anything which being older than my sister I experienced the first was a cause of resentment: piano lessons and a stamp album became issues in Mademoiselle's tortured mind. These were soon indirectly voiced through my sister, insinuations and suggestions which had been carefully instilled like drops in the ear.

I have always been fascinated by violent weather and although I enjoyed the noisiest of storms to the point of deflation when they abated (there was surely some link with the orchestra here), they terrified Helena who would creep into my bed for a story to lull her to sleep. She was imaginative and her special talent for drawing emerged when she was only eight. To the admiration of some of a concert audience sitting in the neighbouring stalls, she drew a sketch of Sir Henry Wood conducting. She also won a verse-speaking prize, reciting a poem called *The Aconite* at the Friends' House in the Euston Road. In time both talents bore fruit. When she left school she studied at the Central School of Art, moving swiftly from drawing and painting to sculpture. Her theatre career occurred beyond the span of this memoir. After a spell at RADA it began with the Gate Theatre Company under Micheál MacLiammóir and Hilton Edwards and went on to great success in New York in Micheál's play *Where Stars Walk*. She was a real trouper and later played Helena in the first production, at the Royal Court in 1956, of John Osborne's *Look Back in Anger*.

*   *   *

I told nobody about Mademoiselle's swipe, nor did Helena, although I was conscious that this was plainly out of order: she had never before laid hands on me. Her method was always far subtler: sending the offending child to Coventry.

Unaware of anything more than her particular sharpness, my mother took this up several times with Mademoiselle who spoke at the top of her voice throughout the conversation and therefore heard nothing that she did not wish to hear. 'Another passage of arms with Mademoiselle,' my mother recorded. 'If I thought she was breaking Angela's spirit she would go.' [SHJ, 3 June 1932] She clearly wasn't, although my father once noticed that my hands, generally as dry and warm as his own, had become uncharacteristically clammy. I offered no explanation. Children always know where the engine of power is running. Accustomed to Ellen's gentleness, he called Mademoiselle 'the Swiss dragon' and returned peacefully to his typewriter.

My undisguised urge to be in the studio made things worse. That was where the music was, where I passionately and constantly wanted to be and where she had no authority. 'You're quite different at home,' said Christine one day at school and I was mortified to have been found out. Although Mademoiselle sometimes went to concerts, unlike the other people around us she had no song in her. (This only struck me years later, long after the truth about her tormented character had come to light.) For around us everybody sang; it was as natural as walking. Once when I asked Ronnie Thurgarland's mother to sing (we had sung to her) and she replied that she couldn't, I looked at her with as much surprise as if she had said she had no feet.[5]

On Sundays we played our pieces for our father since music was not a social asset but serious work. The plan was that after my schooling I would study German and music in Salzburg. He had even worked out that this could be in the care of Eustace Wareing's sister, superior of a convent there. It was only a few years ahead.[6] On these Sunday mornings with my father at the piano a clear path seemed to be opening.

Wilhelm Backhaus came to tea one day and although there were grown-up guests he asked me what I would like him to play. Our house was so bathed in music that it was quite natural for me to ask for something by Mr Beethoven. The name was so familiar that I thought quite simply that he was a friend of the family. That afternoon on my father's lap I heard the Diabelli Variations.

On Sunday afternoon, when Mademoiselle was out and there was a concert to cover, one of us accompanied H. H. to the Queen's Hall while Susie took the other out somewhere else. The following week we did the reverse. I was six when I was taken to the Queen's Hall to hear the London Philharmonic Orchestra newly formed under Sir Thomas Beecham. They were giving Rimsky-Korsakov's *Sheherazade* and my father had told me about *The Arabian Nights*. It was my first encounter with such music and I was transported by the overwhelming sound of a great orchestra in full cry.

Music was not an object of love: it was oxygen, life-preserving, indispensable. After the Beecham experience I began to listen more intently. I could hear what my father was doing at the piano upstairs, weaving strands together, separating them, teasing out new ones. 'Do you know what he does?' I asked my mother when I was in bed with a cold. (As if she didn't know.) I was fascinated to hear him play a tune, do what he liked with it, play it again and then put other little tunes inside it. She was giving me piano lessons and my first pieces were 'French Air' and 'The Bluebells of Scotland' in the Boosey Tutor on the upright piano in the dining-room. 'She tumbles to it so quickly. She gets frightfully excited about her five-finger exercises. She's quite thrilled about the key of C major.' [SHJ, 15 February, 4 March, 8 April 1933] The Jupiter Symphony, the Dissonance Quartet, the Waldstein Sonata, Schubert's great Symphony and the sublime Quintet – what other marvels lay waiting for me beyond the innocent horizon of C major?

A child knows how to protect that private core which harbours caution, secrecy and assumed guilt and I confided nothing of my constant predicament. Our parents were loving and gave us warm and imaginative attention when we were together. I hungered for this in the scrupulously well-ordered domain of the nursery and yearned for the enchantments of their bohemian world upstairs. They wanted the best for us, but following the mores of the time we lived during those years in a dual state. Apart from Mademoiselle's holiday or her day off and the half-hour before bath-time our parents were in their grown-up world where work and play combined; we were then under the laws of a separate fief. Mademoiselle was the one flaw, the single wrong note in a childhood sometimes better than happy, and anyway none of this was to last. Even if she left traces in me I see her only as a severe parenthesis.

But the house itself had a fugitive quality, it seemed to me. I was acutely afraid of loss. Then one day the grown-ups spoke in my hearing of the possible demolition of the Church Street terrace. As one knows now this wasn't to happen but at the time my mother had to console me. Why could I not simply enjoy everything while it was there? she wondered. There seemed to be a discordance, a threat, like unfamiliar sounds approaching. In my recurring dream a woman's face, with a dark complexion and unlike any face I knew, looked up at the nursery balcony from the street below as if waiting for me. She would go away but she would be coming back.

In the rendering of life outside there were perceptible cracks even for those who had not suffered in the Great War, while many of those who had were plainly still there to be seen. Near the street corner I came upon a man sitting on the pavement, his back against the garden wall. The empty trouser-leg pinned back, the small tray of matches and shoelaces, the luminous and triumphant row of medals and the notice EX-SERVICEMAN: the whole picture confused me in its contradictions.

'Sing as we go, and let the world go by,' went Gracie Fields on the wireless and the delivery boy on his bike. It was a song from a film about the cotton-mill workers.[7] Meanwhile Grandpa Hughes, the provider, frowned as he waited for the post from America and the dividends which had stopped coming

*   *   *

Auntie Lena's cottage in Dedham was a rural peace offering from her father after stormy moments. In Belfast Lena Hughes (H. H.'s elder sister) and John Campbell had fallen in love, but F. P. H. would not hear of marriage. So there was none. Did they ever think of eloping? There was probably no money to elope with. With his brother, the poet Joseph, John left for the US in 1912, and for many years the family believed that he had found a wife. I only discovered in the

1970s that he had remained single, as indeed had Lena herself, an outcome which Susie always saw as a tragedy. Lena went further, adopting with a certain hubris the religion long rejected by her father. In old age her younger sister Dorothy recalled their father's grim expression as he read Lena's letter announcing her conversion to Rome, but in spite of this I suspect that F. P. H.'s objections were not entirely about religion (the Campbells and Hugheses were friends after all) but also, perhaps even chiefly, about solvency: the young artist could not yet afford to keep two people. If F. P. H. was confident that Lena would eventually marry elsewhere he had not measured her single-mindedness. She turned to London and music, and became a 'mature' student at the Royal College, studying singing and composition. Then she moved to Dedham and studied horticulture. She was a chronic student, she used to say.

The Dedham household consisted at first of Lena Hughes and Susie's mother, Maria McKernan or Granny Mac, joined after the Wall Street Crash of 1929 by F. P. H. and Ellen. I remember Granny Mac in her eighties, with silky white hair in a bun and the smooth cheeks of a much younger woman. Until her sight deteriorated badly she gardened with passion, in summer sometimes still in the garden at ten o'clock at night, avenging the Irish Famine with English potatoes. Lena trained in horticulture with all the energy and thoroughness she showed in music, and from then on never quite got the soil out of her fingers. United within her were the spiritual and the practical, her competence in almost everything she touched being an expression of this; almost everything, that is, for the grasp of Lena's hand was firm and any domestic breakage she caused was the result of excessive protectiveness rather than limp incompetence. It happened once with a piece of Bristol blue, her sister Dorothy's favourite glass, and there was a gasp of family dismay around the table. It took Ellen's serenity to restore a sense of proportion as she gently dismissed the accident under her breath with, 'Me arse and parsley . . . '

In Church Street, Susie noticed Ellen's hold on children, her calming presence, her low Irish voice and her look of a girl of seventeen as Helena and I, like the five Hughes boys in Belfast, were allowed 'ten minutes of a rough house' before baths and bed. [SHJ, 31 May 1930]

With all her practicality Lena could be extraordinarily vague. She sent us a cat called Tinker believed to be male. My mother took him to the vet who pronounced him female. 'So much for Lena's judgement in these matters,' Susie commented. 'This is the second female pussy she has presented to us as a male!' [SHJ, 24 December 1932]

At table one day the whole family were upbraiding Lena for fretting over some domestic problem which in their eyes was trivial. No doubt for her own good they were urging her to take life more easily. 'You mustn't let the house rule you,' they said. Suddenly I saw her fly from the table in tears. Not only was I shocked to see an adult cry but I was left with a huge sense of injustice.

Serious new plantings had a way of suddenly appearing with as little ceremony as snowdrops overnight – Indian corn, for example, where we could play hide-and-seek – but as well as growing anything which took her fancy Lena started keeping poultry, a new development viewed by Guy, her urbane and elegant brother-in-law, with distaste. But I loved all this, the cock crowing, the hens and their woodwind-practice noises, all part of a firmament of sounds separate from our city life, while ordinary things were transformed like the studio staircase in London by the magic of night. The piano after we had gone to bed arousing a delectable fear at the song *The Terrible Robber Men*; the wind in the poplars along the boundary to Lena's garden; the owl at the back of the house and the distant dog barking at nothing. Rose petals found their way into the bath water and for a time we still used oil lamps with their complicated ritual and hieratical smell. (My mother had no patience for such intricacies: 'I hate all the preliminaries of lamplighting – grabbing at the matches, fumbling with the globe . . . ')[8] There was also the smell of coal, and the hiss when Granny Mac, bending down by the fire, stirred her Sunday stout with a red-hot poker. And in this circumscribed and invigilated little world Mademoiselle's temperament was seriously curbed.

At the back of the house by the shed was a rough area of great promise full of planks of wood, balls of twine, pea-sticks, netting, sacks, bricks and compost bags, objects to be transformed into houses, boats, boundaries. I struggled with a plank hopelessly trying to make a see-saw over a stack of loose bricks. We rode horses on the wooden front of the veranda, with a maid's kneeling mat and the dog's lead as saddle and bridle. With bits of wood we fashioned bows and arrows and fishing rods. Minnie came from the village and worked with one of the cats on her shoulder. We collected black-berries down East Lane for the jam when Ronnie Thurgarland or Mary Codnor came to tea, and we crossed vast cabbage fields to bathe at Flatford in the pellucid underworld of Judas Gap (which we thought was 'Judy's Gap'). Mary's father was a painter, and there were other painters' families round about, the Rushburys and the Munningses.

United in domestic strife and a love of horses, Lena's neighbours Violet and A. J. Munnings lived at Castle House, Dedham. They were known to have quarrelled dramatically over a lemon. One evening coming in from hunting Violet threw off her boots, stretched out on the sofa and started snoring. Her husband threw a book at her but it missed and hit a guest. Encouraged in his youth (perhaps rather rashly) by John Masefield, A. J. wrote verses and songs, including a thirteen-verse ballad which he sang to his guests after dinner. When he was sober he was kind, hospitable and a good listener, he liked talking about books and H. H. found him good company, but there were days when marital discord spilled over.

> A. J. in too happy a condition for perfect comfort. We visited all the horses and the foal. Lena and Herbert saved the situation after dinner with music. A. J. would sing about his long-buried past with 'Julia, Julia, Julia' . . .   [SHJ, 2 June 1929]

> Violet and A. J. came up on horseback to invite us to supper. H. and I went for an hour's walk on our way to Castle House. It was quite perfect.
>
> When we arrived A. J .was still painting in his garden and Violet was upstairs. We waited a while. When she came down she told us that before dressing she had discovered the two colts had walked

into A. J.'s studio and were marching up and down admiring themselves in the mirrors and stopping now and then to look at the canvases.

We didn't have a merry evening. One felt something dreadful in the atmosphere and every subject touched seemed to cause them to disagree bitterly, so that conversation was not easy. They are both unhappy. He talked in a wonderful way about painting farm carts and horses – inspired one might say. It is so easy to blame, but so difficult to know the real truth and whose is the fault.

A. J. walked home with us in the moonlight. The smell of cut clover was divine.   [SHJ, 8 June 1930]

We went to dinner at Castle House. A. J. [Munnings] looked well in spite of his illness. There was a certain amount of cursing of servants and their strange ways.

Afterwards music grave and gay. Lena sang and conversation followed. Tolstoy is Munnings' god at the moment. He talked so much of *War and Peace* that I must read it. He reads a great deal though there is no sight in one eye. [George] Marston, an artist, called after dinner, a gentle fellow. I saw him putting H. to sleep with his soft-voiced theories of art. It was a dry night and we walked home.

Mamma seems better than she has been for ages. [She had just celebrated her eighty-fourth birthday.] We left her easy in our minds. I took with me Maurois' *Les Mondes imaginaires*. I do a good deal of reading and studying but it's all so disorderly and unsystematic that it's wellnigh useless to me. Untidiness, mental, physical and spiritual, is my besetting sin.

I left H. devouring Gerhardi's *Memoirs of a Polyglot* and went to Mass at Brantham. A poor little church with about twenty-three people at Mass. Lena played the organ and Mr Goodchild, a local farmer, Lena and I sang the Mass.   [SHJ, 7 February 1932]

A. J. cursed Violet and she cursed him. We are used to it now and it probably doesn't mean anything. I wouldn't like to be called 'a yapping bitch' but I suppose Violet is used to it and can stand up for herself. Munnings is a great-hearted fellow, a wonderful talker, no doubt a trying husband but nevertheless a great host. Violet is a thoroughly decent sort, but probably only her real self on the hunting field.   [SHJ, Boxing Day 1932]

On Sundays Mr Ellis and his great Wolseley taxi with a running-board took us to Mass at Brantham where we sang the *Missa de angelis*. Afterwards Helena and I were allowed to go on our own to Poyser's farm for the cream, threatened by nothing more than the yapping of a Pomeranian in the yard. On George V's Jubilee night we stood with burning cheeks at Mr Dalton's bonfire while the village band played 'Land of Hope and Glory'.

Printed on my memory is a close-up: my small blunt-ended scissors, forgotten overnight on the lawn and found transformed by sunlight and dew, lying in splinters of glass.

PART THREE

Mainly Musicians

7

Kaleidoscope

Musicians and others pass through London and my mother's diaries as they might through a revolving door. Revered if not exactly canonised today (but very nearly), many of these artists had not yet reached their peak in the 1930s and there are some irreverent snapshots. There was an influx of brilliant Russians echoing the triumphs of Diaghilev – the cellist Piatigorsky, Chaliapin the bass ('being the whole performance, conducting the conductor and all on the stage') and the spellbinding pianist Vladimir Horowitz ('all with perfect ease and every shade of tone colour – a young master') [SHJ, 18 May 1931, 11 April 1932] – but the two Arturs for example had not yet quite conquered the whole of London: Rubinstein ('he had a clever face but not the power to move us') and Schnabel ('who played Beethoven sonatas well and sometimes badly. Badly when he played arrogantly.'). [SHJ, 26 January 1929, 29 October 1932] Even after a successful Queen's Hall recital Susie imagined the sublime Elisabeth Schumann 'going off the platform straight home to fry sausages'. [SHJ, 1 November 1932] Clearly unsoothed, the painter Grace Henry said of Schnabel's pupil Leonard Shures, 'He lifts up all the notes on the piano and throws them at you.' [SHJ, 23 February 1929]

At the centre of musical London stood Sir Thomas Beecham. A performer as much off as on the rostrum, he was brilliant, witty, elegant and autocratic. His whims were indulged and his misdemeanours excused like the pranks of a naughty but very gifted child.[1] He was generous towards his musicians whom he treated as equals and they repaid him with devotion. Having witnessed him in an opera rehearsal at the RCM throw a cushion at a woodwind player, Susie and H. H. were among his audience at the house of the pianist Katherine Goodson.[2]

[He was] full of comic generalities, pontifical nonsense, most amusing but quite frivolous and insincere. All his conversation is for effect. He keeps looking around to make sure everyone present hears him. He's full of temperament and his memory is fantastic. He talked of Mozart and Schubert with adoration and cursed Beethoven and Wagner. He cursed the German singers. He also cursed *Die Meistersinger*. He talked and talked . . . Dora Labette, in white satin and diamonds, contributed to the conversation in a lugubrious suburban voice. She didn't strike me as knowing much about anything but she did strike me as entertaining. We were home at 2.   [SHJ, 14 July 1932]

In 1931 Toscanini was in trouble at home. The conductor Anthony Bernard came to the studio in the afternoon with a strange document said to have been sent to London by Toscanini's son in a parcel of merchandise.

It was about the behaviour of the Fascists in Bologna. Toscanini wouldn't play [their hymn] 'Giovinezza' so they beat him and now he [is] a prisoner in Milan. According to the document they were considering deporting him for five years to one of the islands. Herbert tried to get Massey [of the *Daily Telegraph*] to publish it but A. E. [Watson, the Editor] turned it down because there wasn't enough authority. If [the *Telegraph*] said it had come from Toscanini's son he would be deported at once.   [SHJ, 2 June 1931]

Having refused to play the Fascist hymn before a concert in Bologna, Toscanini had indeed been roughed up by a hooligan who hit him in the face. The conductor was bundled into the car by his chauffeur and driven to his hotel where a black-shirt rabble shouted obscenities under his windows. After he escaped to Milan that night he was put under house arrest, his passport was confiscated and all his visitors listed. Briefed by a minister, Mussolini commented, 'I am very pleased. It will teach those oafish musicians a lesson.' Toscanini did not conduct again in Italy while Mussolini was alive.[3]

H. H.'s chief Robin Legge wrote from the country:

Dear old Elgar drove over here yesterday covered with nieces and dogs – but I was out for a long prowl in the glorious sunshine &

did not see him. He was very shy, Aimée says, & would stay only 5 minutes. He is gone to town today & perhaps you could catch him at Brooks's in St James's St or at his flat.

You know where it is, I am sure. It would, I think, be good if you could get hold of him about our Christmas Music Page – & he is devoted to you and to Suzanne. He will be in town only a couple of days or so . . . [4]

Susie recalled the visit to Marl Bank near Worcester:

Herbert wanted him to talk about conditions in the music world at home. He was perverse to a degree, just like a naughty child, being at the same time hospitable and telling wonderful stories. His house is on the edge of the town with a large garden. His daughter Mrs Blake was there and his dogs very much in evidence.

[SHJ, undated: November 1931]

Elgar told H. H. that his inspiration for the *Nursery Suite* had come from Eddie Morrow's drawing on one of our family Christmas cards.[5]

*   *   *

Susie was selling flags for the Lifeboats at Marble Arch tube station when Dame Ethel Smyth arrived

full of luggage and parcels and with the dear old man's grey velour hat on. She bought a flag and as I was pinning it on I couldn't resist making myself known and in two minutes we were having a great argument about critics. She was talking very loud about Beecham and Bruno Walter and was cursing the critics for not admitting that a woman could compose. We parted friends.

[SHJ, 20 May 1930]

The cellist May Mukle recalled Dame Ethel's drawers descending at rehearsals and how she stopped, pulled them up and said, 'They always do that.' [SHJ, 1 June 1930]

In his Highgate house, once the home of Samuel Coleridge and where Susie often joined in games of charades, J. B. Priestley gave a big party for Wilhelm Backhaus on the eve of his Grotrian Hall recital.

Susie mentions some of the guests – a non-Bloomsbury list which would surely have elicited Virginia Woolf's spite.⁶ The snobs were horrified at Priestley's Yorkshire accent, Virginia calling him 'a tradesman writer' and pouring scorn in her diaries on 'the Roberts and Sylvias'. Walter de la Mare had introduced Priestley to charades which he considered the ideal antidote to the lonely business of writing. Priestley thought of Lynd (who had given him work on the *Daily News*) and de la Mare as the most delightful companions of all the writers he knew. One cannot imagine Virginia in such an irreverent crowd with their *bonhomie* and sense of the absurd. Speaking of Ashley Dukes (drama critic and husband of Marie Rambert), Priestley said to Susie, 'He looks as conceited as I feel.'

> Backhaus enjoyed himself and took a great fancy to Sheila Lynd. Nothing happens at these parties [in Susie's book for 'nothing' read 'no music'] but it's pleasant to see everyone and there is much eating and drinking.   [SHJ, 2 December 1932]

At the recital the following day Freddie Gaisberg of HMV told Susie and Herbert that business was very bad: the slump was making itself felt. 'I thought you were very busy at Hayes,' H. H. said. 'Oh yes,' Gaisberg replied, 'making our coffins!' [SHJ, 3 December 1932]

*   *   *

In the early years when Susie and H. H. were abroad at a festival, a young man often sought them out, following them to a café or down the street. This was Walter Legge, the future impresario and self-styled 'midwife to music', who would later bring into the world some of the most successful recordings of the greatest artists of the century. At the time my parents first knew him he was about to join HMV and work with the brilliant musician and talent scout Fred Gaisberg. This partnership was not a marriage of minds for while Legge was clever and gifted (he had an outstanding memory, aural, visual and numerical) he was devious and often gratuitously unkind. Notorious for upsetting his artists (including Furtwängler), he was later seen reducing his wife the singer Elisabeth Schwarzkopf to tears at one of his sessions. Before he found his true *métier* he had dabbled under

102

the pseudonym of Gerald Young in journalism and musical politics. H. H. refused one of his articles, 'usually damning articles against British singers or conductors. As he is a member of the group formed with Mrs Claude Beddington to support Covent Garden one wonders what game he is up to. Herbert says he has octagonal feet.' [SHJ, 7 May 1932]

> At the Opera Circle in the evening Walter Legge was lecturing on Hugo Wolf's *Der Corregidor*. He tries so hard to imitate Ernest Newman and as a result he is a bore. His lecture was dull and when he began talking of the history of opera, groans went up from the assembled company – more groans when he put on records of Wagner operas. I don't think I want to join the Opera Circle.
>
> [SHJ, 7 May 1932 and 22 April 1934]

*   *   *

The great black American bass Paul Robeson brought his accompanist Lawrence Brown to the studio to try out some songs. Unlike my sister, I hid behind my father's trousers. Robeson was understanding and coaxed my shyness out of me. At the piano Lawrence Brown sang 'Nobody's Knows the Trouble I've Seen' as if shouldering all the grief and pain of his race, and years later Susie recalled how this had moved her to tears. This was the period when Robeson was banned from London's Savoy Hotel in case his presence incommoded American patrons.[7]

*   *   *

Lilian Baylis, 'the Lady of the Old Vic', never knowingly let anything get in her way. An appalling driver but undeterred by the tramlines on Blackfriars Bridge, she drove over them and was incensed when the oncoming tram failed to make way for her. When money for her theatre was short she knew that the Lord would provide, and would drop to her knees in the office to ensure His compliance. She had £15 in the account when in the early days she decided to put on an opera. In the First World War bombing raids were not permitted to interfere with a performance. ('Will all those who wish to leave please do so at once? We are carrying on.') She was stubborn and tactless and failed to put on new plays but drew enormous loyalty from the company who took pay cuts to keep the theatre going. She believed she had direct access to God and to the Bard himself.

Shakespeare, however, had not come easily to Baylis: she had no experience of drama when she took over the old Royal Victoria Hall after the death of her aunt Emma Cons, and it was some years before she felt confident enough. She turned to my mother. 'Miss Baylis asked me if I knew a good Shakespearian producer,' Susie wrote in her journal.

> Andrew Leigh is good, but too gentle. I feared so from watching his crowds on the stage. The principals are so good. Every time I see Esme Church I like her better.   [SHJ, 28 February 1929]

> We set off for the wilds of Stockwell and Miss Baylis's house . . . overrun by members of her Shakespeare Company and her Opera Company, also critics, producers, dancers and friends . . . She is a great woman, forceful and persistent. Mary Terry told me that Miss Baylis had heard a voice within her saying, 'Give them Shakespeare,' and she couldn't forget it.   [SHJ, 14 September 1930]

> At the Critics' Circle lunch at the Café Royal Lilian Baylis introduced me to Marie Ney and discussing her husband said, 'I understand that kind of man. When I was eighteen I was engaged to a man who used to go out and kill lions in the morning and sew on buttons for me in the afternoon.'[8]   [SHJ, 10 October 1930]

Andrew Leigh succeeded Robert Atkins as Director of Productions. (He would be followed by Harcourt Williams, Henry Cass and Tyrone Guthrie.) Although Harcourt Williams was Baylis's favourite director, Andrew Leigh won the friendship and goodwill of all the staff. According to Baylis's biographer both 'believed in compromise rather than confrontation'.[9] Both had a solid Shakespearian grounding.

Although designed to house opera and ballet, Sadler's Wells Theatre opened with a special production of *Twelfth Night* with John Gielgud and Ralph Richardson. There was an overdraft of £15,000. Baylis continued to press for money and she dragooned society women into distributing her green leaflets. She needed all the help she could get and H. H. gave her much support.

> We found Baylis in a bath chair in the vestibule. [She was recovering from an operation]. There were very few people there, mostly from newspapers. I suggested a performance of *Trelawny of the Wells*. As to the Well itself, Baylis's only fear is that some of the surrounding female population might be tempted to drown their illegitimate offspring therein. [SHJ, 30 December 1930]

Just before Christmas 1931 Helena and I had our first taste of the theatre when we were invited to a children's matinée of *A Midsummer Night's Dream* at the Old Vic. In the cast were John Gielgud as Oberon, Leslie French as Puck and Ralph Richardson as Bottom. Robert Speaight played Demetrius and Harcourt Williams, who directed, was Theseus. Much nonsense is talked about small children being too young to enjoy plays or music: one cannot start too early. Susie noticed that we sat quietly entranced, giving the occasional little shout of joy or laughter. [SHJ, 23 December 1931] At tea in Baylis's room we pulled crackers with Puck in his flame-coloured costume attended by a flight of fairies in full make-up. It was magical but it was also quite natural: we were simply migrating from one reality to another over the buns and jellies. For weeks afterwards we played relentlessly at being Peaseblossom, Cobweb, Moth and Mustardseed, jumping noisily off the studio 'throne' in our desperate efforts to imitate the fairies.

We also saw *The Tempest* with John Gielgud in his first Prospero, Ralph Richardson as Caliban and Leslie French as the first male Ariel, superbly naked or very nearly, covered in body paint with a minute thong. Helena marvelled that fairies had belly-buttons. This memorable production under Harcourt Williams inspired Eric Gill's carving of Prospero and Ariel above the entrance to then newly-built Broadcasting House.

*   *   *

Exotics and a Concerto Exhumed

The conductor Albert Coates, once observed eating the biggest dinner H. H. had ever seen, claimed to be 'a sort of envoy of the Russian government with *carte blanche*'. 'He is,' Herbert wrote to Suzanne, 'the Mussolini of music in Russia – his own phrase!' [H. H./S. H., undated 1932] They were to be invited as guests of the Soviet government, Albert said grandly, showing a letter in Russian with its translation into English which he was taking to HMV and which sanctioned the spending of hundreds of thousands of pounds.

We had Albert Coates to lunch. He had asked, 'May I bring Hilda?' and then when I was out telephoned to say he was bringing another lady, Mrs Hessler, Hilda's sister. They arrived a little before their time. Albert flung himself down at once, having embraced us, and went fast asleep. I awakened him and proceeded with lunch. The telephone rang, another sister of Hilda's. I invited her to come along. Lunch was a merry affair. Albert was supposed to be losing weight. He had an orange instead of soup. Hilda Lindas had been to Moscow. Much talk and we asked questions. Albert said, 'The workers are still workers. The scene-shifters at the Opera get a hundred roubles a month – I spend that in a day.' (As I don't know what a rouble amounts to it is difficult to judge.) I asked him about the abandoned children who form bands of fearful scoundrels and raid shops and accost individuals. He said there are concentration camps for them. When they are caught they are beaten senseless, put in hospital and if they recover and don't [illegible] too much they are sent to these camps and trained. They go south in the winter but come north again in the warmer weather. They are terrible to behold – filthy, diseased, almost naked. 'If I see them I give them money at once,' said Albert. They'll stop a lady and demand money and if she doesn't give it they throw handfuls of lice at her. They are eight to fourteen years old, boys and girls. What a subject for a writer. Albert said there is one of them at the Opera, a tenor who had been to a concentration camp.

[SHJ, 20 February 1932]

Amongst the good being done in Russia is the care of working mothers. They are entitled to two months before and two months after the birth of their child, on full pay. It is true that the State may send them to clinics far away, but nevertheless they are looked after. Divorce is no longer easy. Churches exist and people go to them, but they are forbidden. One must work to eat and be educated. A banker's daughter might have to spend an hour in a factory each night to get permission to attend a school.

Albert described a visit to a man called Schmidt who held an important post under the Soviets. Arriving at Schmidt's house Albert said to his host's chauffeur, 'Look after my chauffeur, won't you?' They went in to dinner and presently Albert's chauffeur, the host's chauffeur, cook, gardener, etc. followed, and sat and ate with them. Afterwards they put foxtrots (which are forbidden) on the gramophone, and all danced together.

He begged Herbert not to publish anything political that he had said, otherwise he would not be able to return.

After lunch I thought the ladies looked cold, so we moved to the fire and left H. and Albert talking. They were talking hard when Calvo[coressi] and Ethel came in. Calvo joined them, and Ethel joined us. I could hear some of Albert's conversation, on the subject of Mussorgsky, Rimsky-Korsakov and so forth. Albert announced that the *Boris* [*Godunov*] published by OUP is not the real one, which he has seen and is in the possession of Nicolai Korsakov. Calvo [critic and specialist of Russian music] was silent for the rest of the afternoon. I spoke to him several times but his mind was far away. Evidently this was a bombshell. Albert told Herbert about [Russian] projects for doing *Walküre* with cinema effects. He told him of the ten new opera houses in process of erection with every modern device, whilst in Germany they are closing two hundred. He talked until tea-time, then he and the three ladies left us. Calvo looked unhappy.

Meanwhile Walter Legge, Guy [Pelham Boulton] and the Vanden Heuvels arrived. Walter Legge told us that he is the 'Gerald Young' who has been attacking [Eustace] Blois [of the Covent Garden board] in the *Music Lover*.

In the evening we went to Marie Rosing's. A lot of people including Elena de Frey's sister who speaks eleven languages and works at the War Office, also the actor Ranievsky who recited in French. Before doing so he stood behind me in a corner doing 'mee, mee, mee' with cupped hand in front of nose, to get his voice into the right place.

Olga Alexeeva told me Mrs Cecil Gray's mother (who was married to the Grand Duke Michael) is now about to recover land in Poland belonging to the Grand Duke, and that she will be very rich again.[10]   [SHJ, 20 February 1932]

*   *   *

The Hungarian violinist Jelly d'Arányi lived around the corner in Elm Park Gardens. She and her sister Adila were the great-nieces of Brahms's friend the violinist Josef Joachim whose 1715 Stradivarius Adila had inherited. Jelly d'Arányi inspired composers – Bartók, Ravel, Vaughan Williams, Holst. She played Ravel's Sonata for violin and cello to the composer at a party in Paris where Bartók (with whom she had already performed) was also a guest. She dazzled Ravel through the night with gypsy music improvisations inspiring him to write a work especially for her. He borrowed a copy of the Caprices of Paganini the better to pile on technical difficulties and finished the flamboyant new work just in time. 'Jelly d'Arányi had only four days,' he wrote to a friend. Bartók angrily dismissed the 'gypsy' improvisations as a vitiated form of Magyar music. One wonders what he said when Ravel then light-heartedly called the piece the French for Hungarian gypsy: 'Tzigane'.

The d'Arányi-Fachiri family came in for criticism when the critic Dyneley Hussey brought his own family to a birthday party.

Reserved people are sometimes much less reserved than I am myself about certain things. When I mentioned Adrienne Fachiri [Alexander and Adila Fachiri's small daughter] Mrs Hussey dismissed her at once as 'horribly spoilt' without a thought of all the elements which go to make the child's temperament. Born after nine years of marriage to a Hungarian Jewish mother and

Greek Jewish father coming from families of musicians, one would expect to find something not absolutely docile. And yet Herbert tells me that Hussey is a humorist!

Those thoughts had followed some of Suzanne's musings on the English character:

I told Herbert tonight, we rarely meet English, really English people. The Husseys are the first really English people or should I say very English people I have met for years. I felt he would like to be jolly if he could, but that she wouldn't. They were so solemn somehow. We forget, meeting the people that we do, that England is full of solemn people and reserved people, and people who dare not show enthusiasm even if they feel it. Living in England teaches one that such people, often dubbed dull and pompous, have other fine qualities and make very staunch friends. And yet . . .

[SHJ, 4 January 1930]

Very dull German lesson. Dined at Julie Lasdun's. [. . .] Adila Fachiri talked musical shop and attacked critics and artists during the entire meal. Alexander ought to stop her. He tries but he is not strong enough. Julie was quiet and mysterious.

I called for H. and we went to Basil Maine's World's End studio – Jelly d'Arányi, Mrs Martineau, Frank Howes [later chief] music critic on *The Times* and his wife. Jelly amused us by saying that she and Adila were against cocktail parties. But she begged Basil not to tell Adila that she was having one or two or three. Howes is a dear fellow and I expect Mrs Howes is nice too, if one could penetrate all that Englishness. She doesn't laugh much.

[SHJ, 8, 29 May 1930]

We dined with Adila and Alexander Fachiri. I sat between the Swedish Minister Baron Palmstierna and Huberman the violinist. Huberman has a bonnet full of pan-European bees. He talks well but too much. The Danish Minister and his wife were also there. She is Russian, old-fashioned-looking with puffed hair and high cheekbones. She keeps in close touch with the spirit world. Another guest was Mrs Valentine Fleming. I knew her sister at

RADA but didn't mention it as I understand they held different views and met seldom. Jelly [d'Arányi] was back from her American tour. Adila was full of her approaching recital. I asked about Adrienne. Both Jelly and Adila say that not only is she not interested in music, but she isn't interested in anything.[11] Can that be true or is she receiving the wrong sort of training? She is being brought up a Protestant although Alexander is Greek Orthodox and Adila is Roman Catholic, 'so as to prove,' Adila says, 'that three people with different religions can be in the same family.' But methinks that if none of the three practise their various religions it is equal to having none. Is she bringing up Adrienne a Protestant because she wants her to be English? If the official religion in England were Roman Catholicism would Adrienne not be brought up in that religion?   [SHJ, 14 March 1932]

*   *   *

Lunch with Jo Jones and Paul Henry. We went to his studio and found a Miss Young or a Miss White in possession. I didn't like her, whether it's because Grace [Henry] is a friend or not. Jo and I both felt uncomfortable and were glad to get away after seeing some pictures.

LSO concert, Harty conducting. The orchestra was bad, and even the Brahms Double Concerto with Jelly [d'Arányi] and Beatrice [Harrison] didn't seem well played. Jelly did quite a lot of posing, and before the concerto both soloists fidgeted with their stands and Beatrice moved her chair. The audience tittered – a bad start I thought. I don't suppose there was much sympathy between the players.   [SHJ, 28 November 1932]

The controversial unearthing of Schumann's posthumous Violin Concerto set the musical world talking. Whatever a composer's or a legatee's wishes may be, there will always be interested parties keen to publish, perform, broadcast and generally be seen to be involved with a deceased composer and his work. In this case even spiritualism was enlisted. The composer's last surviving child, Eugenie Schumann, was distressed to watch these developments for she saw the work as flawed and a product of her father's final illness. The manuscript had been sold after Joachim's death, and offered by the Prussian State Library in Berlin to Schott in Mayence for publication. After legal advice Eugenie gave up the fight even before it had started. Germany claimed the first performance, which deprived d'Arányi of a world event.

'This is now postponed,' Suzanne wrote on 30 September 1937,

Palmstierna, late Swedish Minister, Adila and Jelly (according to Palmstierna's book) made contact with Schumann during a seance and Schumann told them to find the concerto and wished Jelly to play it. I can imagine what other fiddlers will think of this! [Richard] Capell [*Daily Telegraph* critic] wrote about it in a sceptical manner last Saturday suggesting that it was no news that such a work existed, and referred to Grove's [*Dictionary of Music and Musicians*]. Apparently Palmstierna found the finished work in the Berlin Museum after great difficulties.

Arrived at May [Harrison]'s flat in Nell Gwynn House ten minutes late. A Mr Phillips of the BBC there to dinner. He's a funny nervous man, most uncertain of himself. They were talking of Jelly, Adila, Baron Erik Palmstierna [former Swedish Minister in London] and the Schumann Violin Concerto. I said it did not surprise me that they had this experience but I thought it should not have been made public, and should not have been broadcast. Phillips said he was very sorry for Jelly as she will not have the first performance. [Georg] Kulenkampff will in Germany and Yehudi [Menuhin] in the USA. Somehow it seems wrong to me that they should break Joachim's will. He said it should not be played until one hundred years after Schumann's death. Phillips had been present at the seances. It is all done with tumblers turned upside down and letters strewn around the table. It seems such an undignified way for the spirit of a great man to communicate.

[SHJ, 20 October 1937]

The Concerto had its London performance in the following February, with d'Arányi as soloist. Suzanne thought it 'an unsatis-factory work, especially the last movement which seems to go on long after it has said its say.'[12] She noticed that the voluminous programme notes made no reference to the seances, but carried an advertisement for Palmstierna's book, *Horizons of Immortality, A Quest for Reality*, which purported to reveal how d'Arányi came to discover the Concerto. In the event d'Arányi surpassed herself and Suzanne found her 'inspired'.

> She wore a beautiful white-gold embroidered brocade with bare back and puffed sleeves and perfect fitting. Her head is fine and she looked so graceful leaving the platform. I feel she is a great artist and lives for her *métier* and through it. She has fire and is not afraid of her instrument. She seems to put into it something of what the Russians put into their voices and something which is racial and cannot be taught.   [SHJ, 7 February 1938]

When I was nine years old I heard Jelly d'Arányi play the Brahms G major Sonata (Op. 78). It was an impromptu performance in the studio with the composer Arthur Benjamin at the piano. With the exile from London and the long musical deprivation of the war I didn't hear this work again until I returned to London as a student and d'Arányi gave it at the Wigmore Hall. Her performance stunned me. Afterwards I stood on the pavement outside, the entire sonata resounding in my head; it had hibernated deep in the cerebral pocket where only music lies. As a child listening in the studio I had been a squirrel piling up my hoard for an unscheduled winter.

And not only the music had left its mark: d'Arányi was one of those musicians who in my eyes embodied everything that made an artist. Besides talent and skill she had passion, imagination and style, the enemies of mediocrity. Being young and naïve I believed that these qualities together with dedication and hard work were enough. I knew nothing yet of the workings of ambition, stamina, ruthlessness or even luck in an artist's career.

*   *   *

Arnold Bax and the Harrison Family

When London went mad about Diaghilev and his Ballets Russes students at the Royal Academy of Music began to give each other exotic names. The composer and pianist Arthur Alexander became 'Sasha' and the pianist Harriet Cohen 'Tania', a nickname she kept for the rest of her life. The composer Arnold Bax, whose discovery of Ireland he likened to a conversion, contented himself with the name 'Dermot O'Byrne' under which in a compartment well separated from his musical life he poured out a stream of poems and stories. Indeed he once declared in a broadcast that Yeats's poetry meant more to him 'than all the music of the centuries'.[13]

Like Irene Scharrer and Myra Hess – 'very small eternally giggling girls'[14] – Bax and Alexander were pupils of Tobias Matthay and neighbours in Hampstead. They were brilliant pianists and outstanding sight-readers, fooling about in piano duets straight from the full orchestral scores of Russian symphonies and *Le Sacre du Printemps*, and never playing from duets 'written as such'. There was no end to their larking about: cutting the long rests, sitting at a ridiculous distance from the keyboard and continuing to play when it was so dark they could barely see.

'Bax and Frontz' (Alexander's invention) were part of a group which included the Farjeons [Eleanor and Herbert], the Hesses, and Arnold's brother Clifford. They met regularly at the house of Frederick Corder who appears to have been more successful as host to a crowd of young people at Swiss Cottage than as teacher or composer at the Royal Academy of Music. Although many of his pupils showed promise, Bax is the only one who really made his mark.

For many years the pianist Harriet Cohen ('Tania') was Bax's muse. Even when their affair hit stony ground she continued to accompany him to musical events and to promote his work, ensuring than nobody but herself gave the first performance, indeed in some cases any performance of a Bax work. She is also known to have helped young musicians and with more skill than she showed in managing her own career but sadly her brittle manner put many people off. My mother wrote impatiently of her 'kittenish ways' and with the pitiless-ness of youth I saw her as artificial, always very chic and striking with her black hair severely drawn back from her face, but flashing a smile like a blade as she took her place in the stalls at the Wigmore Hall.

Watching Arnold's love-life at arm's length was his mother Mrs Ridley Bax or 'Leedle' (a corruption of 'little' as I remember). An adoring mother to Arnold and Clifford, she was a generous woman both with money and advice, if her social energy made her a little too eager to manage other people's affairs. Immensely hospitable, she often filled the house with her protégés and, as Bax's biographer Lewis Foreman describes, strange figures would emerge from their rooms to the surprise of luncheon guests. She lamented the break-down of Arnold's marriage (all the more because she had become to the general consternation a Roman Catholic), and since she con-tinued to see his wife Elsita and the children she refused to receive Harriet. Her sons Arnold and Clifford were always welcome but not their illicit partners.

Arnold and Clifford Bax were very different. I remember Clifford with his white hair and beard sitting beside a majestic Galia Coke at a musical party; there was something regal and Ruritanian about them. One evening when Leedle Bax and her two sons arrived at a London restaurant the head waiter took Clifford's hat and coat and gave him all his unctuous attention. Pointing to Arnold in his rustic tweeds, their mother said with great dignity, 'This also is my son.'

Meanwhile the violinist May Harrison was unhappy. She had worked with Bax in the early years, performed his work and was devoted to him. Sadly she imprudently tried to attract his attention when he was at his most absorbed in both a new affair and another composition. Suzanne, who was an old friend to all of them, dreaded the times when May brought up the subject of Harriet which she knew to be hopeless.

The Harrisons, like the Hambourgs and the Kennedys and the Goossens, were an exceptionally musical family. Colonel Harrison had sacrificed his career in India (where his wife Annie fought off boredom with her piano) in order to return to England and devote himself to the education of his four gifted daughters. Annie had no romantic illusions about music and her advice was practical and robust. She put cheval mirrors in her daughters' practice rooms to prevent them from smiling or pulling faces as they played. May was sent to St Petersburg to study the violin with the great Leopold Auer. At only nineteen for an important festival she 'jumped in' for Kreisler at Auer's request. In Berlin Beatrice was a pupil of Hans Becker and thereafter her cello remained her passion, her 1739 Guarnerius known to all as 'Pietro'. When Tommy Lascelles proposed to her she refused.

Beatrice had become a close friend to Princess Victoria, Edward VII's daughter, a sensitive and very musical girl who was somewhat crushed by the demands of her mother the beautiful Queen Alexandra. She never married. The Harrisons were known for their connections and the royal presence at many of their concerts. Stunned fellow passengers on a train journey peered gingerly over their newspapers as they overheard one Harrison sister casually ask the other, 'Have you heard from the Queen lately?'

Both sisters inspired composers – Delius, Elgar, Bax, John Ireland, E. J. Moeran. Beatrice was coached by Kodály in her Surrey garden, and played Fauré's *Elégie* with the composer. Elgar said to her before a performance of his concerto, 'Give it 'em, Beatrice, give it 'em. Don't mind about the notes or anything. Give 'em the spirit.'[15]

> I went with H. to the Oxf. Univ. Press, a private concert and tea, all works of Dr [Ernest] Walker of Oxford. Miss Murray Lambert reminded me of Kathleen's [?] vile fiddling. Miss [Elsie] Suddaby wasn't bad but Beatrice Harrison was best. But what queer garments. She was wearing a black hat with a dog on it, a white dog.
> [SHJ, 6 November 1929]

Both May and Beatrice gave many performances of H. H.'s arrangements of Irish songs which made up the Kilmacrenan Edition, and for which they and Jelly d'Arányi contributed bowings and fingerings.[16] Beatrice became famous with a wider public when her playing of Rimsky-Korsakov's *Chant hindou* brought a nightingale back to the Oxted woods which bordered the Harrisons' garden. At the first broadcast the locals' sweet nothings in the summer night almost drowned the bird-song. This music became a regular event bringing coachloads of tourists including gardening enthusiasts who insisted on being told the name of every plant. Beatrice became expert in inventing these while the gardener muttered that the birds attracted by the music were eating all the fruit. Beatrice, her violinist sister Margaret and her pianist sister Monica remained in their parents' house, together with sixteen Scotties, other dogs and 'a menagerie of tortoises, fish and birds'. They also adopted a baby donkey who at a bus stop on the journey home brayed with his head out of the taxi window. May preferred independence and settled in Chelsea.

Tania [Harriet Cohen], Arnold [Bax] and Stella Steyn the painter to dinner. Arnold played his new James Joyce song 'Watching the Needleboats at San Sabba'[17] – a lovely thing. We made him play it again and again. Arnold rather prides himself at being a cynic. He's a fine mimic and tells good stories. The evening was gentle and quiet with a lot of piano. Harriet sang a little too. They left at midnight.   [SHJ, 19 April 1930]

Caught the train to Oxted. We went straight to the studio and Herbert and Beatrice practised and practised. Brady the Irish wolf-hound lay across the floor during the rehearsal. He's the size of a pony but a gentle loving thing. He stood up and gave H. a punch in the ribs by way of greeting. I sat by Mr Thayer of Philadelphia at lunch. His passion is cricket. He tolerates music out of a sort of duty but hears it not. He loves his wife and therefore he accepts it, and she loves him and goes to cricket matches. After lunch more rehearsal and many visitors to tea, amongst them Peggy Ashcroft whom the American ladies immediately attacked on the subject of *Othello* and Paul Robeson.   [SHJ, 20 July 1930]

Although Susie didn't record the reproaches in detail one can safely guess that they were connected with the scene, controversial at the time, where Robeson, the black Othello, kisses Peggy Ashcroft, the white Desdemona, in a production which nevertheless ran for 295 performances. Robeson was used to this: from the law firm (he had a law degree) where he couldn't work, to the All-American football team from which he was frequently dropped and London's Savoy Hotel where they wouldn't serve him, he encountered prejudice and insults.

> We were expecting guests at 4 but the bell rang at 3.30 – forty-one guests. Herbert gave out the presents. He and Arnold Bax improvised duets for the musical chairs. The children pulled a huge cracker sent to them by May Harrison whom they love.
>
> [SHJ, 25 December 1930]

*   *   *

Three years later the famous cello and the nightingales attracted a lot of people.

> After a great deal of telephoning we arranged for five cars to go to the Nightingale Festival at Oxted. We got there about 10.30. The garden was crowded, it was dark, there were noises of cars and people talking in the marquee. At first it seemed quite mad but after a while, when Beatrice played in the wood, we heard the nightingales sing quite beautifully. Some of the party got out of hand. We had a lovely breakfast at Lyons Corner House at 6.30 a.m. I didn't feel a bit tired. The country in the early morning mist was exquisite. I was glad I stayed up to see it.
>
> We had some tea and saw the children. For me Sunday was washed out but H. went round to A. J. Munnings.
>
> [SHJ, 13 May 1933]

*   *   *

Heseltine, Gray, Moeran and Ireland

The composer and writer Philip Heseltine alias Peter Warlock (1894–1930) was part of a musical triumvirate which included Cecil Gray and Bernard van Dieren. He was an unhappy man of great talent with a sensitive but disturbing nature. Very witty with a gift for limericks and nonsense rhymes and given to waspish turns of phrase, he was also melancholy, self-doubting, restless and unfocused as if suspicious of life before it had properly begun. He was often helpful to his friends but being also unpredictable he once left Gray, his partner on the journal *The Sackbut*, with a mountain of problems while he took himself off to Paris and then decided to stay there.[17] He enjoyed provoking outrage in the music establishment. Being the product of a conventional background perhaps he had never out-grown a need to shock. Long obsessed by the music of Delius (who acted for many years as a sort of guru), he later shifted his attention to the Anglo-Dutch composer Van Dieren with, in between, a period in the orbit of D. H. Lawrence and Ottoline Morrell which ended in quarrels. Having dabbled in a great many things he found a path for his musical talent when he discovered the Elizabethan manuscripts in the British Museum and drew inspiration from them for his own remarkable songs. When he adopted the identity of the swash-buckling Peter Warlock some music previously rejected found a publisher who had earlier turned it down. Meanwhile behind a Mephistophelian beard Philip Heseltine was able to hide his demons and these he sought out quite purposely in order, he declared, to bend people and events to his will. With Cecil Gray he experimented – and to his lasting damage, many thought – with the occult, with astrology (a horoscope had shown 'a satanic influence'), the tarot and black magic . On one occasion while a naked girl was 'offered' on the altar of a country church a thunderbolt hit the tower and a piece of masonry crashed to the ground.

Peter Warlock might have been more at home in our era with his irreverence, his passion for early music and a louche fantasy side with a touch of *Monty Python* – prancing about in a long witch-doctor's robe with a big black hat, or lying cruciform on the floor of

Carmen Melis and Margherita Sheridan at Bellagio

F. P. H. and Ellen at Canyon Drive

James Joyce and Pat Hoy, Ostend 1929

Christmas Greetings, 1928. Edwin Morrow's drawing which inspired Elgar's Nursery Suite.

Family in the studio, 1929

Beatrice Harrison and 'Brady', Oxted, 1929

Peter Warlock at Eynsford

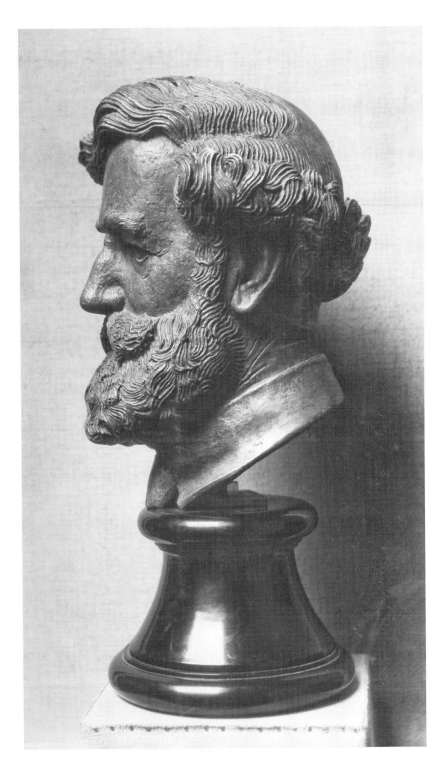

Hilary Stratton's bust of F. P. H., 1932

Celebratory dinner for the first Belisha Beacon,
Savage Club, 17 November 1934

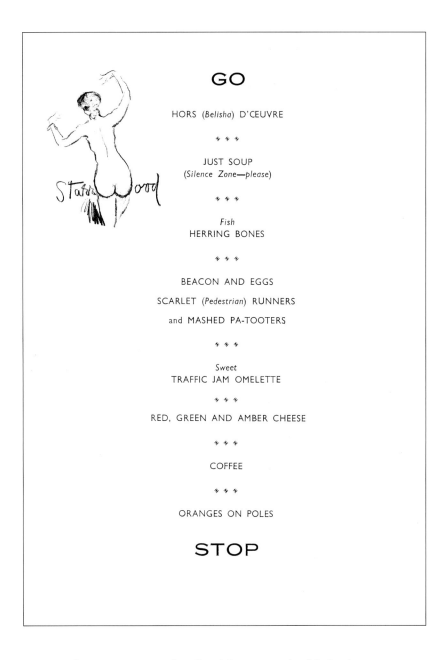

GO

HORS (*Belisha*) D'CEUVRE

❖ ❖ ❖

JUST SOUP
(*Silence Zone—please*)

❖ ❖ ❖

Fish
HERRING BONES

❖ ❖ ❖

BEACON AND EGGS

SCARLET (*Pedestrian*) RUNNERS

and MASHED PA-TOOTERS

❖ ❖ ❖

Sweet
TRAFFIC JAM OMELETTE

❖ ❖ ❖

RED, GREEN AND AMBER CHEESE

❖ ❖ ❖

COFFEE

❖ ❖ ❖

ORANGES ON POLES

STOP

Among the signatures; John ('Jock') Murray (publisher),
G. L. Stampa (illustrator), C. R. W. Nevinson (painter),
'Poy' (cartoonist and in the Chair), Walter Starkie (writer),
Jan Hambourg (violinist), D. B. Wyndham Lewis (author and
journalist), William Murdoch (author and journalist) and H. H.

Ellen and Lena in the garden – a 'Chekhovian group, with Ellen at the samovar!'

Suzanne Hughes

The family at the piano and (*below*) Angela in the studio

Herbert Hughes

Signed menu, Majestic Hotel, Paris, 1929, and (*opposite*)
Granny Mac, Lena, Angela and Helena, Dedham, *c.*1930

A watercolour of 125 and 127 Old Church Street by Tarka Kings

Westminster Cathedral, or again suggesting the renting of caves to flagellants whose shrieks would go unheard.

And yet even Herbert Howells, who described Heseltine as the most satanic person he had ever met, conceded that with the bitterness stripped away he could be gentle and affectionate. After his early death Sir Richard Terry made the distinction: 'a scholar, not a pedant'. Warlock was the first important editor of Elizabethan airs and this brilliant man left a corpus of songs which have long outlasted the melancholia, the scandals and the tragic death.

Susie and Herbert were aware of the contradictions, and Susie, perhaps particularly, of the threatening element in his personality.[18]

I went to a Burlington House concert and heard Italian music while sitting among the Old Masters. Mrs [Hugo] Wortham [wife of 'Peterborough' of the *Daily Telegraph*] showed me pictures lent by her uncle [Julius] Bache of New York. I had a long talk with [Philip] Heseltine – an odd creature with very nice bits hidden – a mass of complexes.   [SHJ, 18 February 1931]

H. H. to Suzanne at La Rocque, Jersey

Chelsea, Sunday 3 August 1930

Darling mine – I had a note from Philip Heseltine a few days ago and he came to see me yesterday. Result we spent practically the whole day together – lunched on pork sausages and red wine in the kitchen – and I missed writing to you. Forgive me! He was on his best behaviour – the sort of person you have guessed he could be: really lovable and rather tragic. We talked music for hours. We talked also of Joyce and I think I have persuaded him to do a song for the volume [*The Joyce Book*] after all. I played him Arnold [Bax]'s, and Moeran's and my own, and he was entirely sympathetic over each. He called mine 'a lovely thing', insisted upon hearing it three times – and thought Arnold's the best song he had ever written. His humility was sincere in presence, so to speak, of Arnold's music; felt he could never approach such beauty himself.[19] He brought a new song in MS – a terribly sad thing – words by a friend of his, Bruce Blunt, who wrote the Carol the *DT* published two or three Christmases ago. He thinks I ought to bring

119

in John Ireland. I dunno. In the middle of the afternoon [Luigi Innes] Meo called and we had a recital of gramophone records, 'Doctor Foster' being encored many times!

Robin [Legge, Music Editor] was acutely nervous at the office on Friday morning – couldn't sit down, and handed me a number of prospective articles to read, which he should have read himself. He was a perfect wreck and nobody apparently knows it but me.[20]

[H. H. to S. H., 3 August 1930]

Bernard van Dieren and Peter Warlock came to lunch. I had never met Van Dieren before. A wonderful talker. His Catholicism interested me, his knowledge thrilled me and his personality I found most attractive. Warlock was off-colour having eaten fish-cakes at a coffee stall the night before, but after a while he bucked up and lost his sickness and his shyness. We didn't finish lunch till 5, and they didn't leave till 7. Herbert had put on some new records and we all laughed heartily at poor old Conan Doyle. He can't say his s's or he says too many. His lecture on spiritualism was mirth-provoking I'm afraid. Warlock seemed to love Herbert's Doctor Foster and Humpty Dumpty, in fact he dubs H. H. affectionately 'Dr Foster'. H. H. sent Van Dieren off with a copy of *Pomes Penyeach*, having extracted a promise that he would be one of the contributors to *The Joyce Book*.

[SHJ, 2 September 1930]

At the proms it was an English night. Constant Lambert had a great success with his *Rio Grande* which he conducted. On the way home we ran into Teddy Schneider and all went to the Brasserie Universelle. He told us John [McCormack] is building a house in Hollywood.   [SHJ, 4 September 1930]

We saw Father and Ellen off at Victoria, a cold wet dank day. I was busy doing nothing very badly all day, in fact slackness betook me. Sir Harold Boulton's chauffeur came for us and we set off for Copped Hall at 6.30. We were in time for dinner.

Copped Hall, Sunday 30 November 1930

Up early and amused ourselves reading and writing – it was too wet to go out. I went to Mass with Sir Harold while H. H. worked. We had the most peaceful day. Herbert finished Little Boats, a lullaby.   [SHJ, 29, 30 November 1930]

What is happening to my German these days? I must set to. How the time goes.   [SHJ, 3 December 1930]

We expected [Augustus] John to lunch but he couldn't come because of his daughter Poppet's engagement. They were having a family lunch.

Herbert and I lunched heartily and went to hear Yehudi Menuhin. The Albert Hall was not full. He played marvellously but that dank cold foggy depressing Sunday-in-the-Albert-Hall feeling was uppermost. Went home to find a message from Augustus and Marie Rosing to say they would both be in after 5. Marie brought Val. They want help for some Russian bass. Augustus arrived with the Joyce drawing. I fetched H. from the Taits [neighbours] and we spent until nearly 8 o'clock talking of Joyce, the drawings, old times. It was rather in the nature of a reunion. A. had to go off for dinner. We went to Maurice Chevalier at the Albert Hall. It was a depressing experience.

Herbert and I went to Cambridge, he to feast and make merry with the Master and Fellows of St John's in company with Claude Guillebaud and I to spend the evening with Pauline. I found her fagged beyond words. She is expected to have a hundred and twenty young men from John's to the house at least once during the term. It seems too much for her.   [SHJ, 7, 8 December 1930]

Called at the Free State Office. Whilst Lena and I were talking to Bessie [Foxe], Kiernan rushed in with a white face to tell us that Peter Warlock had been found dead, gassed in his flat. I was shocked. I telephoned H. H., found that he had gone off on some job. When I left the Office I found all the placards announcing Warlock's death. It seemed so terrible, I couldn't do any more shopping and went home.

I can only remember trying to shop and not succeeding very well. Mrs Philip Rea's party is postponed so I had a free evening. Herbert had a telephone call from Van Dieren who said he had spent the evening with Peter W. and had been struggling with him a great deal, but had no idea he was contemplating such a thing. All his men friends are distraught.

[SHJ, 17, 18 December 1930]

Herbert went to the inquest on poor Peter Warlock and met his mother, Mrs Buckley Jones, and all his friends. The jury did not agree to a verdict of suicide. Strange that he left his money to a Miss B[aker] and not to Miss Barbara Peache with whom he was living. They all speak highly of her and her behaviour. It appears she had been to a dance on the night of the tragedy. It's all strange and sad. A letter was read in which he said to his mother that he regarded Christmas as a time of gloom and preferred to remain in London working.

[SHJ, 22 December 1930]

I met H. H. at the *DT* office and went with him to view the new Sadler's Wells Theatre. On the way he told me that he was to succeed R. H. L. [Robin Legge, Music Editor] and how casual the Editor [A. E. Watson] was about it. After a long discussion about Covent Garden, etc., he said quietly, 'I suppose you know Legge is resigning?' 'Well what about the Music Page?' H. asked. A. E. W. said, 'Do it. You do it anyway, don't you?' That's all.

[SHJ, 30 December 1930]

The Edinburgh-born composer and critic Cecil Gray (1895–1951) was torn between writing music and writing prose – 'a writer and', not 'a writer or', he said of himself. In his youth a heart condition led him to read enormously and he became known for his erudition. Rejected for army service in World War I he moved to London and lived in poverty in a small Chelsea flat. At the Café Royal he met Heseltine and soon became friends with Augustus John, Constant Lambert, Bernard van Dieren and Jacob Epstein. It was there that the sculptor persuaded a puzzled Gray to remove his shoes and socks and muttered, 'They'll do,' Gray's hands, neck and feet were to serve for Epstein's figure of Christ while Van Dieren was to be the principal model.

Pub crawls, roisterous nights and painful sequels convinced Gray that tearing life up by the roots did nothing for his work, and with Heseltine he became involved in a welter of grandiose projects. One of these was a promotional concert of Van Dieren's controversial music. Characteristically this was preceded by a careful antagonisation of the entire London music establishment and although well attended the concert received a terrible slating. Entanglements with writers such as D. H. Lawrence and Anthony Powell brought transparent and often cruel caricatures in fiction and much bitterness in what Gray's daughter Pauline calls 'a dizzy carousel of character assassination'.[21] They were all at it.

Gray's rather unwieldy music was expensive to perform and rarely heard (he was not drawn to small-scale pieces), and he drank heavily, ruining his already delicate health. He had many love affairs and three beautiful wives. The first of these, and the mother of Pauline, was Tata, daughter of Natalie Brasova, morganatic wife of the Grand Duke Michael of Russia who was, very briefly, the last Tsar.[22] Tata, ex-Mrs Val Gielgud and ex-Patou mannequin, shared with Cecil a love of cats and a sense of humour but little else. Continuing to lead her own life she eventually moved on to another marriage, exposing Pauline to the perils of her two successors neither of whom made a tolerable stepmother. He was too kind to women, Gray rated, for his own good.

Working for the *Daily Telegraph*, with H. H.'s blessing he spent a few days with Sibelius while Tata visited her father Sergei Mamontoff, director of the opera in Tallinn. The Finnish composer detested journalists and musical talk but Gray made a success of the meeting by adroitly steering their long conversations in other directions. Before he left, and possibly planning a biography, Gray asked Sibelius to tell him something about himself. The great man answered, 'J'ai un membre énorme.'[23]

Took the children to tea at Cecil Gray's house. Pauline is now 2½. His beautiful Russian wife very friendly. She told me about Warlock and how he quarrelled with his lady (Barbara Peache) and locked her in the bathroom, and she being quite a calm and cool person, simply took a bath! Natasha Gray spent the evening with her and when she [Barbara Peache] went back in the morning she found him dead. Evidently this has upset Gray very much. He suffers from heart, liver and nerves and has threatened suicide himself. She said he shouldn't drink but she can't go on nagging at him to stop, especially as she likes it herself. She has become great friends with Sidonie Goossens and they are going to Le Touquet together. Angela had heard Herbert say something about Natasha's relationship to the Grand Duke Michael and in the middle of tea suddenly asked her, 'Are you a Grand Duke?'

[SHJ, 22 May 1931]

Bernard van Dieren and his wife came to lunch. He talked about the difficulties of trying to come to any arrangement with the BBC about a Delius concert. The BBC asked him to approach [Sir Thomas] Beecham, after which they denied that they ever intended to do a Delius concert other than *A Village Romeo and Juliet* with Adrian Boult conducting. Van Dieren looked ill and exhausted.

[SHJ, 26 January 1932]

I wrote to Mamma and asked her for news of Dedham – nothing from there for a fortnight. No doubt Father [F. P. H.] is worrying over finance. It's a pity at his age to have to bother about it.

May Harrison was very pleased with the *Three Folk Song Studies* which H. did specially for her. [SHJ, 2 March 1933]

I'm reading Ibsen's plays at the moment – *Rosmersholm* and *Hedda Gabler*. Ibsen's technique is of immense interest. They are just ordinary people speaking in the most ordinary way, and yet he makes it all intensely dramatic and one is eaten up with curiosity to know what is going to happen next. I'm still reading Baker's *Dramatic Technique*. [SHJ, 3 March 1933]

On my way to meet Herbert and Lionel Hale at the Café Royal I saw all the posters announcing the closing of the New York banks.

[SHJ, 4 March 1933]

In the afternoon we went to the Delius concert. Beecham conducted. I was glad to hear the Hassan [incidental] music. At the theatre one can never hear it properly with people chattering. Mr Chenhalls let me look at the score of *Appalachia*. I felt I was holding some priceless material in my hands – the texture of the music is exquisite.

We visited the Van Dierens and found Arthur and Trudy Bliss there too. Van Dieren was looking ill. He wore a splendid maroon velvet coat and sat on his hunkers. Trudy said that if things go from bad to worse they will have to give up East Heath Lodge [Hampstead] and maybe go and live in the country. I said I dreaded the country. Things look very depressing all round, and the American situation is bound to have its repercussions in Europe.

Frida [van Dieren] is a most sympathetic person. He is a very sick man and I feel that she keeps him alive just by being herself.

[SHJ, 5 March 1933]

'No man I have ever known,' wrote Cecil Gray in his notebook, 'gave so much or asked so much in return as Bernard van Dieren.' About Frida he wrote, some pages further on, 'Disinterested altruism is the rarest of virtues. The only person I have ever known to possess it is Frida van Dieren. She has always been willing to give everything without any hope, expectation or desire of getting anything in return.'[24]

Some people slip easily into a drinking fraternity as did (in Herbert Howells' words) 'the Warlock gang'; others, like the young William Walton, find the 'convivial pressures' too great.[25] When the composer and music publisher Hubert Foss vacated a cottage at Eynsford in Kent, and it was taken over by Heseltine and his fellow composer E. J. Moeran, the tiny house and the surrounding pubs became a focal point for a great number of people more than happy to join in – among them the composers Arnold Bax, Cecil Gray, Constant Lambert, Lord Berners and C. W. Orr, the baritone John Goss, the poet Robert Nichols and the painter Nina Hamnett. On offer besides the drowning of troubles were Heseltine's wit, his arcane knowledge, his schoolboy pranks and, more seriously, his musical influence which was generally recognised as well as his often generous help.

Even when recovering from riotous weekends Heseltine found the peaceful setting a boon for his work. For Moeran on the other hand the rackety life was more destructive. As a despatch rider in the First World War he had suffered a head wound. Pieces of shrapnel had lodged too near his brain to be removed surgically and a steel plate was fitted into his skull leaving him prone to headaches, disorientation and irrational behaviour. Initially alcohol may have served as a painkiller but in the Eynsford circle it took hold of him and since he was shy and fiercely self-critical the proximity to the brilliant Heseltine damaged his confidence, leading him to recall later that at Eynsford his inspiration dried up. Only when distanced from that group did he return to form and produce after a long and painful gestation his G minor Symphony. Herbert Howells never forgave Heseltine for his part in the ruin of Moeran. Part of Moeran's tragedy is that unbeknownst to the public his strange behaviour stemmed not always from alcohol (which he avoided at certain periods) but from his disability. Fears of insanity hounded him at the end of his life.

Like Bax, whose music (like that of Ravel, Fauré and Vaughan Williams) influenced him, Moeran loved Ireland. In his early years his music evoked the lonely fen country; later Irishness took over. He set several of Joyce's poems, including 'Tilly' for *The Joyce Book*. He believed that Yarmouth fishermen took their songs into the 'back kitchens of Cahirciveen'.[26] He was perhaps happiest in the West. (See letter to H. H., pages 161–2.)

Another artist both stimulated and damaged by his boozy association with Heseltine was the brilliant and multi-talented composer, conductor and critic Constant Lambert who in Anthony Powell's words 'moved with perfect ease in the three arts'.[27] An unrevealed diabetic, his addiction to drink would lead tragically to his death at the age of forty-six.

The same threads run through all the accounts of this period: the disturbing nature of Heseltine's personality and the sinister atmosphere he engendered. The poet Robert Nichols spoke of the Eynsford house having a 'taint': 'one felt in it a spirit which seemed to darken the soul.'[28]

At the time of putting *The Joyce Book* together, H. H. wrote to Susie in Jersey

I telephoned to John Ireland on a wave of inspiration and made him spend the evening with me – from after dinnerish. I played him the songs from *The Joyce Book* and made him read *Pomes Penyeach* to make his choice. He got terribly excited over several of the lyrics – after having pleaded, very naturally, that he couldn't undertake to set any particular poem to order – and immediately selected one called 'Tutto e Sciolto'. We had an enormous talk, a real gak-gak, and played the piano together & solo. He is full of his new Piano Concerto which is to be done at the Proms in about six weeks. He loved my '[She Weeps over] Rahoon' (or so he said) and made one or two criticisms in detail that interested me: two beats extra in one bar, different cadence for the voice.

We talked of the College, of [Sir Hugh] Allen, Vaughan Williams and so on; enough scandal and gossip to fill the pages of the *Daily Express*, and afterwards we went into the Chelsea Arts Club for a nightcap. And so to bed, not too late.

This morning to Robin [Legge]'s. R. very quiet and gentle, Aimée being out shopping or something. Leaning again very much on my opinion. Passed on another article in MS for my verdict. Talked of writing one or two reminiscences of the eighties in Leipzig. He retailed one story of Mahler and I told him frankly it was so good that he ought to do it in eight hundred words. And so he will. It was a very funny story of musical and political conditions of that time, with Aimée as prima donna in a little provincial theatre.

Tonight I am calling at the Euston Hotel to take J. J. to the Proms. [William] Walton is conducting *Portsmouth Point* and [Sir Henry] Wood is doing Arnold [Bax]'s 1st Symphony. J. J .not much better, but glad to be invited to hear some music, poor soul.

I have written at least another one hundred words about Nohant![29]

All my love, Herbert. [H. H. to S. H., 14 August 1930]

Over a meal that autumn Ireland was in one of his unhappy moods: he clearly felt he didn't get the recognition he deserved.

> John Ireland came to supper and talked so much about himself and his music that we could have wept. Queer, strange unhappy creature. I told Herbert I was sure he had had a bad unsympathetic mother, from what he related. [SHJ, 12 October 1930]

Ireland, who was another Chelsea composer (his *London Pieces* were inspired by walks along the Thames Embankment), had indeed been unhappy and lonely as a child. His mother was an invalid and he, being the youngest of the family, was delivered up to sadistic bullying by his elder sisters and beatings by his brother. His refuge was music and he bravely auditioned for the RCM at the age of thirteen. His organ teacher, Sir Walter Parratt (who some years earlier had taught Herbert), mocked the young boy's clothes in front of a class of girls but Ireland managed to put the ogre in his place. Astonishingly he became an FRCO (Fellow of the Royal College of Organists) at the age of sixteen. Sadly, throughout his life a pessimistic streak bedevilled his relationships. Congratulated after a performance of one of his works he would mutter grimly that it wouldn't get another performance for years. He was brusque, but he was also kind. Discovering a talent for the piano of one of his choristers he accompanied the boy home to Cheyne Walk to urge the parents to let him have lessons. When he found out that the mother, a widow, couldn't afford the fees he offered to teach the boy himself. By one of the quirks of the honours system Ireland was never awarded the knighthood he could well have expected.

*   *   *

Genes

Besides the Harrisons a number of other musical dynasties, the Goossens, the Kennedys and the Hambourgs, drift in and out of Suzanne's journal.

Lauri Kennedy was leading cellist in the BBC Symphony Orchestra under Adrian Boult. His wife Dorothy was an excellent pianist and his cousin Daisy a gifted violinist who at one time surprised the clients of the Regent's Palace Hotel by leading an all-male orchestra in a series of Beethoven concerts. She was married first to the pianist Benno Moisewitsch, and later to the poet John Drinkwater.

Lauri was unhappy under the BBC régime.

> We had an evening with Lauri and Dorothy Kennedy at their house in Regent's Park. All during dinner he related to us how he is caught up in the BBC machinery. He has to play thirty-six hours a week for forty-eight weeks a year. He is called sometimes three times in one day. He says they are all dog-tired and can't give the performances they should. As leader of the cellos he has to turn up to all rehearsals and play under bad conductors just the same as any hack, and he never has time to practise his solo work. It's despairing. He wants to leave and yet fears that there isn't enough work outside unless he goes to the USA. And he has only just come from there to make his home in London. There is much wrong with the BBC, but who can right it? Boult can't, Lauri says. They want to have the finest orchestra, but how can they, when they treat their musicians like factory hands. Lauri says he can't remember what he was playing the night before.
>
> [SHJ, 16 January 1932]

A few months later the Hugheses and Kennedys met again.

> Daisy Kennedy wants them to form a Kennedy Trio with her. Lauri is tired of the BBC. If Beecham would only start his orchestra with [Albert] Sammons, [Lionel] Tertis and Lauri as leaders, he could work at ensemble playing and solo playing in his spare time. The BBC is drudgery of the worst kind. We listened in to some modern music – Křenek's *Theme and Thirteen Variations* and fragments from Alban Berg's *Wozzeck*.   [SHJ, 13 May 1932]

Lauri and Dorothy's son John was principal cellist in the Royal Philharmonic Orchestra. He is remembered as a flamboyant character, given to doing 'whirlies' with his cello in rehearsal. His wife Scylla was a pianist and their son Nigel is the unique and superbly musical Kennedy of today.

The composer Eugene Goossens, Eugene III in the musical dynasty, and his sisters the harpists Sidonie and Marie were familiar figures, but Léon, the oboist, was the Goossens we saw the most often. He lived in World's End Studio with his second wife Leslie Burrowes, principal dancer with Margaret Morris at the Little Theatre in Chelsea. When in later life they settled in the country Léon told Suzanne that the Great War had given him his first taste of an outdoor life like a first taste of freedom: until then he had been closeted indoors, a slave to hours of daily practice. On the Somme in November 1918 Léon had been hit by a high velocity bullet. This passed through the shaving mirror in his pocket but was deflected by the silver cigarette case which had been a present from Dame Ethel Smyth to his brother the conductor and composer Eugene Goossens III.

Another musical family was the Hambourgs. Mark, the eldest of six children, was a pupil of Leschetizky and in Busoni's opinion the most talented pianist of his generation. His violinist brother Jan made a number of arrangements for his instrument and also bought and sold works of art. Jan tended to be 'long' (as they say in Ulster) on his various activities. When after the Second World War he died in a Spanish train in the company of his two violins and a Botticelli the local mayor ordained a state funeral with all the trimmings including plumed horses.[30]

> I met H. at 6 o'clock and we went together to the *Sunday Times* Book Exhibition at Grosvenor House. I only wished I had more time to inspect the books, but we wanted to listen to Starkie's lecture at 6.30 p.m. We met the Murdochs and with them that horror Jan Hambourg. He sat next to me and I felt myself getting into blind rages every time he opened his mouth. He is so smug, conceited and egotistical. He knows everything, speaks all languages, has had a finger in every pie according to himself. He is the perfectly oiled and highly-polished bore. H. was going on to the Savage Club with Billy Murdoch, Starkie and McCaffrey, and when I heard Jan ask Billy if he could join them my heart sank for H. and I said to myself, 'His evening is spoilt.' And it was. After the

dinner to Hore Belisha at the Savage [see illustration] where he was ragged about his new traffic regulations, beacons and so forth, they returned to Murdoch's house. Jan Hambourg brought out his two Amati fiddles, took off his coat and to an audience consisting of [Walter] Starkie, H. H., McCaffrey and the Murdochs played his new edition of unaccompanied Bach. H. came home early, bored and exhausted. Jan . . . talks incessantly about himself and his Bach. He just set upon them and no one could get a word in edgeways.   [SHJ, 17 November 1934]

Boris Hambourg was the cellist of the family. Like his parents he settled in Canada where he was a founder member of the Hart House Quartet.[31]

Galia, their sister, lived in Carlyle Square. She was attractive as I remember, warm, funny, anxious and generous. She once remarked, 'All Russians are cruel unless they have Jewish blood in them.' [SHJ, 8 March 1938] Susie observed Galia's preoccupations with amusement. Her marriage to the Hon. Reginald Coke gave her an entrée to society and this she was determined to exploit to the full. She appears in the journal which I shall pick up on 10 March 1930.

I took my first lesson in German conversation at the Regent School of Languages with two girls, one middle-aged woman and one elderly lady.

In the evening we dined with [Irène] Poldowski at the Eiffel Tower restaurant to meet Guy Marriner, a New Zealand pianist. Altogether an odd evening. I think the pianist felt somewhat out of it as he departed at 11 o'clock. Nancy Cunard was dining with a very black gentleman called Henry [Crowder] with whom all seemed to be on familiar terms. Napper Dean Paul, Nina Hamnett and others drifted in and out. Later on we found ourselves in a breakfast room (Night Club) run by Napper – all very dull and depressing. I can't see what Irène sees in it all. The dark gentleman sang and played the piano badly without the marvellous negro rhythm and voice. We were glad to get home.

Cunard shipping heiress and daughter of Maud 'Emerald' Cunard (who had a famous liaison with Sir Thomas Beecham), Nancy was known for her wide circle of friends and lovers and her scandals. She was currently living above the Eiffel Tower restaurant with the African American jazz pianist Henry Crowder but her mother was having them followed by detectives and the proprietor Stulik eventually asked them to leave. (Margot Asquith, arriving for lunch, asked Emerald, 'What is Nancy up to? Is it dope, drink or niggers?') But Nancy had a serious involvement with literature, published several volumes of poetry and briefly (with Henry's help) ran the little Hours Press in Normandy, printing works by Ezra Pound, Norman Douglas, Samuel Beckett and others. She also produced a withering pamphlet on her mother, for which Thomas Beecham declared that she ought to be tarred and feathered. In another role she worked energetically for refugees from the Spanish Civil War, and later joined SHAEF as a translator. She died in Paris in 1965.

On a quieter note, following the Eiffel Tower evening, Susie records the first performance of Arnold Bax's Third Symphony at the Queen's Hall under Sir Henry Wood, 'very well received'. [SHJ, 10 March 1930]

Herbert's birthday (16 March) and the day of the party. It was a good night, ending at 6 a.m. We had the *Toy Symphony* with the critics playing the toys and John Barbirolli conducting. [André] Mangeot and his quartet, [W. W.] Cobbett and May Harrison and Lauri Kennedy responsible for the strings. Basil Maine caused much amusement with the cuckoo. Barbirolli entered into the spirit of it. He once stopped them all and made the critics play alone – the effect was absurdly funny. After that the quartet played Fauré's Piano Quintet with Mannheimer at the piano. This was wonderful. Hugh Campbell sang [H. H.'s] 'The Spanish Lady' somewhat nervously. James McCafferty, Herbert's find, sang superbly. Lena sang. [George] Zucco even recited. Basil [Maine] sang at the piano and Peggy O'Neill whispered a little song too. Violet managed beautifully all alone. She's a wonderful little girl. We slept from 6 a.m. to 10 a.m.

In the afternoon went with H. to Steinway's to hear a twenty-one-year-old unknown Hungarian pianist Miklos Schwalb – a wonderful lad – fire, poetry, poise, technique, everything in his playing and so exciting. A real musician, no money though. Had tea with Jenny Simson in her studio, William Steinway present, a charmer.   [SHJ, 10,14,16,18 March 1930]

Called on Galia [Coke née Hambourg] and Luba Hambourg. They talked of the party and Lena's singing. I asked them to be interested in Miklos Schwalb and they promised to bring some likely benefactors to hear him play.[32]

German lesson in the afternoon and in the evening went with Bessie [Foxe] to see *The Damask Rose* at the Savoy. The music is Chopin's mutilated by Clutsam, book by Clutsam and Robert Courtneidge. Poor Chopin. I think he'd feel this more than his illness. Thieves are put in prison, and as the mother said in *Mixed Marriage*, 'There's them that do worse and they do be put in Parliament.' Bessie hated it too.

Ogden came and whisked us off to his underground den of mystery in Soho. He put on James Joyce records, speaking 'Anna Livia Plurabelle'. Glanny [Stephen Glanville] was fascinated but I think Galia and Luba didn't know what it was about and Jenny looked frightened.

We went to Kettner's and had cocktails as Glanny's guests. Galia asked him to lunch but he couldn't stay, alas. He was in such good form, just like a child let out of school. Galia amused him by saying, 'Do lunch with us. You see I'm a rich widow now.' Then she added, 'You must think me common to talk like that.' 'On the contrary,' said Glanny, 'I think it most uncommon to be so frank on a first meeting,' and so on. She liked his pretty wit and he was taken with her I'm sure. Herbert, Luba, Galia and I had lunch at Kettner's and a long talk. We tried to persuade Galia that people, parties and invitations don't matter. She worries at being 'left out' as she calls it. I tell her that thinking of these things makes them happen, and anyway so little is worth worrying about.

Dined with the Macnaghtens in their new house in Park St. Beverley Baxter and Mrs Macn. sang *Tosca*. The music was the sad part of the evening, alas. Malcolm S[argent] took us home in his two-seater. He told us that Mrs Sam Courtauld sent a bill to Sir Hugh Allen for a seat at her last concert.

[SHJ, 25, 27, 29 March 1930]

*　　*　　*

Spent an evening with the Smithson Broadheads at 38 Cheyne Walk. Galia and Luba [her sister] were there. Galia was as ever warm-hearted and confiding. She had presented Becky Sieff at Court and was offended that she hadn't been given a suitable memento of the occasion – a diamond or two. Dear thing, she's like a jackdaw. Luba is as ever soft, sentimental and invertebrate.

Léon Goossens was there with Leslie Burrowes the dancer. She was at St Idesbald three years ago with the Margaret Morris Summer School, and since then she has been studying at Dresden with Mary Wigman. Léon told us that he and Fay[33] had parted company and it's obvious that Leslie Burrowes attracts him enormously. It was significant that when Edie the hostess asked her to dance she kicked off her shoes, asked Léon to play his oboe and they both improvised – first a slow movement, then a scherzo. [SHJ, 28 June 1932]

*　　*　　*

Sunday 20 November 1932 (my birthday)
We went to Yehudi (Menuhin)'s concert at the Albert Hall. He played concertos – Bach, Mozart and Elgar – and as an encore unaccompanied Bach. Packed house. Afterwards we went to tea with Julie Lasdun to pick up Anna Pearce's brooch which she had discovered caught in the net of her evening frock! Galia and Luba were there with Jan Hambourg over from Paris especially to hear Yehudi . . . [Jan is] a 'paycock', always showing off. It was amusing to see Galia coaxing a cheque or promise of one for Stella out of Miss Marks (of M. & S.). She put on the poor mouth, 'Poor Stella has to wear Luba's old clothes. Her husband's out of work,' and so on. I suggested to Galia that she ought to get some of her smart and influential friends to give Stella's husband a job.

8

Crossed Lines and Dislocations

Like all people working at home H. H. had his share of disruptions. Often they came from anxious singers. Although he was successful in broadcasts and recordings and performed H. H.'s songs most beautifully, the singer James McCafferty had problems.

> All during lunch [he] went into details about his diaphragm, his abdominal mind, his solar plexus. I laughed outright until the tears ran down my cheeks. Herbert laughed and then McCafferty himself laughed. Just for a few minutes he seemed normal, but he returned to the subject of himself and his voice and no matter how we tried we couldn't get him away from that – it's an obsession.
>
> [SHJ, 2 December 1932]

Another singer in the same line, although not blessed with the same talent, arrived unannounced protesting all the while that she didn't want to disturb H. H. Susie was tempted to say, 'Well if you don't then why don't you go home?'

> She began before H. came in and continued for about thirty minutes talking about all she had learned through Henry Wendon's muscular trouble. 'Our tongues are attached to our shoulder blades, rhythm is square, oblong or circular', etc. Herbert pulled her leg all the time shamelessly. [SHJ, 5 January 1930]

A neighbour, Willie Jaffe, came to tea the same day as the singer Laelia Finneberg. He turned to her and said, 'Will you tell me why it is that singers are always so fat?' Susie was mortified but Finneberg took this well. [SHJ, 28 November 1929]

> Mrs Finneberg, the prima donna's mother, and I had tea at the Piccadilly. She talked of Laelia and her singing, her plans, her

proposal of marriage from a rich Warsaw surgeon, her career in general. I had to keep a straight face when she told me she didn't like London but wanted to be abroad again as she missed the intellectual set. Anything less intellectual than Mrs Finneberg would be hard to imagine. When I asked her what she would do if Laelia married the surgeon, she said with great firmness, 'Oh, he would have to take me on too.' Now I wonder if the surgeon knows that? [SHJ, 14 April 1932]

The actress Máire O'Neill (Molly Allgood) telephoned H. H. about her disputes with her husband Arthur Sinclair (also formerly of the Irish Players), and Susie wondered how they had ever managed to live in peace. She had memories of her American tour in 1922 and the digs with the warring Allgood sisters.

I told Bess Tait [the miniaturist and a neighbour at 137] about the tour and said how I hated rows. Bess said, 'I like a good brawl now and then.' I can picture her standing up to it. Her cook once said when she swore at her, 'Oh Ma'am, you have a lovely flow!'
[SHJ, 29 May 1932]

Living a few houses away Bess missed the row which awakened us all in the small hours on a winter's night and came from next door at 127 (the other part of our house). Some dispute with our tenant Joy Vinogradoff had brought her brother the actor Robert Newton in a taxi to Church Street. There were screams and bangs and blows, a vase was broken, a telephone flew across the room and their mother Marjorie Newton was so frightened that she called the police who arrived in force. They stood helpless in the front garden and were not allowed to leave until they had escorted Robert to his flat. Robert Newton and his dog marched off and everyone went to sleep again. [SHJ, 20 January 1932] The next day Susie received a letter of apology from the unhappy Marjorie, anxious for the reputation of the family enterprise, the new Shilling Theatre in Fulham.[1] There were nine policemen in the front garden, Mademoiselle reported with relish. Helena and I were spellbound.

Susie and Eleanor Hoare spent an afternoon at the house of Mme

Visetti, the American widow of a controversial RCM teacher, Albert Visetti.

> Fearful, dreadful, terrible singing, painful, unhappy singing, bad, wicked singing. Julia Chatterton's folk songs were performed but I couldn't get any idea of what they were about. It is very dangerous to fly to foreign parts, hear some songs and make pianoforte arrangements and call them folk songs. I felt a brute saying I thought them nice because I didn't. How can an Englishwoman get a hold of Yugoslavia on a holiday – it must be in one's blood or else one must have genius. Eleanor's comments afterwards were rich, if not kind and appreciative. 'My friend Edna Ryan had lessons from old Visetti and developed varicose veins in her neck. Did you ever hear of such a thing?' said she, etc. We had tea at Fuller's after the reception.   [SHJ, 31 March 1930]

A few days later there was a strange evening at the house of the designer Oliver Bernard.

> I rang up the Oliver Bernards and asked if we were expected to eat beforehand and was told not to eat, so we didn't. We arrived at 8.30 p.m. and at 9.25 p.m. food was announced. We were ushered into the dining-room and there was the table with a few sandwiches and cakes sitting on it. We were ravenous and I got the giggles and kept on laughing immoderately when anyone made the least effort at humour. [The architect] Sir Owen Williams was there. His stories and conversation made us forget our hunger. Oliver was himself. He had just danced on a brand new Corona typewriter in a rage and it had retaliated and bitten him.
>
> Herbert thinks the sandwiches are part of Dora's Christian Science.
>
> A Miss Davis who is in *Bitter Sweet* told a story of a girl in the company who drowned some kittens and not knowing what to do with them took them in an attaché case to Hampstead Heath. As she was walking along trying to make up her mind where to deposit them a car drove up, out jumped a man, seized her case and drove off. I'd have loved to see this face when he looked at the loot!   [SHJ, 6 April 1930]

Susie's old friend from student days, the painter Jo Jones, lived in London hotels between journeys to Spain and Africa where she painted gypsies. It was gala night at the Constance Hotel.

> Nothing could be more pathetic than the sight of the solemn residents all sitting at their little tables, some of them alone, wearing the most absurd paper hats and not a smile on any face. Jo and I hastened over our food and vanished to her room.
>
> [SHJ, 17 January 1933]

Susie enjoyed recording quirky incidents and eccentricities, from George V's crease down not the front but the outside of his trousers at a Royal Garden Party, to the Princesses Helena Victoria and Marie Louise walking up and down smoking in the street during the interval of a play ('What would Queen Mary think of these bachelor girls?'), and the concert under the racehorse owner Sydney Beer, 'a sporting event with an audience to match and a shout of "Well played!" from a portly old gent as if it were football.' [SHJ, 20 July 1933, 9 July 1934, 24 January 1933]

After a Critics' Circle dinner when all the younger people were scattering to look for cars and taxis Susie caught sight of the seventy-six-year-old George Bernard Shaw walking away with the light step of a man of twenty. [SHJ, 9 December 1932]

Hugo Wortham ('Peterborough' of the *Daily Telegraph*) gave a dinner for the French restaurateur Boulestin. Hugo was a good host if laboriously sacerdotal over the wines. He had a long face which Susie found attractive 'when it makes up its mind to laugh'. Boulestin condemned all cocktails except gin and Dubonnet and all wines except fine champagne. The conversation moved on to meat. Susie heard that Australian meat was frozen for twenty-one years. 'Was it a good year?' asked Boulestin. Neil Grant of the *Cape Times* came up with a story about the *Manchester Guardian* journalist G. H. Mair when he worked for the Foreign Office.

> He had to entertain some Swedish pastors one day, and on another some Portuguese boxers, but he made a mistake. He gave the Swedish pastors the programme intended for the boxers – cabaret

turns and so on – with the result that the Swedes were delighted and at once became England's allies.   [SHJ, 17 January 1930]

J. B. ('Johnny') Morton was 'Beachcomber' of the *Daily Express* and creator of such characters as Lady Cabstanleigh and Professor Strabismus (whom God preserve) of Utrecht. Like most Irish priests Susie encountered and like Kiernan of the Free State Office, Johnny Morton fed my mother's appetite for argument, usually around 3 a.m. With priests it was the subject of censorship; with Kiernan it was all the recognition he felt Protestants were getting in Dublin to the dismay of the Abbey Theatre directors, etc. With Johnny it was usually France, religion and morals. Sadly she didn't record the inflammatory subject under discussion after a cocktail party at his sister-in-law Kay Vanden Heuvel's.

> When all had left I began arguments with Johnny Morton. I fear me he is a gasbag. He talks such utter nonsense about life, morals and religion as if he had been brought up under a pot. His nice wife Mary looked furious that one contradicted or challenged him in any way. Every time I meet him I seem to disagree most violently with his theories. I hate it when people extol one virtue above all the rest and talk as if they themselves were perfect. How can ordinary people judge their neighbours or condemn them? I never forget the boys' [Susie's brothers'] story of the difference between going to confession in Paris and Dublin. In Dublin the priests were lenient on drinking but severe on those who coveted their neigh-bours' wives; in Paris the boot was on the other foot. I was home at 9 o'clock and read until I fell asleep.
>
> [SHJ, 30 October 1930]

Johnny gave Susie a lift in a taxi after a party. While they were stuck in a Piccadilly traffic jam, Susie caught sight of the lawyer Albert Ganz and told Johnny, 'That's the man who has all the Berlioz letters. He can't get his own book published and won't let anyone else see them.'

Immediately Johnny put his head out of the window and screamed

'What about the Berlioz letters?' and then drew quickly in. Ganz looked about mystified while we slid on Chelseawards.

[SHJ, 16 May 1933]

Johnny Morton was an unconventional gardener, Susie noticed years later.

[He] decided to burn his field to rid it of weeds, and proceeded to do so with matches, box after box, igniting each blade and calling for more and more boxes. He worries continually about what is happening to the flowers through drought or bad weather. He hasn't the fatalistic temperament that makes for a good country dweller.   [SHJ, 7 July 1938]

Albert Ganz, son of Adelina Patti's accompanist, was a fellow guest at a dinner given by the conductor and composer Frederic Austin. 'Mrs Austin is all depressed,' Susie wrote. 'I think she would be happier in Surbiton playing bridge.'

After dinner when I was 'left alone with the ladies', they talked in that awful disillusioned way about life and marriage – it gave me the blues. I was glad when the men appeared and conversation took a more interesting turn. Mrs O'Neill played Scarlatti very well. Ganz seemed to offend his hostess by stamping with excitement when on the subject of the Musical Copyright Bill. I believe the servants slept beneath. He's a nice unconventional creature and amused me by telling me among other things of a composer or writer complaining to Oscar Wilde that there had been a conspiracy of silence among the critics on the subject of his [own] latest work. 'What do you advise me to do?' he asked Wilde. 'Join the conspiracy,' said Wilde.

   Ganz also told a story related by [the tenor] Parry Jones about John McCormack having cancelled his passage on the *Lusitania* [sunk in the Atlantic in 1915]. I told Ganz I had never heard this and I would be more likely to credit it had it not been told by another TENOR!!!   [SHJ, 30 March 1930]

When the editor of *La Revue musicale*, Henri Prunières, came to lunch and the other guest was Mrs Samuel Courtauld the conversation was part English, part French. Mrs Sam started complaining of her treatment by the Philharmonic. Prunières who only half understood and didn't realise she was talking about her own troubles said, 'We have many such women in Paris who think they only have to give money to get all the power they want.' Happily Mrs Courtauld's French was no better than Prunières's English and the gaffe went unnoticed. [SHJ, 28 November 1929]

*   *   *

Mrs Claude Beddington was the Linda Snell of musical London.[2] Guests were invited to a musical evening of 'Spring Blossom and Birdsong'. Under the list of bus numbers was a request to bring 'distinguished overseas guests of British origin'. Any delay in replying brought an imperious reminder from Mrs Beddington that she was an extremely busy hostess.

Leaving Eleanor Hoare's At Home, Mrs Beddington said she had five other parties to go to. 'Well you had better hurry up,' answered Eleanor, unperturbed. 'This in the softest Irish voice imaginable,' Susie noted. [SHJ, 11 December 1929]

At a concert there was no escape.

Ma Beddington, looking like a witch, leaned over and said, 'Scuola di Eduardo Germano,' three times. I pretended not to hear and she said, 'Don't you know Italian? That means "School of Edward German".' She is a perfect fool.   [SHJ, 7 October 1938]

During the thirties the Covent Garden Opera House was already a boiling pot of quarrels and intrigue as if the nightly drama on the stage was infecting the boardroom. Who held the power? Colonel Blois? Thomas Beecham? Ethel Snowden? What was happening about the finance? When would British artists get fair treatment? But worse than all this was the incompetence.

These nights nobody is thinking about Covent Garden and it is their own fault. They don't bother about the press, they don't send seats for repeat performances, they don't give their news, so no wonder they are quickly overshadowed when important concerts [like Toscanini's presented by Lionel Powell] take place. [SHJ, 2 June 1930]

'The staging was as poor as ever,' Susie commented after *Rheingold* with Heger conducting. The proscenium curtain was so low that from the box the Rhine maidens were invisible while the machinists could be seen running up and down pulling wires. The following day with *Tristan* (under Beecham) the performance was better but as for the lighting one could have thought that anyone standing around was switching on anything. And in the last set Olczewska had to move a boulder in order to get into position beside Isolde at Tristan's death. [SHJ, 10, 11 May 1932]

*   *   *

Dislocations

As Music Editor on the *Daily Telegraph*, Robin Legge had introduced an innovative and readable music page and a new, less crushing style of music criticism.[3] He was known to his staff as 'Father Robin' and had long been a friend to Herbert. 'A bit of difficulty and you are on top at once,' he wrote to his junior during one crisis. 'I wish I had your patience.'[4] Now, however, fatigue, illness and personal problems had made him unpredictable. '[Robin] was acutely nervous at the office on Friday morning, ' H. H. wrote to Susie, ' – couldn't sit down and handed me a number of prospective articles to read which he should have read himself. He was a perfect wreck and nobody apparently knows it but me.'[5] H. H. covered for him most of the time, and when ill-health finally obliged Legge to resign, H. H. succeeded him. 'You do the work already, don't you?' the editor Arthur Watson said gruffly, announcing the promotion and the £250 salary increase.

A large music staff produced the weekly page, including Hugo Wortham (later 'Peterborough'), Basil Maine, Rollo Myers, Ferruccio Bonavia and Stephen Glanville, who became a close friend. The newspaper's Assistant Editor was Oscar Pulvermacher. Energetic and autocratic, he was well known for placing his relations in strategic posts.

From letters and diaries it is clear that H. H. and Pulvermacher did not get on; things might well have turned out differently for my father had he consented to pay court to the Assistant Editor and speak well of his singer daughter. Pulvermacher was a supporter and friend of Malcolm Sargent so that when Barbirolli became conductor of the Hallé Orchestra Pulvermacher showed his feelings by contemptuously leaving Barbirolli (who had taken the trouble to bring him a message from the New York correspondent) waiting in the hall like a telegraph boy.[6]

H. H. was to pay, for Pulvermacher was unforgiving and above all he had the ear of the proprietor, Lord Camrose. When H. H., over-tired at a concert, fell into the classic journo's trap of misreporting a name (a singer in this case), Pulvermacher pounced as if waiting for this excuse.

In Jersey the holiday atmosphere evaporated. Susie was in such torment while H. H. waited in London that even I realised that something was wrong: 'aged six and wanting to take it all on herself without knowing what it is'. Just before going home I developed a temperature, a diversion which kept my mother busy.

After days of suspense Camrose refused to relent: the assistant editor had won. The task of breaking the news fell to Glanville. He telephoned Susie, H. H. being at a BBC lunch at the Savoy, and they were both almost too upset to speak coherently. H. H. came home to be told the news and there was a moment when she thought he was going to faint, but he composed himself, wrote a few letters to friends and took her to the cinema. For years this supremely forgettable film with Greta Garbo as Mata Hari lingered unpleasantly in their memory.

'Remember you have friends,' Glanville had told H. H., and the letters started pouring in. Ernest Newman said he would have made the same mistake and 'the monstrous injustice of it made [him] disgusted with the profession'. Percy Scholes wrote from Switzerland about a similar accident he had had on the *Observer* and how the editor J. L. Garvin had told him not to worry: the paper would pay up if there was a court case. The Critics' Circle became involved; a group of musicians would have lodged an official protest if H. H. had not dissuaded them. Arthur Hinton showed him W. J. Turner's abusive and libellous notice of a concert by the violinist Arthur Catterall. Although he had to apologise in a further issue Turner didn't leave the *New Statesman* for that.

In the weeks and months that followed fellow journalists called at Church Street, among them *DT* colleagues shocked at the resignation, complaining that Pulvermacher, the 'snake in the grass', was undermining all departments and poisoning Camrose's mind. Bonavia rejoiced that his son Gabriel's scholarship to Cambridge meant less time as a journalist. '[Bonavia] is longing to get away from the *DT*. They pile work on him and give him no extra money. A thankless job.'] SHJ, 19 December 1932] Glanny urged H. H. to contact J. L. Garvin; Dulanty reported that Beverley Baxter would like to have H. H. on the *Daily Express* but Beaverbrook would have to be won round, and 'he [was] interested in neither the theatre nor music'.] SHJ, 1 December 1932] 'I sell newspapers as another man sells potatoes,' Beaverbrook said to Susie at a dinner.

'I can't go on,' Susie wrote, exhausted by her narrative,

At least I want to go on, and not back. H. is well out of it. He is 50, full of music and energy and with twenty-one years' experience as a critic.

Lena has been up for the night, full of compassion as she always is – a rock, a shelter, a port in a storm.

[SHJ, 21 September 1932]

Lunch with Trudy and Arthur Bliss, both of them horrified by the action of Camrose. Stayed with them until nearly 4, met Robert Lynd on the doorstep and went back with him. Got home at 1 a.m. Like everyone else they think Camrose was wrong, and Robert quoted literary errors made by big men and which were allowed to pass unnoticed. Sylvia is sad as [her daughter] Sheila has left home and is living on her own with a job at Gollancz. The house is too small and probably Sheila felt cramped with so brilliant a mother. They are alike. The dark one is still at Oxford.

[SHJ, 16 October 1932]

John McCormack was in London at this time for an Albert Hall recital. He and Lily had taken Moore Abbey for another nine years, but they said that now de Valera was in power they didn't want to stay in Ireland.[7] John had a packed house for the recital, and sang four of H. H.'s songs, 'The Forlorn Queen', 'The Spanish Lady', 'Little Boats' and 'Kitty My Love'.

*　　*　　*

The studio after breakfast.

'I must go to the office.'

'Why?'

'So that you can have your Post Toasties.' (Pause.) 'We are poor.'

I wasn't convinced. Poor? The man in the carol gath'ring winter fu-oo-el. The half-dressed children I had seen in Battersea . . .

H. H. was thinking aloud, his brain a soup of heavy ingredients, the Slump, the lost job (he was working out his six months' notice), the search for a new one, the temptation to throw in the London towel and go native in the west of Ireland. From a host of journalists reports were coming to him of the charged atmosphere at the *Daily Telegraph* and of regrets and incomprehension at the change of music editor, but any small satisfaction to be had from this was quickly neutralised by anxiety. Through Hugh Campbell he joined the *Saturday Review* for a weekly musical column but he would have to find more work. Should they let go of the house?

For a time little changed.

Saw Mlle and the children off to Dedham. I had a few words with her about her severity with Angela. Strange woman – so fine and so loyal and yet so odd, so intelligent and yet so silly.

[SHJ, 22 December 1932]

After [Christmas lunch at Dedham] we heard the Empire broadcast and after the crackers there were the presents. Helena and Granny Mac pulled crackers – a lovely picture, eighty-five pulling a cracker with five. Angela would stop opening her parcels to read a book. I have a picture of her in my mind sitting under the tree reading *The Child's Garden of Verses* with crowds of unopened parcels beside her.

[SHJ, 25 December 1932]

A funny tea party. Christopher Salmon brought Vasalakis, a Greek pianist who lives in Paris and plays very badly. Eustace Wareing came too, and a Miss Sheen who wants to write something about the studio for *The Queen,* also Julie Lasdun. Afterwards we went to the Maresco Pearces. Olga Lambert[8] regaled me with stories of the Savoy Ballets – Tilly Losch's season put on by her husband in a last effort to win her back. Rows, intrigues, doped singers. Lifar pretending to be unable to dance because he didn't want to dance with Markova. Edward James slapping his face, and so on. Constant Lambert being called in at all kinds of odd times to fix disputes.

H. and I went to the Café Royal for a snack and then so to bed.

[SHJ, 21 July 1932]

Dined at the US Embassy. Sat between David Garnett and Noël Coward. Coward is conceited beyond words and talks incessantly about himself and his brilliance. I liked talking to David Garnett, especially about Lawrence whom he knew so well. There was a Lord Amherst there, a flying man and adorer of Coward's. Somehow Coward's type brings with it the kind of professional atmosphere one would like to avoid.   [SHJ, 25 July 1933]

On the Sunday Clarice, Isabel, Major and Mrs Quigly came to tea, also a German friend, Hagen something. He was all for Hitler, though disapproving of the Nazi treatment of the Jews. He was for sterilisation as well. I suggested that there might be another side to it, and that the Germans were too willing to be ordered about, and that officialdom gone mad would be worse than their former state. He said he thought England would finish up with a dictator. I advised him to see a Cup Final and a Grand National before making up his mind about the English character.

[SHJ, 26 July–1 August 1933]

[Dedham] Beautiful weather and quite a lot of amusing things to do. I swam at Belle Meadow and also at Judy's Gap [Judas Gap] with H. H. and Lena and Margaret Clover. Then Jimmy [Field] took us in the Bentley to Frinton. It was hot and we bathed in the evening and had our picnic by moonlight!

On the Saturday Margaret Clover invited us to her house. It was a poor evening. H. was very bored with the male members of the party. He spoke with horror of the desecration of the countryside by jerry-builders. Mr Foster, who is supposed to be an artist, took the opposite view. H. gave up the ghost and lapsed into brooding silence. Harold Clover called Mr Downes 'Mr D.' all the time. Mrs Downes hardly spoke. Mrs Foster seemed kindly and pleasant. We played cards and at long last Ellis came to fetch us.

We also went to the Daltons – it was pleasant enough. Munnings and Maurice Codner were there making merry. Little Mr Dalton sings comic songs efficiently and Mrs Dalton smiles all the time without expressing herself one way or the other. A. J. Munnings sang his song 'Julia' in truly bucolic manner.

On Sunday night we went to the Munnings. Maurice Codner is staying with him. Before dinner Codner told us that he had been questioning the butler as to his birthplace and that he had answered that he was born in a mews in Richmond, whereupon Munnings shouted, 'He was born in a bloody manger like Christ!'

A propos of jerry-builders at Dedham, Munnings has bought up land and knocked down some hideous bungalows to preserve his view.   [SHJ, 4–14 August 1933]

For the fiftieth Jubilee of the RCM, H. H. accompanied Beatrice Harrison in four arrangements of his, 'The Bard of Armagh', 'The Siller Crown', 'The Blackbird Reel' and 'The Lament of Fanaid Grove'. Afterwards there was a party at the Lynds, where Susie mistakenly called the recently promoted 'Lady' Squire 'Mrs'. Larry Morrow had done the same thing and been sharply reprimanded. 'Silly bitch,' said Priestley. [SHJ, 6 July 1933] With James Bone and Dulanty, Susie and Herbert followed Paul Patterson of the *Baltimore Sun* to his suite at the Savoy where they sang songs in a semicircle in front of the window as they watched the dawn break over the Thames and Cleopatra's Needle appear above the trees. 'London at her most bewitching,' Susie wrote. At 6.30 a.m. bacon and eggs were wheeled in. H. H. took me to school as usual.

The pot was kept simmering with songs for Boosey, work on Seán O'Casey's *Within the Gates* and in Dublin the music for a film. 'Indefinite and chaotic' was how H. H. described this new experience to Susie, with the producer Brian Desmond Hurst continually changing his mind and the crew on edge, although there were fine actors in the cast – Sara Allgood, Arthur Sinclair and Cathleen Drago – as well as good singers and dancers. The Gresham Hotel management was amused to have stars and potential stars parading through the corridors and lolling in the lounge into the early hours. For H. H. irritations were alleviated by the company of friends such as Walter Starkie and the poet F. R. Higgins, a follower of Yeats (with whom Higgins collaborated), who later became a director of the Abbey Theatre. 'I have found my poet,' H. H. wrote to Susie; the two men were looking forward to working together.[9]

> H. is happy about some of the work, notably the ceilidhe scene and the tracks made with the double quartet. The experience has taken a lot out of him. Being an artist he burns himself up, using too much fuel, frets and fumes over his work if he is opposed or wounded in any way. Working at his music in his own studio a happier or more placid musician doesn't exist, but working with people of such a different outlook – and especially film people who seem to be rude, crude and mad – gets him into a highly nervous state. I tell him he's like an instrument hanging on a tree and that all the winds play on! [SHJ, 2 July 1934]

At the trade show they were amused to see the names of Hurst and the producer Clifton in Gaelic. 'What weird people they are.' [SHJ, 31 October 1934][10]

Never long depressed and with the film job over, Susie and H. H. took a trip down the Thames, and tried out the new Wembley Pool like children let out of school. They spent a week at Knocke and noticed that the French and Belgian papers gave more European news than the London *Times*.

> It made us wonder if the FO censors the news or discourages giving too much space to foreign entanglements, so as to avoid

war panic . . . Abroad they expect war. You see pictures of all
nations practising mock warfare on sea, land and in the air, while
their statesmen are bleating on about peace.

[SHJ, 30 August–6 September 1934]

During 1934 violence was rumbling like the first intimations of
the cataclysm to come: the Night of the Long Knives in Munich (the
Nazi wiping-out of dissidents),[11] the murder of Chancellor Dollfuss
in Vienna, the assassination of the King of Yugoslavia.

At Charterhouse we were all watching the Field boys in a cricket
match[12] when suddenly there was a commotion. I saw my father
stretched out on the ground and people milling around calling for a
doctor. He returned to London that night under medication. His own
doctor told him to rest but he was in pain until the early hours. All he
complained of was a troublesome digestion and he continued to live
at the same pace as before.

Taking his work with him Herbert and Susie stayed with the
publisher Daniel Macmillan and his wife Betty. Susie swam in the
river, her feet tickled by a water-rat; soothed by the lapping water H.
H. was busy at the O'Casey score. Dan put mottoes over bedroom
doors and H. H. found on his dressing-room mantelpiece: 'Obedient
wives govern their husbands.'

*   *   *

'These are days of anguish for you,' H. H. wrote to Susie, who was at
her mother's bedside in Dedham in the spring of 1935.[13] He was in
Chelsea working as usual and we saw him every evening in the
studio but all I could think of, delivered up to Mademoiselle in my
mother's absence and watching the slow movement of the minute
hand on the wall, was Please God make Granny Mac die or get
better so that Mummy can come home. H. H. sent Susie titbits of
news, the concerts, the musicians, the cat ravishing the cigarette
holders and breaking them with his teeth, Walter Starkie lecturing
on gypsy music, dinner with Jock Murray at the Café Royal, the ink
spilt on the studio carpet . . .

To Suzanne Hughes

Chelsea, 19 February 1935

Darling mine – [. . .] Helena is buzzing round me as I write and I find it difficult to be quite articulate; Angela is trying to write a note to enclose with this. Helena has now been telephoning to the Tower of London (apropos of a remark of mine about punishment) and has started to smoke a Craven A. This sound pretty crazy I'm sure but it is part of the game trying to write to you at News Time in the studio . . .

A retrospective exhibition of Ambrose McEvoy's work was held that winter at the Beaux Arts Gallery in Bruton Place.

Chelsea, 13 February 1935

My darling – I deserted all work this morning on purpose to have a look at McEvoy's 'Susie' and spent this afternoon & evening writing and typing my Berlioz review for the *News Chronicle* which goes by this post.[14] That McEvoy picture is enchanting: not of course a 'likeness' of you, but you spiritualised in an altogether uncanny way. A curious thing happened. I went in search of the manager of the Gallery and found him sitting at a desk in a funny alcove off a staircase. I wanted to know the price of the picture (if it was for sale) & the name of the owner. The price was only 40 guineas and the owner Mrs McEvoy . . . I told him that it had a special attraction for me, and why, and although I said I was absolutely broke I might pawn something or steal something to possess it – all a little flippant, as you can imagine. He said very courteously, after a little talk about McEvoy's tremendous gift, that he'd speak to Mrs McEvoy. Then I signed my name, at his suggestion, in the visitor's book, and when he saw my name he burst into a terrific monologue on my Irish folk song arrangements, told me that he had met me once in his own studio, thousands of years ago, whither I had been brought by Eric Gill. He himself is a sculptor (probably out of business now) called Lessauer.[15] I think he is probably a French-Canadian, for he talked of French-Canadian folk songs.

But that picture, Susie, is quite uncanny, reproducing something

of Mamma and something of Helena, and very few people in the
world would guess who the sitter was.[16] I enclose a poem Helena
has just learned at school. It is called (as you may decipher) the
Baby Seed Song.

All my love, and whisper a little word to Mamma for me.

Ever, Herbert.

The Joyces came back into the picture:

> Miss Weaver has just this moment rung up to say that Lucia Joyce
> may call here and try to borrow money on the pretext of wanting to
> go to Ireland. She implores me not to lend her anything, that Joyce
> gives her just enough for her needs from time to time. Apparently
> Lucia is being exceedingly 'difficult' and Miss Weaver is being
> responsible for her. Poor Joyce!
>
> [H. H. to S. H., 8 March 1935]

At a period when mental illness was still often referred to as 'nerves',
Miss Weaver was too discreet to tell Susie just how 'difficult' Lucia
had become. While successive doctors made attempts at diagnosis
and treatment the Joyce circle, and especially Joyce himself, were
bewildered at the unpredictability of her behaviour. By turns
childishly wilful and wildly inventive, she was often destructive
and violent. Joyce saw her as a gifted artist and hoped to give her
confidence, but her tragedy, a disaster beyond all their efforts, was
her shattered mind for which no cure was found. She spent the last
years of her life in St Andrew's Hospital, Northampton, where she
had been a patient from 1935–6, not long after Miss Weaver's call to
my father. She died in 1986.

*   *   *

At John Murray's they were fêting Walter Starkie's *Spanish Raggle
Taggle* and William Murdoch's *Chopin*.

> We were drinking our cocktails in a room which reeked of Byron
> and Sir Walter Scott . . . a fireplace where the Memoirs were burned,
> and a glass case full of Byron relics and Scott's walking stick in a
> cupboard. It all seemed full of reverence, but one can't help feeling

that during a writer's lifetime and after his death the publishers all get far too much of the profits – alas!

[SHJ, 6 November 1934]

*   *   *

Mademoiselle's efficiency had been the lynch-pin securing my parents' peace of mind but the structure was loosening. Most of the unpleasantness occurred out of their sight behind the nursery door but now our governess was sometimes caught out. She was respectful to my mother but took not the slightest notice of any serious criticism. While admitting that she had a bad temper, she believed that having different natures my sister and I ought to be treated differently, and confessed that my mother's apprehension made her even more severe with me.

One afternoon in early summer I was practising at the upright piano in the dining-room, Mademoiselle at my elbow. Suddenly I received a violent slap across the face (not all that easy when you picture where she was sitting). Had I given her some lip, or was it just a wrong note? In that fraction of a second when her hand was in its trajectory to my cheek, my mother came through the door.

She was angry as I had never seen her. 'You must go. Now!' she hurled at the governess.

Later that evening, light-headed, unburdened and free, and blissfully swinging my sandalled feet in the downstairs lavatory, I repeated like a mantra, 'She's going, she's going, she's going, she's going . . . ' And go she did. At the last minute there was an *apologia pro vita sua*. Mademoiselle revealed that all her life she had been bitterly jealous of her elder sister who had had all the advantages.

There was little more to be said.

PART FOUR

Angst

9

The Light and the Dark

Mareillen from Cologne opened the curtains in German and in the nursery no word of English ever passed her lips. She was, although I was too young to recognise it, very sexy. She had dyed blonde hair and wore a seersucker dress and when she walked along the pavement in front of me holding Helena's hand her well-rounded bottom oscillated, a sight I found vaguely repulsive. She was immensely capable and in her care we made all sorts of little objects, ending with the most complex and splendid advent calendars. I don't remember her ever being disagreeable, but she had an unnerving habit of running her thumbnail sharply down my spine if she caught me slouching at the table. She was keen on gymnastics and after a Sunday swim we lay on mats doing exercises. The bristle hurt my back. I would much rather have climbed the rope. But these were the years, although I didn't know it, of 'Strength Through Joy'. I think I made Mareillen pay for my experiences with Mademoiselle because I remember having to write out – how many times? – 'Ich muss immer höflich sein.' (I must always be polite.) It could be said that I was doing my bit for the war effort four years in advance.

A particular scene has survived from the summer Mareillen was with us. It was my birthday, a shimmering June morning and the whole family at breakfast in the garden, and my father gave me my first fountain pen. No rite of passage gave more pride than this little blue bakelite Conway Stewart nestling in its case with an elegant pencil and which I was carrying off to school.

Mademoiselle had already given us notions of German to my mother's great satisfaction, so that now under Mareillen we were beginning to handle the language quite well in our limited way. At Christmas she wanted to go home to Germany but her father wrote to warn her that she might then be caught up in the Arbeitsdienst and prevented from leaving the country again. (The Nazis had been in power for two years.) But Mareillen was already very taken with Hitler as she told us and Weinachten was always important. I don't think it was because she was unhappy with us that she left at Christmas, never to return. She must have been homesick although she had made some friends in London, among them a certain Mr Fox. Later I often wondered if the mysterious Mr Fox was a London fascist, a member of the Fifth Column or simply a young man driven mad by Mareillen's luscious curves.

F. P. H. died suddenly the same summer. H. H. came into the nursery that morning, went straight to the window and stood silently looking down at the lime tree and the sunlit street. Awed by the news we said nothing. 'I must get into black,' he said, to himself and not to us. Then he quietly turned on his heel and was gone.

*   *   *

I had always known that Ireland was what made us different, but the first sight of that coast gave my ten-year-old eyes the kind of shock which earlier the orchestra had given my ears. Up to this I had known only inhabited places, wheels and footsteps in London streets, cottages scattered along blackberry lanes and the voices of nannies and children on English Channel beaches. Here a fine Olympian pen had drawn a long slow rhythmical line defining the contours of this waiting landscape. Everything visible seemed to express great age as if worn down by nature: no crevices, no asperities, no jagged edges here. As the MV *Inisfallen* incised her path up the River Lee in the morning sun a single white cabin stared riverwards, a dab of white like a painter's afterthought. The train journey to Kerry took most of the day.

The Chelsea house had been temporarily let. After planning the future like a young couple in a small Tite Street flat our parents had moved to Kerry for H. H. to complete the series *Irish Country Songs* – four volumes for the four provinces. At one point anxiety and desperation had driven him to consider a job as cinema organist. He and my mother had gone to the Empire Cinema in Leicester Square to observe the technique of Sandy Macpherson. As a career move it would have been a disaster: the music selections imposed by the management would have driven H. H. mad after a week. In the end they went to Ireland and he returned to his little black notebook.

The house above the market town of Cahirciveen belonged to a farmer called Duffy. Sonny, a fourteen-year-old from a neighbouring farm, came to the house with a little brown donkey. We called her Brenda after the patron saint of Kerry. She had cost our mother fifteen shillings, her gear one pound; it had the very strong smell of new leather. We took turns riding her, one on her back, the other on a bicycle, and she had a habit of rubbing our bare legs against the rough stone walls along the road behind the farm. The rest of the time she was in a great field which melted into the mountain, its summit often invisible in the mist. Here she kept company with a herd of Kerry cows, the breed with the short legs which make them look as if they are standing in very long grass. When we called her with a splendid litany of names from the bottom of the field she came quickly to bury her mushroom nose in our hands. Her official treat was a cardboard box of oats up the front steps; unofficially she created havoc among Mrs Duffy's hydrangeas.

Bridie Clifford came to give us Irish lessons in the morning, starting with TÁ AN CAT AR AN SAC with the strange new vowels. We learned to read a little and to say the Our Father and Hail Mary in Irish.

Annie helped in the house. With her high colour and curly black hair she had the physique of a livelier person than she turned out to be and her milk puddings resembled seascapes with rocks. When the *Hindenburg*, a gleaming silver fish, flew overhead, she gasped, riveted to the floor, 'It's mowvin!'

Beyond the ruin of Ballycarbery Castle was the White Strand. On our four bicycles, Helena's doing four revolutions to our one, we rode along the dusty untarmacked road to bathe in the cold wild water of the Atlantic, the haunt of gannets and cormorants. Next stop America, the mirage for the coffin ships.

In a hired boat with Mr O'Sullivan and Mr Conway who had a hound's-tooth jacket and fur in his ears we crossed to the rocky slate Skellig Islands. Landing could be difficult with 20-foot Atlantic waves and in bad weather visitors were winched ashore. The larger island,

Skellig Michael, had a working lighthouse and two keepers whose provisions arrived from the mainland every fortnight. They kept a goat and had tried to keep rabbits but the creatures had turned green. High above the rocks were remains of the beehive cells where the monks were starved by the Vikings. The smaller island with its great arch, Little Skellig, was entirely white with gannets. These birds, some with a six-foot wing span, had won a battle with the seagulls.

The governess era was over and there were just the four of us. Mrs Duffy's dining-room table was covered with a cloth of fringed velour, which had tassels at the corners, and surrounded by ornate high-backed chairs which H. H. called our Chippendales. A robin flew in through the window and perched on the piano-lid while he was working, but most of the time he was out searching for singers and songs. One of his sources was Mrs Coffey who had a small house up the mountain and large number of grown-up children, one a priest, some in America. I was awed by her dignity, the bareness of the interior and the extraordinary strength of her tea. One singer recommended another and we soon had a great number of friends: the O'Sullivans at the Station Hotel, Ellie O'Shea and Tom Griffin. Michael Morley who worked at the Cable Station on Valencia was permanently, or one might say definitively engaged, judging by the number of years it was taking him to decide to marry his Bridie. In Waterville the Huggards ran the Butler Arms where the day's catch was displayed on the lobby floor. Father Keane was a handsome young priest who taught us how to cheat at Thirty-One, the local version of whist. Suzanne, always one for arguing with priests, scolded him for shining his torch on courting couples in the hedgerows.

Our coal merchant was Battie Sheehan, a genial character of louche appearance and an air of hovering neither within nor totally without the law. He was always irreproachable in his dealings with us: Suzanne had to call at the shop repeatedly to get the coal bill out of him. It would be churlish to suspect that we were being mysteriously subsidised but everybody knew that he conducted a war of attrition with the local police, the Civic Guard. At Christmas he sent them a parcel labelled POISON.

The Puck Fair at Killorglin is a matter of three days in mid-August: the gatherin', the fair and the scatterin'. We drove there each day, returning late falling with sleep.

Every year in honour of the stampeding goats who warned of the approach of Cromwell's army, a billy-goat is tethered with food and water on the higher of two platforms erected in the market-place. On the lower level are the folk dancers in saffron kilts. The goat is ritually crowned while below the scaffolding the townspeople and visitors mill about among the horse-traders, the sheep and cattle fair and the singing and drinking. I watched an old woman sitting pensively on the edge of the pavement, smoking a clay pipe. H. H. wrote in his notebook and we brought home ballad sheets.

We had the freedom of the countryside where a mountain slope would suddenly be lit up by *ga gréine,* a sunbeam escaping through cloud. Yeats's 'trembling light'. Silent during the week the roads were alive on Sunday mornings with the rattle of carts bringing families to Mass. In Mrs Duffy's trap we drove across the bridge to the disproportionately large church dedicated to the Liberator, Daniel O'Connell. According to local lore there were fifty-nine licensed premises up the main street. Every time we passed with Brenda someone always came out to pour lemonade down her throat.

One morning just before the end of the holidays I found I had left my shoes downstairs overnight. As usual I slid down the banisters on my stomach but barefoot and top-heavy I took a plunge into the stairwell and, breaking my fall on the opposite banister, ended on the hall floor. I woke up in bed.

'Where am I?'

'Really! How *could* you?' Helena was more put out by the melodrama in my question than by my misfortune although she did concede that the noise had made her drop her hairbrush in fright.

With a fractured wrist and a continent of a bruise along my left side it was goodbye to riding Brenda or the bicycle or to games in the garden. Mrs Duffy made me a present of a formidable iced cake which was placed beside my bed but which we never managed to finish. It couldn't be put in the bin where she might find it, nor could we bury it in the garden below her windows, so the plan was to drop it into the river where like so many Irish products it might be carried to America . . .

At dusk H. H. took it down to the bridge wrapped in a brown paper parcel and flung it over the parapet.

'Well, has it gone?'

'It's floating.'

* * *

A change in our fortunes came in New Year 1937 when H. H. was appointed editor of the new *Boosey & Hawkes Gazette*, with an inaugural number due to appear in two months. For an experienced journalist it was not only familiar ground but a more creative job than any he had yet tackled from an office desk and one where he had a free hand among friends in congenial surroundings. 'I am just waiting for a conference with Leslie [Boosey] and a young woman composer,' he wrote to my mother from 295 Regent Street.

> Arthur Benjamin has just walked through, after asking for you, or rather of you.
>
> All I've done today so far is to talk a bit, go out and get some money from the Savile to pay this week's rent and the wireless licence, meet Howard Ferguson, [Gerald] Finzi and Gabriel Lavelle at the Bolivar. The sad news came that Harold Samuel is dying: . . . I was terribly depressed, for Harold is someone I have always wholeheartedly admired. Isn't life bloody? The longer one lives the more one must get oneself accustomed to death, tragic or natural . . .
>
> Actually I did more today than said at the beginning of this ramble, for I made out a skeleton design for the *Gazette* and L. A. B. [Leslie Boosey] was mighty pleased . . . Today my desk had more furnishings – a blotter (to taste) and a big diary! The whole business is rather fun – touch wood!
>
> God love you, darling. Sleep well.
>
> Ever, H. H.   [H. H. to S. H., 12 January 1937]

Our next temporary home was a flat at 11 Regency Square, Brighton.

Why Brighton? I don't remember asking this question, probably because this sunny flat with its balcony and the oblique view of the sea had a charm which put it beyond any queries and we knew we were going home to Church Street in the autumn. In the meantime we were amused to see our father turn into a commuter like any businessman, going up to London by train every day. My sister and I settled into a life of boarding at Kensington and holidays in Brighton, with the prospect of watching George VI's Coronation procession the coming May from the Regent Street office.

During this time friends began to wonder what had become of H. H. Why had he disappeared from Chelsea? The composer E. J. Moeran, who was clearly unaware of this, wrote from Valencia, Co Kerry, sending the score of his revised trio for violin, viola and cello 'for your own personal amusement'. [1]

I am still more or less laid up, but the plaster of Paris is coming off this afternoon, so I hope to be walking about again soon. At the moment, I have not been outside the garden gate for 5 weeks

I propose visiting England as soon as I am able. Where do you live? I only have a Sussex address which Ellie O'Shea gave me just before I got hurt, but that was before you had taken up your appointment at Boosey & Hawkes. Have you a London address as well? I was under the impression you had let the Church Street establishment.

I can give you no Cahirciveen news, as I have seen nobody lately. I do know that the influenza epidemic has been particularly active there; nearly everyone had it, including Tom Griffin. I also hear that Batty Sheehan continues to remain temperate. Father Sugrue died from pneumonia and was buried ten days ago at Cahirciveen. Danny Creedon of Kenmare is also defunct; he collapsed in the street & died of heart failure.

I am happy to say that I have succeeded in falling out with that impossible crowd of British Imperialists at the cable station here. First of all they threatened to be a nuisance with their invitations to frightful evenings of bridge, etc. But they have come to the conclusion I am rather an outsider ('not a sahib') so now I am left in

peace. I gather they do not approve of my IRA acquaintances &
friends & look upon me as a sort of blackleg.

Tell me how to find you when I come over to London.

Yours, Jack M.[2]

Another friend, the publisher John ('Jock') Murray, had also lost
track of Herbert. 'My dear H. H., You are a TRUMP,' he wrote from
Albemarle Street,

for sending me those Irish songs. I shall try to sing them to myself.

Besides a trump you seem quite invisible. Are you so Irish now
that I have to eat berries before being able to see you? I'd do even
that if I knew where to get them and what kind.

By planning or incantation we must meet again. On Wednesday
if the winds are fair I go to America but winds again fair I get back
at the end of May.

Gratefully,

Jock G. M.[3]

There was to be no meeting.

One weekend Helena and I were told that we couldn't go home
because H. H. had 'laryngitis'. I wasn't very sure what this was. Anything with 'itis' at the end commanded respect; I had no itises that I
knew of. A week went by, and the following weekend it was the same:
we stayed at Kensington Square. Flora Campbell took us to see the
film *Elephant Boy* on the Saturday, and on Sunday we had lunch with
Mrs Bax in Cavendish Square where she kept an unharmonious
parrot. In the evening we returned to the convent to find, unusually,
two choir sisters waiting for us at the top of the steps when the door
was opened. 'Your father has been very ill,' they said. 'Has he had an
operation?' I asked. This was the most alarming medical condition I
could possibly imagine.

On the Monday morning my sister and I were taken to an empty
classroom. Mother Alethea said gently, 'Your father has gone to
Heaven.' I stared fiercely at the window sill. That is all I remember.

It wasn't until September that Susie opened her diary again. She
went back over the last months, the tiny flat at 41 Tite Street where

Helena begged her to make no plans for Sundays 'just so that we could all be together and read and draw and talk and listen to the wireless', then later H. H.'s return in the evenings to the Brighton flat.

He gave [the children] all his thoughts. Their drawings were kept for his criticism. He helped them with their music. He answered their innumerable questions . . . He did not seem to want them to go to bed. Did he have some instinct that he would not be with them for much longer?

I must stop now and continue later

Then she strides bravely into the account of H. H.'s short illness: how he had attended Jimmy Tait's wedding in spite of feeling ill, the fearsome speed at which the fever was followed by double pneumonia and the specialist's warning of what to expect. At 9 p.m. on May 1st, 'Herbert slipped away and all was grief.'

Sleep left me altogether. I went over all that had happened and all the strange feelings we both had had even before H's illness. The sadness which would come over us when he was working at the old songs. Sadness that came from within him and which he could not explain. Sadness we felt on hearing the Elgar Violin Concerto on the Sunday before he died. [Antonio] Brosa was playing and I felt it so terribly that I left the room. We were dining with [C. K .] Ogden that night. As he had specially invited the children we allowed them to stay up. It was meant to be merry but I could not shake off the feeling I had. When we came home and were alone I asked Herbert why he thought we had such strange feelings. I wondered if it was something Brosa himself put into the music, with the Spanish war going on. Herbert said, 'No. It is as if Elgar were sending us a message.'   [SHJ, 29 September 1937]

In the course of working on this memoir I found a passage, written nearly forty years after the events described, by the critic Neville Cardus.[4] He was writing of Elgar's Cello Concerto. 'We do not appear so much to be hearing as to be overhearing music which has the sunset touch on it . . . telling of Elgar's acceptance of the end. The bright day is done and he is for the dark.'

10

Palliatives

'One aches all over for want of the rest of oneself,' Susie wrote of a painful moment brought on by a second meeting with the solicitor and the renewed sight of the dark passage in Coleman Street. To compound the gloom she learned that the Belfast family firm had been swallowed up by J. Arthur Rank. Homeless still and jobless, disposing of H. H.'s remaining possessions, fetching his books from the Savile, she was in a state of suspense, taking refuge in Harrods to pass the time.

> A pouring wet day. Prowled about, had my watch strap mended. Sat in the Banking Department for a bit and smoked. Saw Mrs [?] who lives at the Cromwell and regrets she cannot now live in the S. of France. Not my type at all. I hid behind a newspaper and smoked a cigarette. What these South Kensington dwellers would do without Harrods Banking Dept., I know not!
>
> [SHJ, 28 October 1937]

The two things I remember most of the weeks immediately following our father's death are my incredulity and the pain I now found in music. Everything was going on normally around me at school and yet everything had gone awry as if the solid, compact earth had fractured under my feet. If I was just old enough to realise that I had lost the person who the most willingly gave me his attention, who the most patiently answered my torrents of questions, I was still too young to measure all the rest which had disappeared with him. In one sense we were now set apart from our school friends but the veneer of English education around us prevented us being aware of this. I had no idea how to respond to sympathy from strangers and when the French teacher approached us in the garden with the most florid of condolences, I was embarrassed – a truly English condition.

My mother and Lena, now rarely apart, came to fetch us in full mourning, my mother in what I realise now was a very elegant outfit with black silk stockings which in those days were seen only on widows. I disliked this badge of disaster and hoped fervently that none of my schoolmates was looking. Separateness was to be avoided.

We spent the summer holidays of 1937 in Findon Valley, a suburb of Worthing where to H. H.'s horror Lena now lived and where she could comfortably look after Ellen. We had some music and Lena sang in the Worthing Ladies' Choir. It was a warm and affectionate household and everything was done to please us children but for our mother the contrast with Chelsea was deeply depressing. It was as if fate was underlining the alteration in her life. While she took great care that Helena and I could enjoy the seaside, the boating pool and rides on the Downs, she looked up balefully at those hills, dreamed of the Continent and took refuge in books – Hazlitt, Maupassant, Tolstoy, Turgenev, Katherine Mansfield. I myself was reading *Jane Eyre* and Granny Ellen who remembered every page kept the fires of suspense stoked up each supper-time as I told her how far I had got. When I had chickenpox my mother read me *David Copperfield* in an effort to stop me scratching my spots. That to a certain extent it succeeded is an extra tribute to Dickens.

The arrival of Alfie Wilfie created a diversion. Helena and I had found him on a Woolworth's counter among a heap of other tortoises and to save him from asphyxia we bought him for sixpence as a present to Auntie Lena. In his excitement he misbehaved on the bus home and had to be put into two bags. We were keen to see what would happen at the house. Lena was intrigued, to Susie's relief as she recorded. Barney the Irish terrier sniffed at him and walked away; the cat ignored him completely. We christened him Alfie Wilfie after the initials of the family solicitor. Put in a warm spot in the garden with lettuce and milk he grew bold enough to walk round the border and back. Susie was amazed by his speed on the ground and thought he must be a descendant of the tortoise who outstripped Achilles. Mr Solder, a neighbour, brought him home from his wanderings on a copy of the *Daily Telegraph*, but one day, possibly meeting another tortoise – there was by that time a fair number in the neighbour-hood – Alfie Wilfie went off and didn't return.

Suzanne was looking for a flat.

'It will be in Chelsea.' (Longish pause.) 'Or Bloomsbury.'

Bloomsbury? The name scratches at the brain but fails to stir the heart and at the age of eleven Bloomsbury meant nothing to me. Susie had always found that part of London depressing but she must have seen it even with all its murk as the antithesis of the Sussex seaside town.

> To me the Sussex village or the suburb like Findon Valley are equally and utterly impossible. People seem to live into themselves with their dogs and cats and occasional relations to stay, but there is no communal life, no hospitality, no open houses as we under-stand them in Ireland. The local pub I expect is the only place where one would get a little conversation. Long ago there was a church which all attended, and now there's nothing but the cinema! [SHJ, 12 October 1937]

Mass Observation was a study initially set up by two young men from Cambridge, Tom Harrisson and Charles Madge, to gauge the effect of the Coronation of 12 May 1937 on the British people. Soon nobody in the street was immune to the approach of the researcher with his notebook and pencil, and on the whole people enjoyed this, Susie among them.

Mass Observation

1 Overheard in Harrods. A woman saying, 'Foreigners think English-men have no guts because they let their wives do what they like.'
2 Overheard in Derry & Toms ladies' boudoir: Daughter (while doing over-elaborate hairdressing) to meek and mild mother: 'You ought to tidy yourself now you have the chance.' Mother (weakly): 'I did.' Daughter (ignoring this): 'Nothing makes Granny so livid as looking as if one came out of a rag-bag. It quite spoils tea.' Mother: (No reply.)
3 Waiter in cocktail bar said to me apropos of work: 'When you work

for yourself you don't mind how hard you work. When I had a café on Lavender Hill I used to work late every day, and on Sunday I used to experiment with cakes. I wasted a lot of money that way, doing it all wrong, not flouring the roller and all that.' I can picture him producing indigestion *en masse*.   [SHJ, 29 October 1937]

Susie dreamed one night that H. H. had told her to look for a flat 'near Hugo Wortham', 'Peterborough' of the column 'London Day by Day' in the *DT*. He had moved house and she didn't know his address. She put the incident out of her mind.

At intervals while the builders were working in our new home, a flat at 64 Redcliffe Square, she took a room at the Lansdowne Club, coming to life in London as she saw old friends like C. K .Ogden or Jo Jones or treated herself to the little Berkeley cinema in Lansdowne Row. Walking through London she found that she was looking about her more often, noticing details which would have escaped her earlier. 'I find myself getting intimate with inanimate objects. I get pleasure from gaping.'

One day she ran into Hugo Wortham near the square. She discovered that he had moved to a flat not far away, and then she remembered her dream of months earlier.

With Lena's help Susie moved into a first-floor flat at 64 Redcliffe Square on 4 November 1937. 'I went through dreadful times,' she wrote,

drowned in loneliness and sorrow. The sight of all the familiar things sometimes making me glad, sometimes making me want to die. The children's delight in their new home rewarded us for all our work. Such joy at finding old toys and bits of dolls' clothes and books and teddy bears' hats . . .

A pea-soup fog. The children did charades. Helena was on the top of her form, dressed in an old frock of mine with chiffon tied round her head as a prima donna. Angela announced, 'Madame Catalena will now sing La donna e immobile,' whereupon in broken English Helena sang Three Little Kittens and Three Blind Mice, all this with the aid of gramophone records and noises off – most effective.

What a slough I am in . . . I have got things done – a new letter-box, two new dustbins, a key for the char – but all this I have done as if in a dream.

When the radiogram and piano are in, and Herbert's [memorial] concerts are arranged, and when I have answered all the letters and decided about the music, when the carpet is on the stairs and my name on the door, then I will begin to 'live' in the place and try to write. Whether what I have to say would be of any interest to anyone is another matter. But at all events a course of reading and writing would help me find peace.

[SHJ, 21–26 November 1937]

A few days later she had lunch at the Café Royal with H. H.'s brother Freddy. His resemblance to H. H. fascinated her and she stole glances at him when he was unaware. At the Polytechnic Theatre she saw *Victoria the Great* and was surprised at its effect on her:

For the sake of the children I must pull myself together and try to get back my enthusiasms and tastes. I feel my life is over, my happiness lost, gone with Herbert everything which was worth while. Yet there is so much to be done for the children.

[The painter] Vivian Forbes, who had come from Paris to attend Glyn Philpot's funeral (he had been arranging rooms there for himself and Glyn for Christmas), has committed suicide with an overdose of sleeping tablets. Distraught creature – what an end to a talented young man. But he was not normal. I am and I have children, sweet friends and a perfect family. I can argue with myself and promise to make efforts. And yet I find myself with no urge, no ideas, no flavour. Music, on the other hand, gives me solace and brings back the happy past in a way that isn't painful . . . Anyway, *Victoria* gave me a jerk and I made a vow to find my way through this dark forest . . . The children loved Herbert and will always love his memory but he and I had an affinity. It was more than a happy marriage, we were as one. Can I ever learn to travel alone again?

[SHJ, 29 December 1937]

On November 25 Susie was saddened to hear of Lilian Baylis's death. 'The Lady of the Vic' had written to her immediately after H.

H.'s death. Clearly she was another friend who had been puzzled by his long absence from London.

> We loved him . . . he has been a splendid friend to our work and we have missed your visits very much . . . We should love to see you and if the Vic can help your girls to love Shakespeare, please give us the pleasure of having them as our guests in the coming year . . .
>
> [May] the kindness your husband has done to so many be returned to you a hundredfold.
>
> Your sincere & deeply sympathetic friend
>
> Lilian Baylis.[1]

Susie was all the more enraged by St John Ervine's obituary in the *Observer*.

> He wrote much praise . . . but also wrote that she was ungrateful and when people no longer served the Old Vic she had no use for them. Never was there such a mis-statement. She never ceased to be grateful to Herbert, after he had left Fleet Street, for what he had done for the Vic. [SHJ, 28 November 1937]

> Went to St Martin-in-the-Fields to the memorial service to Lilian Baylis. The place was packed. Began with the Prelude to *Lohengrin*, Lawrance Collingwood conducting. John Gielgud read the lesson and after other prayers and hymns Father Andrew spoke of her faith – immovable – and told funny stories of the Old Vic. At a performance of *Hamlet* an old woman leaned over to another and said, 'Them 'amlets 'ad a lot of trouble in their family.' The service ended with the 'Awake' chorus from *Meistersinger*, which seemed odd to me. If ever anyone was an old pagan [Wagner] was! Saw many people I knew but got away without meeting anyone.
> [SHJ, 1 December 1937]

In spite of a biting east wind the first anniversary visit to H. H.'s grave at Hove was enlivened by Eddie Morrow who had designed the stone and took us back to tea with his companion Lottie. She told us he had set the various objects on the table to give the appearance of work. He always did this when someone was coming. They were not going to get married since everybody thought they were brother and sister and marriage would, she said, create scandal. They were contemplating a move to a country cottage near Uckfield at 12/6d. a week but with no water. Susie advised them against this. Better live in a tent or caravan, she thought, and be done with civilisation, but half measures might be abominable in illness. Eddie fiddled unproductively with the radio (thrown in with the flat for £1 a week). After much turning of knobs he said, 'I can get everything but I can't get something.'

That night Susie dreamed of H. H., at the piano in the studio. He told her he had dreamt about herself and Parnell. 'Not me,' she had corrected. 'It was Mamma [Granny Mac] and Parnell.' 'So it was,' he had said, 'I skipped a generation.' After that she got up, ate an apple, read *War and Peace* and went to sleep again.

A few weeks later I had something to tell my mother.

'I was with Daddy one day and a man called with papers to be signed. I saw Daddy sign his name and when he was going to write "occupation" I thought he would write "composer" but he didn't. He wrote "musician". I asked him why and he said, "I like to be known as a musician." '

What a strange remark for a child of ten. I now understand why for days I couldn't decide what wording should go on Herbert's memorial stone and when finally I put 'musician' I felt happy about it. It had come from him.   [SHJ, 26 May 1938]

After a long period of parched gardens there was rain at last. Birds and rabbits on the Downs accompanied Susie across the Gallops to Mass at Durrington. She thought of an In Memoriam notice she had read in *The Times*. 'To the beloved memory of Jane and Walter Williams who lived such beautiful lives on Bromley Common'. 'They sounded like rabbits,' she said to Eddie. 'Can't you see them nibbling?'

The Downs haunted Susie. On Easter Monday she recorded a walk in bitter wind up the sunless slopes of Cissbury Down.

Angela and I talked of how we disliked the Downs when the sun did not shine. They are ominous. They draw you on, further and further to your doom. Sunless even, the Irish mountains in the wildest places are lovely. Their desolate treeless beauty, stark and lonely, affects you in quite a different way. Is it the soil? Here we are on chalk. Does chalk depress you or not? Think of the Aran islanders! Their walks are taken on granite.

Angela and I began a poem: 'From Cissa's Ring I gaze below . . .' We walked around the Ring from a sense of duty, frozen to the marrow.   [SHJ, 18 April 1938]

Our neighbour on the floor below the Redcliffe Square flat told our mother that Helena and I made her chandelier tremble and her china rattle, which was true. This woman was to be dreaded since she talked at great length 'of nowt', but Susie quickly discovered congenial neighbours on the floor above. Humphrey Higgens, a master at St Paul's School, was described by Susie as an Eton communist rather as if he were an interesting species of plant. His wife Peg was one of the twin daughters of the poet Laurence Binyon. The Higgenses told Susie of an evening entertaining the High Master of St Paul's whose wife's attack of hiccups lasted all evening although she tried to pretend that all was well. Mr Higgens said, 'Why didn't she ask for a glass of water?'

I thought to myself, 'How very English, the headmaster's wife trying to suppress the hiccups and nobody showing by word or look that they were aware of it.' That's another story of how the British Empire came into being.   [SHJ, 7 March 1938]

Higgens occasionally complained of the conditions of his work.

'I now know why he is peevish,' she wrote. 'He feels the grind . . . That is what makes him a Communist and an atheist. Atheism comes from being bored by the C. of E. from early youth. I was amused at the anxiety he showed about his potatoes. Peg had to go up while they were having sherry and put them on. True he was hungry. How people differ. Herbert would not have interrupted the conversation for potatoes or anything else. In fact had we been visiting a godson (as they had) he would have insisted on celebrating the occasion by dining out! But then he was extravagant, but it was

fun always, never, never dull. However I like my upstairs neighbours
very much.   [SHJ, 8 March 1938]

Susie's natural buoyancy saw her through difficult moments when
even among musician friends, or perhaps especially then, and going
home alone afterwards, she felt Herbert's absence like physical pain.
Then she would turn to her journal.

'Why I do this I know not. I feel in a way that it tidies my
very untidy mind.' [SHJ, 8 February 1938] There had been a dis-
heartening concert at the Wigmore Hall, where May Harrison had
played Moeran's Sonata with the composer at the piano. For the
usual reason Moeran was 'all every way' and Susie wondered how
May kept the shape of the work.

The arid aftermath of a cocktail party left her unwilling to face
going home.

She ate at the Club and overheard two men at the next table.

A   Whatever you say about Havelock Ellis you can't call him
    shallow!
B   I had a lot of imagination when I went to public school. I could
    draw and write poetry and all that, but it was knocked out of
    me . . . [Long pause during which the other did not speak.] But
    I don't know if that wasn't a good thing . . .
                                    [SHJ, 24 January 1938]

The diplomat Robert Vansittart, son-in-law of General Heppenheimer, Susie and Herbert's American 'foster father' of 1922, wrote
to Susie having just heard of Herbert's death. He had just lost his own
father. 'Van's life now belongs to the State and his friends now rarely
see him, alas.' [SHJ, 17 January 1938]

As head of the Foreign Office he was famous for his suspicions of
Germany's intentions but his warnings had fallen for the most part
on deaf ears. His lucidity was an embarrassment to the government
(Chamberlain had him kept under surveillance by MI5), and he
was replaced at the time of this letter. His successor, Sir Alexander
Cadogan, caused less trouble and Vansittart was given the vague post
of 'Diplomatic Adviser' which meant little or nothing.

One of our most loyal friends was Clara Evelyn, pianist, actress and singer who had been a double scholar and a fellow student of H. H.'s at the College at the turn of the century. If he ever dared mention this, carelessly pinpointing her age, she kicked him under the table.

A child prodigy given to reading a novel on her lap while practising, Clara angered her piano teacher Marmaduke Barton when she accepted an offer from George Edwardes to join the Gaiety Girls. Thereafter she sang in many musical comedies and was reputed to have been a merrier widow than even Lily Elsie. J. B. Priestley confessed to Susie that he had long been in love with this 'last of the postcard girls'. She was an excellent pianist with magnificent hands, large for a woman but long-fingered and loose-jointed, able to cope happily with the most demanding scores. She could accompany herself when she sang Richard Strauss's *Ständchen*, although she rarely if ever practised. In her nineties she appeared on television with Hughie Green on *Opportunity Knocks*, playing a Chopin Scherzo and Raff's *La Fileuse*.

H. H. nicknamed Clara 'Litigation Lizzie' for her tendency to go to court. Early in her career she was able to buy a house with the proceeds of a successful case over the loss of a part in *White Horse Inn* for which her name had already been publicised. In a property matter she was less lucky: her adversary Baroness de Busch was a match for her as Clara gamely admitted afterwards. This exquisitely groomed woman, delicate as a piece of Sèvres, had made her entrance in court dressed as a bag lady – without make-up, hair askew, wan and desperate, a pathetic figure winning the sympathy of all including the judge. But in other matters Clara knew how to bend bureaucracy to her will. Separating her St John's Wood house into flats she simply marked the doorbells Night, Day (her married name) and House-keeper. Years beyond the span of this book we became close friends and I remember her as unique. She had a rich sense of humour (and the wickedest laugh), enormous generosity, utter professionalism and she was a true musician to the tips of those supple and powerful hands.

We often walked across Kensington Gardens and Hyde Park to

173

reach Clara's house in Westbourne Terrace, Susie astounded at the number of people sitting in their cars by the Serpentine, 'all shut in'.

> Lunched with Clara [Evelyn] . . . She suggested the stage again for me but I said that even if it were possible I would not do it. It wouldn't be the right background for the children. Then she said writing. It is so easily said, but to do anything worth while one would have to work very hard. The words for so much fail me.
>
> She knew Herbert so well that I was glad to be with her. She had met Priestley in Egypt and [they had] made friends. I reminded her that he called her 'the last of the postcard girls'.
>
> [SHJ, 30 September 1937]

> Clara spoke of the children. Said Helena was heading straight for the stage and Angela was musical, played like an adult. She would love to teach her. I felt she was really sincere.   [SHJ, 7 October 1937]

The painters Jo Jones, the friend from Vicarage Gate days, Barbara Watson[2] and Luigi Innes Meo and the pianist Ivor Newton were constantly in touch. Susie was at her most light-hearted with Jo; they were like truanting schoolgirls.

> Jo and I walked all the way to Martins Bank in Whitehall. In Regent Street we passed every kind of extraordinary person, insane-looking, smart, peculiar, comic, tragic. We laughed a good deal at our own observations. Jo had heard from her brother in Bombay. He was taking his Freemasonry very seriously and visiting the biggest and oldest lodges in the world. I said I could picture him riding on a goat in Bombay and Jo said she was sure he would betray all their secrets.   [SHJ, 14 October 1937]

They went together to J. B. Manson's private view at the Wildenstein. Susie introduced Jo to Maurice Lambert who told them Constant had separated from his 'funny exotic wife' Flo.[3]

> Maurice disliked her intensely. I said I thought she was very attractive like a marmoset. He said Yes, she could be admired in a cage. He made equally rude remarks about the offspring and said

it was a mistake a young man makes once in his life . . . [the actor] Robin Farquarson was also present. I heard him stutter in his inimitable fashion, 'I l–l–like these p–p–pictures for wh–wh–what they are n–n–not.'   [SHJ, 15 October 1937]

At dinner with the Norths, Katherine told a story of her father, the actor Horace Hodges, taking his leave after a very grand party. On leaving he thanked his host most profusely and the little man was very nervous and said excitedly, 'Yes! But who is going to pay for it all? That's what I'd like to know!'

The Abbey actress Máire O'Neill (Molly Allgood) had a flat in neighbouring Redcliffe Gardens,

> on the square, at the very top. Went up with her. She looks very old
> and bedraggled. Seeing her depressed me. I wish I could like her.
> I can sometimes, in bits. Her humour is wonderful, she has a
> generous heart, but her foul language puts me off and I always
> remember how unhappy I was with her and Sally in summer 1921!
> Molly and Sally by right of talent should be at the top of the tree,
> but lack of character has kept them down in spite of their great
> gifts. The back street element has never been eliminated.
>   [SHJ, 20 October 1937]

C. K. Ogden, translator and consulting editor at Kegan Paul, was the inventor of Basic English and founder of the Orthological Institute. His 850-word system was intended as an international auxiliary language and had the support of Neville Chamberlain and Winston Churchill.

'Had a meal by the pool,' Susie wrote of an unpromising evening but her old friend Ogden came to the rescue.

> Felt at the end of my tether and was just going to go in despair to
> the Berkeley cinema when Ogden phoned and asked me to meet
> him at the Escargot. I had an entremets with him and we talked.
> He nagged at me about God in his Heaven, taking – it seems – my
> Faith as a personal insult. He has got religion on the brain – in fact
> he is all brain. H. H. used to say he was an intellect on two legs.
> Nevertheless I always find very clever people very stupid in some

175

ways. They do not live enough – in fact they are not in close contact with life itself. Anyway it is better to be nagged at by Ogden than to be miserable and lonely as I was before I went out. He is a good friend. [SHJ, 30 September 1937]

Waiting for Ogden to ring me back I went downstairs and saw the Viscountess Snowden pacing up and down the lounge obviously waiting for a much-belated guest. She looked so vulgar and domineering and could not conceal her impatience, watching from the window and in the front hall, really blocking the passage. I ate at the pool and decided to go to bed early and read when Ogden phoned. We met at Prunier's. I had coffee and a liqueur while he ate. Spent a truly delightful evening with him. We spoke of education. He is very much against the School Certificate and said exams were the greatest nonsense, that matric was easy to get if it were needed later, and so on, with all of which I agree. He says children ruin their eyes and their health and it is quite unnecessary. He was in a gay affectionate witty mood, the mood I like best.

I teased him about his various houses and flats. He has each for a different reason. Montagu Street for Gerard Manley Hopkins, Gordon Square for Basic English and so forth. I asked about the upkeep. He says he never has servants, people who raise dust. The windows must always be kept shut to guard against dirt and dust. He says his place never needs cleaning nor do the beds need making. I asked about rubbish. He says he has none. 'What about tea leaves?' I asked. He said, 'I buy *The Times*, not to read of course. I wrap the tea leaves in it, and drop the package into the yard below. It is collected by the dustmen. All these women who come in, upsetting the dirt and bringing cleaning things, are impossible, and one can never find anything after they have gone.'

On the way back [to the Lansdowne Club] we disagreed about which was Wimborne House. He thought it was Beaverbrook's at first. We sat in the Adam Room referring to *Who's Who* and Court Circulars and looking up streets and amusing ourselves generally like small children until 1 a.m. We had called in at the Royal Societies Club to collect his letters on the way – such a depressing place especially after the Lansdowne . . . How right H. H. was when he insisted on me keeping it on. It has been a haven . . .

I asked Jo to come round. We laughed a lot in my room. Jo said it was a cell. When I put enamel on her nails (Barbara Gould Koral) she said I was a procuress.   [SHJ, 23 October 1937]

'Heaven help the poor journalists,' Susie wrote of the merger of the *Daily Telegraph* and the *Morning Post*, 'swallowed up by Lord Camrose.'

I remember Ernest Newman saying the hardships were terrible when amalgamation took place. Pulvermacher will be in his glory.

On the way to the Escargot (I walked all the way) I passed a place in Bateman Street, Chez Joe's, and saw about a dozen very black men going in – all very well-dressed and handsome. Musicians, cocktail-shakers, boxers or what I wonder? Soho seems to me more sinister than it was, yet it has great fascination. How I love London!

I have just read the new *DT & MP* [*Morning Post*]. The leading article 'A Welcome to our New Readers' admits to a very guilty conscience, pleads 'cruel necessity'. I don't like the expression 'strictest scrupulosity'. I said to Ogden that I was sorry for the three-quarters of the staff who were thrown out. He says they were such impossible stupid fellows that they were only getting what they deserved. Hard words!   [SHJ, 30 September 1937]

'Qui s'excuse s'accuse,' she commented, hearing of the Assistant Editor Pulvermacher's denial that H. H.'s departure from the *DT* was of his doing.

If H. H. had taken up with P. and his family all might have been well, but H. was too sincere. Well no newspaper man can hurt him now and his music will be heard when they are all forgotten.

[SHJ, 19 March 1938]

Eustace Wareing, the Berlin correspondent, was equally irritated by Pulvermacher.

When [Eustace] sends the best of good stories they are cut out, and when the same stories appear in *The Times* he is reproached for not having sent them to the *DT* . . . I have a horrid feeling Pulver wants him out, and this is the beginning of his funny trickery.

[SHJ, 10 January 1938]

During supper at the Café Royal with Larry Morrow (who had announced himself on the telephone as 'our uncle with the pink beard'), Susie noticed Liam O'Flaherty sitting opposite reading *Le Populaire*.

Larry says he doesn't understand French and that this was a pose! John Gielgud was sitting beside us. He ordered a glass of coffee and sat in solitary state gazing around and being much gazed upon by all. One man came up for an autograph which the great actor willingly gave. It seems odd to come to the Café Royal close on midnight alone for a glass of coffee when one could easily have it at home. He was evidently putting himself on view. Had a taxi home against my principles but it was past the hour for such principles.

[SHJ, 12 March 1938]

Larry Morrow asked Susie to help him with research on Irish harps for a Harp Festival in the north of Ireland. With a sharp eye on her bookshelves he said, 'You have all the material.' She didn't produce the work as promptly as he would have wished and on the telephone he said to Helena, 'Bawl "HARPS!" into Mummy's ear.' The project helped her postpone writing anything of her own, although the journal kept her writing anyway. Her lack of self-confidence led her to procrastinate further by joining a correspondence course in creative writing. Her life was far from empty and she continued as before to take interest in people from all walks of life, observing them with a writer's eye, drawing much amusement from their appearance, foibles or weird pronouncements. She was grief stricken, desolate but never, ever bored. How could one be bored when there were books to read?

Wisely she stayed in London, not too far from her old haunts and her friends. And observing the friends of friends was half the fun.

Dined at Harriet Cohen's – a lovely studio in St John's Wood. People came in after dinner including a very brilliant woman doctor and her husband, also a doctor. The woman had the most enormous hand which she kept spreading out fanlike under her chin. Her face was big too like her hands, with big eyes, big mouth and big teeth. I didn't see her feet as she sat on the floor and they were tucked in. Her husband seemed like a curly lamb beside her.

The episode of the smouldering Steinway diverted me. Wetzler dropped his cigar into it. When I first saw the smoke arise I thought his music must be extra special. It came faster and more furious just as Mrs Peter Latham was being most intense about Mr Wetzler's double and triple fugues. Dr Carr fetched tools from the car, undid the piano and removed the cigar.   [SHJ, 2 June 1938]

Susie was finding her way, learning to be two parents. Helena still had a child's directness and charm but I was turning into a demanding adolescent. Obsessed with ballet I insisted on joining the advanced class midweek which entailed yet more bus journeys. Susie sighed and complied. (Although I was the right size and shape, heaven knows that even if I had been admitted to a senior ballet school, orthopaedic problems would soon have seen me out of the door. Dancers like singers have to be a minimum of two-hundred-per-cent fit.)

After my father's death I became convinced that I would now also lose my mother. If she was five minutes late collecting us at Kensington Square I would stand at the door, peering through the grille, listening for the familiar determined step on the pavement to confirm that she had not been run over. After weekends at home I insisted on returning to school on Monday mornings rather than Sunday nights to avoid the sight of her disappearing alone into the darkness. Again she complied, although when Monday came not always in the best of tempers on account of the very early start.

How it tries my patience. I must beware of losing it with [the children]. It could become a habit and how I hate nagging females. Herbert never spoke a cross word to them and he would be quite shocked to hear me do so. In that he was like his father, always sweet to children.   [SHJ, 31 January 1938]

If my sister and I had both become anxious, Helena's fears were different. When we took a taxi she would watch the meter in anguish and offer her pocket money to pay for the journey. She showed a budding talent, preparing a delicious cold lunch one Sunday, not wanting to disturb our mother, while I sloped off to the nursery to read *David Copperfield*. [SHJ, 17 July 1938]

Susie suggested an afternoon walk near Cissbury but we grumbled and made excuses so she went off alone. For hours there was no sign of her and we became very worried, doubly so when we saw Lena's anxiety. It seemed an eternity before our mother returned and later I told her how frightened we had been. She had visited Barbara Watson at Washington and they had gone to look for whitebeam on the Downs. There was garlic in bloom, and primroses and cowslips. 'A heavenly place where one is shut off from the horrors of the contractor.' Being mostly farmland and private grounds it couldn't be spoilt.

> Arrived back to find my absence had caused consternation. A. and H. and Lena had been searching for me. The children had expected me to take them out for a walk. When I said to Angela, 'But you grumbled, so I thought I would go alone,' she said, 'But I expected you to make us go anyway.' Which shows she will have her grumble and obey afterwards. [SHJ, 27 April 1938]

Back in Redcliffe Square there had been bad behaviour.

> I put A. on my balcony to do her homework and tried to cope with Helena who by this time was running riot. After an unpleasant quarter of an hour I managed to get her to practise and after that to do an imposition. I threatened to take them from 23 Kensington Square. It all blew up so suddenly, a storm but not in a teacup. When all was calm again I took H. with me to [the grocer] Rapson's, leaving Angela practising. On our return I found the door open and no Angela! H. and I searched the flat and then fell to debating what to do next when the doorbell rang. I went down to find Bill Orton on the doorstep and Angela seated majestically in his car. There was guilt in her majesty. I scolded them both. Bill took all the blame and made amends by helping me fry the sausages for lunch. He had to go back to Heston aerodrome by 3 p.m.
> [SHJ, 2 July 1938]

While Susie was struggling in her personal limbo she was also beginning to write stories. She finished two which failed to satisfy her.

I am at an impasse. Reading without absorbing, writing with a mind wandering over hills and dales, but it has helped to keep my mind off the haunting misery of H.'s illness and death . . . These days I think of him as alive – his voice, his laughter, his piano-playing, his gentle affectionate ways and his whimsical humour . . .

[SHJ, 8 April 1938]

Passing our old house on her way to Maresco Pearce's, Susie noticed that the new tenant had knocked out two windows on the south side and closed up the red door. Windows on the garden side, she was told, had also gone.

Maresco told me he had collected the blue tiles from the day nursery [the William De Morgan fishes]. The stockbroker Mr Briscoe had torn them out and they were lying in a broken heap in the garden. Maresco saw the lovely blue gleaming and penetrated with the aid of a workman and removed them. He is going to put them up in his house and have a special tea party with the children. What memories the blue fishes awoke in me! What will Herbert think of Mr Briscoe the stockbroker?

Went to the Library and then home to bed. [SHJ, 1 April 1938]

Wanting us to keep in touch with Ireland – 'I should hate [the children] to grow up without any real understanding of their country' – Susie planned a return to Cahirciveen in the autumn of 1938, her courage boosted by the presence of H. H.'s sister Lena and their brother Freddie and his family. The particular magic of our first visit with H. H. could never be revived but there were many people to see. Alarmed at this plan, concerned friends in London had advised Susie to make a complete break with the past, cutting it out ruthlessly. She had no intention of doing this.

'I feel I can only go on by being almost the same, as if Herbert were coming in in half an hour . . . I wonder if they feel like that because they have no faith in the life to come?'   [SHJ, 14 July 1938]

In Cahirciveen we were welcomed by all the friends who had known our father.

'I am very sorry for your trouble,' they said, often quoting his words, and ending, 'Lord have mercy on his soul.' Susie found this hard at first but their feelings were expressed with such grace and tenderness that she became used to it.

> These rough boys and men in Cahirciveen, labourers, farmers and fishermen, have all the elegance of manners that the English try to acquire through expensive education and even then don't always succeed. We are a different people and it is well that [the Irish] are now free to run their own country. They will like England better for it.   [SHJ, 2–19 September 1938]

There were trips to Derrynane and Glenbeigh, to Ballaghisheen Pass and to Waterville, to Coonana and Cahirdaniel, always with friends and often staying late, with Lena feebly protesting at the time. 'Good for her to cease being a slave to the clock,' thought Susie. The Butler Arms, Waterville, was packed with English visitors there for the fishing. Michael Morley was with us and his situation had not changed one iota in two years. At dinner Helena said, 'Why don't you marry the girl and be done with it?' He seemed unsurprised.

People sought out our mother as if to leave her no time for sadness. Friends took us to see their friends in a chain of hospitality. It amused her when the scholar Donal O'Sullivan showed her an invitation in Irish to a garden party at Vice-Regal Lodge. 'Thirty-five years ago,' he said, 'I was fined for having my name in Irish on my card, and now look at this!'[4]

We took up our Irish lessons again with Bridie Clifford and much of what we had learnt two years earlier came back to us. Our cousin Desmond started teaching me to drive. He had joined the University Air Squadron at Cambridge, waiting-room for the Battle of Britain in which he was soon to shine as one of 'the Few'. (His signature is on the open page in the Book of the Few at the Imperial War Museum.) We all went to the Cahirciveen Races and carried picnic baskets to wild beaches, bathing again heroically in the cold Atlantic. But above all we found Brenda.

In the two years of our absence our little donkey had acquired a reputation. After we had left two years earlier, the head of the Civic Guard, the 'Super', had taken her to amuse his children but she wanted none of it and threw them off her back. In the end she was sold to James O'Connor, a local farmer, to draw his milk cart. 'Don't let the children near her,' Susie was warned. 'She'll bite and kick.' But we took no notice. We re-engaged Sonny to care for her as before and went to the field on the Valencia Road where she was kept among O'Connor's cows. When we chanted our ritual litany – Beautiful, blissful, bashful, bountiful, beloved baby Brenda, the Belle of Cahirciveen! – she trotted down towards us to bury her nose in our hands. 'Caressed, brushed, fed upon sugar and carrots from Lena, stale bread from the hotel cook and oats from Ryan's', she became quite frisky, breaking into little canters and her version of a gallop. Helena rode her in triumph through Cahirciveen. My legs were too long.

PART FIVE

Emergency

11

The Munich Waiting-Room

Because we were London children notions of world events were blown towards us like leaves on the wind from street hoardings or casual glances at the *Evening Standard* as we managed to postpone our homework. The Abdication had been a dramatic moment. Girls in my class who had heard Edward VIII's broadcast came to school the following morning with serious faces, some no doubt piously borrowed from their parents. And we all knew the jingle:

> Hark the herald angels sing
> Mrs Simpson's pinched our King.

The Spanish War with the bombings and executions made lurid headlines in all the papers. We were aware of the Red menace (there were prayers after Mass for the Church in Stalinist Russia) but it was confusing nevertheless. 'Franco is like what Mosley would be if he got the chance,' C. K. Ogden had told Susie. While she was meeting writers who sided with the Republicans (many had friends in the International Brigade) at the convent there was an influx of Franquist refugees. One night there were screams from a Spanish girl having a nightmare. 'What was she shouting?' I asked Isabel Quigly who was born in Spain. 'Don't kill him!' she said.

There had been one of the many spats in Parliament between the Prime Minister, Neville Chamberlain, and Winston Churchill. Being a child conformist I assumed that the Prime Minister was probably right or he wouldn't have the job. 'No,' my mother said flatly. 'Churchill is right.' He had just said, 'This famous island [is] descending incontinently, fecklessly, the stairway which leads to a dark gulf.' Gradually Susie's attention was turning from her own problems to the dangerous world situation although, like most people, she would have preferred not to think about it.

The comments of the French diplomatic journalist Geneviève Tabouis regularly printed in London newspapers were followed closely but often with the attention given to a fortune-teller. Her views didn't make pleasant reading. To predict the annexation of Czechoslovakia after Hitler had walked into Austria was not far-fetched, but Tabouis also seemed to know the secret workings of all the chancelleries of Europe. Hugo Wortham said she must fly around the Continent overnight on a broomstick. The same evening on the subject of our education he said, 'I think it's a good place to bring them up. The lies they tell them are less harmful than the lies they are told in other schools.' [SHJ, 24 March 1938] 'Dear cynic,' Susie commented.

> I have nothing to show for the time since 8th June except visit to [Belgium], social engagements, Angela's twelfth birthday and my own little party. When and what am I going to write?
>
> Worked all day writing – very displeased with myself. Read some George Meredith in bed.
>
> Nothing particular except Wars and Persecutions. Cooked breakfast for myself. Find I have been forgetting altogether about food at times – a bad principle.
>
> Worked at story for G. M.[1] I get some ideas here and there but all is chaos in my head alas! Maybe I am gone beyond redemption. Still the struggle of trying to overcome weaknesses adds zest to life. I like having my back to the wall.
>
> Made myself a dinner of Beautiful River Trout grilled with sherry and butter, followed by salad and gooseberries and a glass of wine.
>
> [SHJ, 11, 12, 13 July 1938]

We attended a lecture on Air Raid Precautions in the Recreation Room at Kensington Square.

> Lt Commander McKenzie, ARP officer for Kensington, told us all about mustard gas, gas masks, air-raid shelters. The children looked amused as if it were all a joke, laughing heartily when he said that a person suspected of contamination would be seized, stripped and washed forthwith. The gallant sailor himself was a

little florid man with blossoming nose. He has either been gassed or burnt by the gas experiments which he frequently carries out, or else he is fond of the bottle. I think it is bad luck when the effects of alcohol come out instead of going in. I remember Mamma always saying when we joked about a person's expensive complexion, 'Poor man, it may be indigestion.'

[SHJ, 1 April 1938]

Lena and I listened to Verdi's *Requiem*. I wonder sometimes if I am right to listen. I love the music but the work nearly tears the heart out of me. The haunting *Agnus Dei* will be with me for a long time – the sadness of life. I felt like fading and dying from the overwhelming sadness of things. [SHJ, 27 May 1938]

'News of Czechoslovakia is not so disturbing tonight,' Susie wrote as fears of war advanced and retreated.

Last night it seemed as if war was imminent. Czech soldiers shot two Sudetendeutsch crossing frontier on motor bicycles. France declares she will go to aid of Czechs if they are attacked.

[SHJ, 20 May 1938]

She finished *War and Peace*, commenting that she could now under-stand how Tolstoy came to be regarded as a prophet.

The worst of reading deeply is that one realises the depth of one's own ignorance. This wonderful book should have done more than anything to stop War. One can see no hope. The hopes for Peace after the Great War have long since vanished.

[SHJ, 30 May 1938]

In June our mother accompanied us on a school visit to Huy in Belgium.

[In Huy] soldiers were very much in evidence, in fact they awakened us this morning with their tramp tramp tramping under our windows. Four abreast, they were led by a bugler. I watched them with a kind of shocked fascination. Although they are not very smart they have a serious air about them that English soldiers do not have.

[In the UK] one feels it is mostly showing off, but [in Belgium] one felt that at any moment war might burst upon them. The bridges are guarded by toy soldiers with fixed bayonets standing beside camouflaged sentry boxes. The registration of foreigners is very strict and the police are always on the alert for spies.

[SHJ, 22 June 1938]

There were rumours that Germany was mobilising and the hotel proprietor said that they expected war 'that weekend'.

After the annual Corpus Christi procession at 23 Kensington Square Susie was not ready to go home. Her unreadiness brought out a Syngian idiom, among other things.

Walked into Kensington Gardens along Flower Walk to Restaurant. The beauty of it all and the loveliness of the evening and I walking alone made me so sad I wanted to die. However instead of dying I had salmon mayonnaise and lager under the trees. Nowhere else except abroad could one find such a scene – tables full of happy people eating and drinking with their friends in lovely surroundings.   [SHJ, 16 June 1938]

European news full of tension. Don't like it.

These nights I have been reading *Quel Amour d'enfant* by the Comtesse de Ségur aloud to A. and H. as they sit drawing in bed. 9 p.m. is time for lights out. I will make a book of drawings. Helena presented me with a v. good caricature of Hitler.

[SHJ, 18 August 1938]

Then at the end of September the Munich crisis was upon us. Susie agreed to let us go away with the school.

Awful day. Hitler-Chamberlain talks. No one knows. ARP have begun orders for gas masks. They are digging in all parks to make shelters.

Children and nuns left in the afternoon – a heartbreaking sight, thinking one would never see them again. Angela broke down at the station. Helena was excited at the change. Mother Clare looked exhausted.

Dined with Flora [Campbell] and listened in.

[SHJ, 27 September 1938]

Spent a demented day. Went to Mass at the Cathedral, Cardinal Hinsley, Monsignor Elwes and many others assisting at the High Mass for peace. Walked all the way home. Laurie and Jim [Field] came at night to offer us the Mill House, Kettleburgh and a car to take us. They were going to join the Navy, and Jimmy Senior to go back into the Army.

News came through late of the success of Munich talk between Daladier, Hitler, Mussolini and Chamberlain but I went to bed knowing nothing and expecting the worst.

[SHJ, 29 September 1938]

On 30 September Neville Chamberlain returned from Munich waving the piece of paper which was supposed to ensure 'peace in our time'.

News that war has been averted. Germany gets what she wants and when she wants it and the Sudetenland is to be occupied piece by piece from October 1st–10th. Went to stay with Clara and we listened in to Chamberlain's welcome at Downing Street. We were going to go out but instead stuck to the radio.

[SHJ, 30 September 1938]

Of the two weeks at Cottesmore Hall I remember little more than a claustrophobic atmosphere due to living more intensely cheek by jowl. I hoped it wouldn't last. As for my friend Christine, un-accustomed to boarding she was so incapacitated with misery that her parents rescued her and took her back to London. We stayed longer, driving back with Isla Mitchell and her daughter Benedict in an open-topped car, singing Deanna Durbin numbers ecstatically at the tops of our voices, drunk with the joy of going home.

As an end-of-half-term treat, my sister being at a tea-party, my mother took me to the Ballets Jooss at the Old Vic, a treat beyond all expectations. (Dress-circle seats at 4s. 6d. as she recalled tidily.) I have never forgotten Jooss's ballet *The Green Table*. The table is centre stage, covered in green baize and surrounded by the diplomats in conference. They discuss, agree, argue, passionately disagree and finally rage, drawing revolvers from their pockets and shooting at each other. Death now stalks the town, picking out his victims. This was Jooss himself, impressive as the walking skeleton. At the end we return to the green table. The diplomats shoot in the air to celebrate peace and the talking then resumes.

A prizewinning ballet first produced in Paris, *The Green Table* related initially to the 1914–18 war. The revival in 1938 of this modern Dance of Death was apt and frightening.[2] And, supreme irony, this comment on war was the masterpiece of a German choreographer, albeit one who was annoying Hitler.

12

The Green Table

And here we are – just as before – safe in our skins;
Glory to God for Munich.

Louis MacNeice, *Autumn Journal 1939*

Lena's new flat in a Georgian terrace in Worthing was only a short walk across the gardens from the Odeon cinema. This was surely no coincidence for Lena was a screen addict whereas our mother rather grandly called the cinema 'a bastard art', or at least she did until she changed her mind. That point was reached later when she saw first *La Kermesse héroïque*, and with the influx of other French films *Sous les toits*, *Carnet de bal*, *Hôtel du nord*, *Le Million*, *Le Jour se lève*, and later the sublime *Les Enfants du paradis*, then her objections faded away. During lunch Lena, trying not to look over-keen, would suggest a film to fill an empty afternoon, setting Helena and me wriggling in our chairs. These were the great years of Hollywood comedy – Katharine Hepburn and Spencer Tracy, William Powell, Gary Cooper and James Stewart.

On an autumn evening in London we were on our way to see the film *Pygmalion*.[1] We were walking with our mother up Redcliffe Gardens when at the junction with Brompton Road a taxi swept too fast round the corner and knocked us down, just like that – one, two, three. Helena and I quickly picked ourselves up with only a bruised forehead and a twisted ankle between us. Suzanne lay inert on the edge of the road. Passers-by comforted us and took us into the little chemist's shop. I wanted none of this, only to know that my mother was alive. When the ambulance arrived she was gathered up and hidden from our sight by a screen of professionals as we sped to the hospital. Helena and I were taken to Kensington Square and the school infirmary. Our mother was diagnosed with concussion and lost her memory for some weeks. I believe her life was saved by that splendid coil of hair at the back of her head.

During the spring of 1939 Helena suffered from a persistent cough of the sort which made people turn round when we sat on the bus. Suddenly one summer afternoon in Kensington Square she shivered and complained of an aching back. She was carried off to hospital with a temperature of 105 degrees and pneumonia. Taken home she was quickly put on a course of M&B 693. These were the first sulphonamides and they made her very sick. We heard later that the consultant had told our GP, Dr Coyne, 'Give her as much as you like, she couldn't be worse.' We were now separated for the first time in our lives. At half-term I was sent to Worthing where Lena did her best to distract me while hiding her own fears. In those days the illness developed until it reached a crisis when either you died or you recovered. On the crisis Tuesday Lena took me to the cinema – they were showing a film with Shirley Temple, a potboiler called *Just Around the Corner* of which, thinking my sister might die, I took in absolutely nothing, there being nothing to take in, anyway. At tea-time the telephone rang with the news that Helena had come through. She had been saved by these drugs. Two years earlier, when H. H. was fighting the same illness, they had not been available.

When Helena came home honey-coloured after recuperating at the seaside, even with all the changes and limitations to our family life we had an unforgettable summer. Why in 1939 did everybody seem to have plans? An Old Girl had made a bequest to the school for refurbishment (we were shown the architect's drawings) and we were to have a proper theatre with raked seating and a gold curtain, perhaps also a swimming pool. There seemed to be no end to the amazing projects. The English superior had modernised the school uniform and there was even talk of being allowed, O Babylon, to wear shorts.

In my class the secret Scarlet Pimpernel Society added some spice. Mooning as usual I was a late adherent but we were to have a solemn meeting so we all went to tea at Wetherby Gardens with Daphne Speir ('jumpers and skirts' we were told rather in the same tone as 'black tie'; jeans were not yet part of the politically correct wardrobe).

I think Daphne may have confused a swearing-in ceremony with an exorcism: it was held in a darkened room with a candle and a prie-dieu and a Bible; only the bell and the demons were missing. We were to swear loyalty 'without changements'. The word seemed odd but Daphne was half French. We had all taken names from the Orczy novels. I was Viscount Holt of Frogham, alias 'Froggie'. I still don't know what the purpose was. I must have been mooning.

On summer evenings, long after we were supposed to have settled down to sleep, I would cross from my cubicle to the window-seat and, safely behind the curtain until the light was spent, read from the *Baroness Orczy Omnibus* as the late trains clattered by near Pontings.

Much of our life was centred on the garden. It was here that we ate our penny Cadbury bars at morning break, where we escaped to play tennis, where Our Lady of Lourdes turned a blind eye on our doings from the peaceful obscurity of her grotto at the end of the lawn. There was a vegetable garden and a shed where one of our classmates, Kathleen Binder, showed us her appendix in a bottle. It had that blanched look of dead things. My mother was horrified when she heard of it, but then she was never attracted to clinical details. At a fête, Captain Eyston, world champion in his *Thunderbird* at Salt Flats, Utah, gave rides in his saloon round the garden at a shilling a go in aid of the Crusade of Rescue.

The feast of Corpus Christi in June was the high point of the year, with the procession through the garden, the priest in the gold vestments of the great feasts of the Church carrying the monstrance with the Blessed Sacrament along the path, while throngs of parents and children watched from the lawns. It was a cosmopolitan crowd. Mixed with the English and Irish were Spaniards and South Americans, Germans, Austrians and French, exotic-looking mothers and aunts, many in chic hats, a strong whiff of Schiaparelli blending with the piety as they watched the solemn ballet of little girls in white and the rose petals strewn at the rhythmical snap of Mother Isabel's spectacle case; by tea-time her cheeks had the flush of great occasions. On the other side of the wall the whirr and clatter of the underground trains almost drowned our hymns which floated, their resonance failing, on the dust and haze. At the end, when our goodness had expired, we turned the garden hose on the little boys of the St Thomas More school next door.

I recall that summer of 1939 as a time of anticipation, like waiting for a party. Perhaps this was simply the approach of adolescence. Although and because the shape of our family had changed our mother gave us all her attention. Home life was delectable and with the stimulation of a capital city humming outside those confines I felt quite civilised and a mite sophisticated. I was nearly thirteen.

One area had remained fallow since our father's death: musically I had been marking time, allowed because I was 'musical' to do pretty well what I liked in that domain. With my father gone this was not what I needed, but even this gap was filled that summer by Dorothea Aspinall, the new visiting teacher from the Royal College of Music in Prince Consort Road near by. She had a pale skin and auburn hair and the gentlest manner. The work was unforced and I gained confidence. Working at my piano was like sailing a little boat, so smoothly did it go.[2] But war was coming and in my small world what followed was like the obliteration of a theatre set, the accidental darkening of a stage by a clumsy electrician in the wings. While the set was visible and because I was very young, life seemed to hold no obstacle, everything secure like a ground-bass to my alleluias.

*   *   *

The Grand Hotel at Berneval near Dieppe was run by Monsieur Lambert, his wife and two sons André and Claude. A holder of the Légion d'honneur, Lambert had lost a leg at Verdun and often left its successor on the beach when he went to swim. Sometimes he left it off altogether. 'La jambe de Papa lui fait mal.' ('Papa's leg is hurting.') Claude would explain. There was a *buvette* on the beach selling bread, fruit, chocolate and wine. My choice was baguette, a bar of chocolate and a glass of white wine, preferably all together. At the pâtisserie on Sundays after Mass the rum babas were my favourite and all hotel meals were a delight. I had never before handled the complexities of a globe artichoke and Mme Lambert's had a sauce out of fairyland. At boarding school during the war I remembered Mme Lambert's sauce and always wondered what it was until as a newly-wed in Paris I made it myself – a *mayonnaise mousseline* – and the fairyland bit was the white of egg.

I played tennis with a boy of my own age called Peter Barclay. His annoying habit of putting a top-spin into his forehand meant that he nearly always won. Afterwards we had a glass of grenadine at the local café. In the evenings the table-tennis room in the garden was cleared for dancing to records by Jean Sablon or Charles Trenet. One song with Maurice Chevalier went:

> Ça . . . vaut . . . mieux que d'attraper la scarlati-ne,
> Ça vaut mieux que d'avaler d'la mort-aux-rats . . .

This song accompanied the *jeu du tapis* (the mat game). Everyone turned in a full circle holding hands and when the music stopped the dancer in the centre laid the little *tapis* in front of a chosen one of the opposite sex and they both knelt down on it and solemnly kissed each other on both cheeks. Then it started again with the second dancer. It was all very decorous.

There were entertainments and competitions and Suzanne who was an excellent swimmer won a bottle of champagne for catching the decoy duck at sea. At the end of a fancy-dress party, a professional actor, a middle-aged Parisian, suddenly made a surprise entrance at the dining-room door, costumed and made-up as Adolf Hitler. Briskly, giving the Nazi salute, he goose-stepped to the opposite corner and went out as fast as he came in. The room froze.

Over the hotel, anxiety was beginning to hang like the threat of rain. English guests cut short their holiday, first the fathers, then whole families. We saw our friends disappear and with them the Saturday matinée atmosphere. On the village telegraph posts notices for general mobilisation appeared in old-fashioned print topped by the two crossed flags. On 3 September we went to Mass as usual, picking up our *babas au rhum* on our way back. At the hotel the fourteen-year-old Claude who was sweet on Helena was standing on the *perron*. He said, 'Ça y est.' ('That's it.') We knew war had started.

Until five o'clock that afternoon the French residents were hoping for some last-minute miracle. Then we heard the radio bulletin. For both our countries the war, the phoney war, the *drôle de guerre*, had begun.

The Grand Hotel took on a new identity. Instead of the pock-pock of tennis balls, the scratchy gramophone records and the banter of aperitif-time there were black-out fabric, newspaper and sticky tape and space had to be found for new people, relations of the Lamberts from Paris and refugees from eastern France. Sitting in the garden was a large group of women of all ages, some with small children. Many were crying, three generations of women the oldest of whom had known not only one but two previous wars with Germany. After the buttoned-up departure of the English it shocked me to witness this adult outpouring of grief and fear. 'They know about invasion,' my mother said.

We left Dieppe in a darkened ship, not knowing what time we would leave, the captain being under sealed orders on account of the danger from U-boats. In the event we sailed at about three in the morning, disembarking at dawn at Newhaven where everybody around the harbour had a purposeful air: no families, no loiterers. A hospital ship lay at anchor. Along her gleaming white hull was a broad green stripe interrupted at the centre by a huge red cross designed in vain hope of protection from the enemy.

PART SIX

Return

13

Putting in an Appearance

Each time I pass the house I quicken my step, deliberately casting off sounds and images of fifty years ago, but this late afternoon my thoughts are a couple of streets further. An old friend is struggling with the loss which will soon claim her own life. It will be her turn for hospital screens and lines and monitors and her friends will say afterwards that she died of a broken heart.

'Never pass our door without knocking,' Eve and Maurice always said to me.

'How did you do it?' I asked. 'Always the same, always together.'

'Inertia,' Maurice said laughing.

They belonged to the generation before mine, young in the First War and active in the Second. Few of their contemporaries are still around but now and again you pick out the face of a survivor like an unfamiliar plant trying to pierce its way through the AstroTurf of present-day Chelsea.

A quick look up at the studio window and I notice a new coat of paint (at one time the pillars were modishly picked out in black). I have often pictured the successive tenants: a foreign executive on a short-term contract, a minor diplomat perhaps, an American lured to the spoils of prodigal London, a best-selling writer of horror fiction – who knows if those Dracula pillars were not his fancy?

A hot summer's night after the war. Along the lamplit street I am on my way to the Fulham Road. A man is sitting at the open studio window, listening to music which nearly reaches me but is not loud enough to be recognised. The word 'hi-fi' has appeared and I think of what he is missing, sitting there alone under strip lighting. But perhaps he is not as disconsolate as he looks; perhaps he is simply waiting for his lover . . .

How could Susie bear to pass the house bereft of its live music? Her step is determined, steadfast. She keeps going. 'When you are both launched I shall be happy to go.' I don't protest: such an eventuality is too remote to think about. August 1939. We are in Normandy at the descent into war and we return to England in a darkened ship. Soon all change: anyone for Liverpool? How can one imagine war doing any good? But our mother reads those German letters and with the danger around she has barely time to dwell on her loss. For us children, 'safe in our skins' in damp Shropshire, little comforts arrive – a pot of jam, a cardigan, letters in the familiar rounded hand, written at night perhaps. Her handwriting resembles her, round and firm. 'Your mother has only you now,' the nuns remind us. At night the hiccuping German planes are on their way to Crewe, Coventry, Liverpool. In a tin hat on Littlewoods' roof-top our mother is on fire-watching duty. Her colleague collapses with a heart attack and she is alone as they carry him away the night the Bon Marché burns down. Meanwhile in London an unexploded bomb wrecks the Redcliffe Square flat. ('How devastating!' an acquaintance had remarked of our new address.) Many of our books are beyond repair – books and the piano, but not ourselves. We are lucky: a girl we knew was buried for four days in Bramerton Street. There are near misses, when a Mozart quartet at the College prevents my riding into the crash of a V1, and when the Guinness buildings are destroyed, down at World's End . . .

As I turn the corner into the sun I nearly collide with a youth carrying a Walkman and shambling ahead of me in baggy trousers, his laces undone. A well-dressed blonde with an Alice-band loses control of four designer carrier-bags, staggers across the street and drops her keys.

Town leaves are heavy with August dust. In Elm Park Road past our vanished side entrance I find the garden door open to the street. In a Portakabin two builders have mugs in their hands. I ask them about the owner.

'Yes. The German millionaire.' An Ulster voice.

'I lived here as a child.'

'Would you care to look round?'

We cross the garden and go up the stairway. The foreman sits in a narrow passage, a young man with Maori looks, long wavy hair and neat khaki shorts. Perched on a high stool, one leg stretched side-ways, he puts down the receiver and turns to greet me unsurprised.

The basement with its fashionable arrangements has something of an out-of-hours health club. In an empty room the present owner seems to be divining my thoughts from a blown-up photograph propped against a radiator. He looks like an unentertained host whose guests have overstayed. At the top of the staircase, elephant grey and narrower than I recall, Evelyn De Morgan's great studio has lost the U shape which protected the farthest end, the tip of the upward stroke, hidden from the door, the corner with my parents' big divan. Like an uninvited visitor a new staircase now erupts in this private space. I reflect that this was probably where I was conceived.

It is early morning and I am in my parents' big bed, holding one of the little Lunéville cups which are too shallow to keep the tea warm. What do we talk about? Heaven knows, but H. H.'s thoughts turn to his work and soon he slopes off to the piano an arm's length away to go over last night's pencilled notes.

Witness to the refurbishments, a sixties' retro mirror hangs for-gotten like an unwanted gift. The floorboards have been gloss-painted, grey again but with the narrow red stripe of the Dracula Club.

Floorboards in King's Road . . . The gaps between them under the piano stool send up an icy draught from the empty shop below. Fingers stiff with cold attack 'Dr Gradus ad Parnassum' before I run for the bus to Prince Consort Road. At the Albert Hall steps, off the number 9 from Barnes, Herbert Howells laughs, 'We are both late for your lesson.'

A brass player is noisy in the next room. Philip Jones of the future Brass Ensemble. Seeing my tweed suit, Howells says, 'You look very county today.' I register the small chip left by who knows what patronising remark delivered too early in life. I'm not good at handling chips and ignore it. Unlike his colleagues he has something of the faun about him – a faun and an artist, with his attention to women, his careful speech, his sharpness and his exquisite script. This I celebrate by passing on my father's creamy pre-war manuscript paper as Howells works on his Hymnus Paradisi *in memory of his lost son. What music would you like to die to? he asks. For him it has to be Schubert . . .*

The move to London and my mother's lower-paid job have nevertheless meant a home and access to music, so it is back to Chelsea at a strange time. Flowerpots and a breakfast table appear on the little terrace above the empty shop. With a night raid shreds of paper from the fire-bombed paper mills float above the Thames like a gale of incandescent autumn leaves. The shoemaker Lansdell and his wife are local heroes, digging people out of their houses at all hours. On his nightly rounds a friend in Civil Defence keeps an eye on our maisonette above the abandoned vegetable shop –'Amalgamated Fruiterers' with the little orange trees, symbols of vanished abundance, at each end of the old sign barely legible for dust. Awaiting electricity and a boiler we clean by torches and candle-light and wash in front of the gas fires. In Barbara Watson's Tite Street studio during a pause over the tea-cups the voice of the painter Luigi Meo is raised in a Goya-like evocation of a bombed shelter and coffee-coloured corpses. It is so grotesque that we laugh.

Passions and Messiahs, the discovery of chamber music, work with May Harrison on Bach's Musical Offering, *playing with friends in the holidays, poaching violin or oboe parts on my flute – Hausmusik or the platform it is all the same to me. In my hands so many hours a day the cocuswood barely strays from body temperature. Waiting in its case it is a live thing breathing, ready to collude.*

Mozart's profile speaks across the orchestra desks: Stephen D., sensitive, complicated, angry and imbued with music. Up Queen's Gate on our bikes he shouts, 'SHUT UP!' at exploding exhausts. Shared concerts, new scores, poetry discovered. Slim volumes on the underground and afternoons which do nothing for arpeggios: summer days evaporate. The unbesmirched might be safe from the world but it isn't because we are children. Or very nearly which is worse, and ripe for all the shocks.

Music through the week, the return to London of foreign names, and yet one moment stands out when I play with the Boyd Neel Orchestra in an Exeter church. Kathleen Ferrier is singing in Bach's St Matthew Passion. What is it about this voice, at ease with itself at any pitch, its colour sometimes dark and fearful, that can pour all the sorrows of the *world into, 'Erbarme dich'? When that voice answers the filigree violin a thread broken for me by my father's death comes very near to being rejoined.*

Our nursery below with its balcony is unchanged. Behind this room, above the garden, is the little study where during the Great War William De Morgan tried to continue writing and where around the tiled fireplace he had set his frieze of hungry-looking fish. These tiles were to survive intact only as long as did our own household, and possibly only as long as the pear-tree just outside which Susie had likened to a bride. A pregnant bride heavy with fertility and improvidence, this tree now long gone shed her blossom inside the room, on the window-seat.

When after we had left the house Maresco Pearce recovered the tiles thrown into a heap of rubble by our successor, Susie wrote 'What will Herbert think of Mr Briscoe the stockbroker?' 'Will think', not 'would think'. Advised by a well-meaning friend to make a clean break with the past she disagreed, wanting to feel that H. H. could come home at any minute.

Maresco's son the architect John Pearce inherited the house at 117 Old Church Street. When it was about to be sold at his death the fish tiles rescued by his father were still displayed in the dressing-room. Efforts to remove them failed: they disintegrated. Initially set up in his own house by their creator, they had been successively enjoyed by a musician and his family, discarded by a stockbroker, saved by a quick-witted painter, preserved by his son a hundred yards down the street and were now simply too fragile for another adventure. Their entire fate, like the most significant part of our family life, had been played out within one small acre of Chelsea.

Down the steps, through the garden and past the Portakabin, I thank the foreman and leave. Out in the street to my surprise I feel nothing at all. Have I been scoured, bleached, cleaned out? I have just emerged from a place which operates a new and unfamiliar currency with its own rules, its own constraints, a currency which is now being minted in a frenzy all over this city. Leaving this altered house is like leaving a foreign country.

A souped-up Lamborghini draws up along the kerb with its windows down, the bass thumping hard and as many antennae as masts in a harbour. Soon it will be gone and the summer evening will take over and voices float up again from neighbouring gardens.

Notes

Chapter 1 Chelsea 1915

1 The house was a wedding present from Halsey Ricardo to his daughter Anna and his son-in-law Maresco Pearce.

2 The *Echo* of 10 April 1885 reported that the owners of 125, 127, 129 and 155 Church Street were prosecuted for 'keeping disorderly houses'. Nos 125 and 127 had been known until 1867 as nos 1 and 3 Bolton Place. After World War II the street was renamed 'Old' Church Street to distinguish it from its Kensington namesake and in homage to the original Chelsea Old Church destroyed in the Blitz.

Chapter 2 Goodbye, Belfast

1 In Patrick Kavanagh's *The Green Fool*, 'Hughes's millmen' appear briefly in a mock-heroic incident. Penguin Books, 1975 edition, p. 109.

2 Harry Plunket Greene, *Charles Villiers Stanford*, London, Edward Arnold, 1935, p. 256.

3 Ivor Newton, Herbert Hughes BBC Memorial Broadcast, 9 October 1953.

4 Herbert Howells, *Essays in English Chamber Music 1966*. Cited in Christopher Lambert, *Herbert Howells, A Centenary Celebration*, London, Thames Publishing, 1992.

5 *Songs of Uladh* was published in Belfast by W. J. Baird. Some of the songs appeared later in Herbert Hughes's *Irish Country Songs*, published by Boosey & Co from 1909.

6 Stephen Gwynn, *Experiences of a Literary Man*, London, Thornton Butterworth, 1926, p. 257.

7 Mary and Padraic Colum, *Our Friend James Joyce*, London, Gollancz, 1958, pp. 223–4.

8 Coole Park, September 1906. *The Letters of W. B. Yeats*, edited by Allan Wade, London, Rupert Hart-Davis, 1954. Cited by N. Saunders and A. A. Kelly, *Joseph Campbell, Poet and Nationalist 1879–1944*, Dublin, Wolfhound Press, 1989, p. 39.

9 W. B. Yeats to Lady Gregory, 14 March 1905, *The Collected Letters of W. B. Yeats*, edited by John Kelly and Ronald Schuchard, Oxford University Press, 2006, Vol. 4, p. 56.

10 'Fenians' was the common name for the Irish Republican Brotherhood (IRB), a separatist secret society which appeared in the late 1850s and was committed to armed insurrection.

11 W. B. Yeats to Lady Gregory, 11 November 1905, ibid., pp. 221–2.

12 F. S. L. Lyons, *Culture and Anarchy in Ireland 1890–1939*, Oxford University Press, 1979, p. 130.

13 Ivor Newton, BBC Memorial Tribute to Herbert Hughes, 9 October 1953.

14 Fiona MacCarthy, *Eric Gill*, London, Faber, 1989, pp. 75–7.

15 Spike Hughes, *Opening Bars*, London, Pilot Press, 1946; and *Second Movement*, London, Museum Press, 1951.

16 Sir John Lavery, *The Life of a Painter,* London, 1940. Cited in Keith Jeffery's *Ireland in the Great War,* Cambridge University Press, 2000.

17 Friedrich Nietzsche, *The Dawn of Day*, translated by J. M. Kennedy, Edinburgh and London, T. J. Foulis, 1911.

Chapter 3   Au Revoir, Dublin

1 Ambrose McEvoy (1878–1927), English painter, protégé of Whistler and friend of Augustus and Gwen John. This watercolour ('Susie') now hangs in the National Gallery of Victoria, Melbourne. See H. H.'s letter, Chapter 8, p. 150.

2 To correct one of many biographers' errors, Suzanne, not yet eleven, had not 'been to a dance'. (Herbert Gorman, *James Joyce*, London, John Lane and the Bodley Head, 1941, p. 69.)

3 Charles Stewart Parnell (1846–91). Home Rule MP for Meath, President of the Land League, leader of the Irish Parliamentary Party, half-American (Protestant) figurehead for the Irish

peasantry. Able politician falsely accused of complicity in the Phoenix Park murders (1887) and subsequently vindicated. Seen as the greatest Irish leader since Daniel O'Connell. Cited as co-respondent in MP Captain O'Shea's divorce petition and subsequently deserted on all sides, especially by the Catholic hierarchy. He later married Katharine O'Shea. His fall was seen by Yeats as the Fourth Bell in the series of 'deep tragic notes' of Irish history.

4 H. H. to M. McK., Chelsea, 13 November 1921.

5 R. F. Foster, *W. B. Yeats – A Life. Volume 1: The Apprentice Mage 1865–1914,* Oxford University Press, 1997, p. 311.

6 H. H. to M. McK., Chelsea, 15 January 1922.

7 H. H. to M. McK., Off Cherbourg, 20 January 1922.

8 General Heppenheimer's son-in-law was the diplomat Robert Vansittart, later Lord Vansittart.

9 On this occasion Koussevitzky declared that he believed Coates was the best Wagner conductor in the world. [SHJ, 26 January 1938]

Chapter 4   Ireland in London

1 Joyce studied German, a language he disliked, only in order to translate Gerhart Hauptmann's plays.

2 Besides Nora Joyce the others were the art expert Robert Langton Douglas and Violet and A. J. Munnings.

3 *Finnegans Wake*, Penguin Edition, p. 550.

4 ibid., p. 431.

5 From H. H.'s Preface to *The Joyce Book.*

6 *The Collected Letters of W. B. Yeats*, edited by John Kelly and Ronald Schuchard, Oxford University Press, 2006, Vol. 4, p. 56n.

7 Besides H. H. (who set 'She Weeps over Rahoon') and Arthur Bliss (who chose 'Simples'), the other contributors were C. W. Orr, Herbert Howells, Bernard van Dieren, E. J. Moeran, Albert Roussel, George Antheil, Roger Sessions, Edgardo Carducci, Arnold Bax, John Ireland and Eugene Goossens.

8 Long believed to be by Haydn but now credited to Leopold Mozart.

9 Ochone! Pillaloo! Och I'm kilt!/May the quilt/Lay light on your delicate form, / When the weather is hot / But my love, when 'tis not, / May it cradle you cosy and warm / Nic norum ni roo, / Nic norum ni!

10 Mary and Padraic Colum, *Our Friend James Joyce*, London, Gollancz, 1958.

11 Stephens told Robert Lynd that he believed only in cocktails and God.

12 Produced at the Royalty Theatre in 1933, *Within the Gates* ran for only a month. In New York the work was more successful, with Lilian Gish as the Young Whore. In Boston the play was banned.

13 Dierdre McMahon, *Republicans and Imperialists, Anglo-Irish Relations in the 1930s*, New Haven and London, Yale University Press, 1984, p. 58.

14 McCormack had taken out US citizenship in 1919 having applied in 1914. This was seen as dereliction of duty and led to abusive mail. Ironically his last and most faithful audiences were British.

15 Suzanne remembered Hugh Kennedy 'as a little red-nosed boy with purple hands, fair hair and a navy ganzy in Sister Francis Xavier's infant class'. [SHJ, 2 January 1930] It is of him that John Stanislaus Joyce, the writer's father, said, 'He had a face like a child's bottom, well-whipped.' R. Ellmann, *James Joyce,* Oxford University Press, 1959, paperback edition 1965, p. 70.

16 This is probably Comyns Beaumont, elder brother of Gerald du Maurier's wife Muriel.

17 And like many Irishmen he didn't.

18 V. S. Pritchett had never seen 'such a measure of infinity poured into a single shaggy suit of Irish tweed'. V. S. Pritchett, *Dublin*, London, The Bodley Head, 1967; Hogarth Press, 1991 edition, p. 19.

19 Clandillon, *Songs of the Gaels*, Oxford University Press, 1927.

20 Clifford Bax, *Some I Knew Well*, London, Phoenix House, 1951, p. 88.

Chapter 5   Immersion

1 H. H. was working on a biography of Chopin.

2 And alien tears will fill for him/Pity's long-broken urn,/For his mourners will be outcast men,/And outcasts always mourn. Oscar Wilde, *The Ballad of Reading Gaol.*

3 Edward Gordon Craig (1872–1966) was the son of Ellen Terry and E. W. Godwin. Actor, designer and innovator, he wrote copiously on theories of theatrical production but was more appreciated in Germany and the States than in Britain.

4 Predecessor of the Sadler's Wells Ballet, the Camargo Society was founded in 1930 to develop British ballet. Among the founder members were Arnold Haskell, Edwin Evans, Constant Lambert, Maynard Keynes and Lydia Lopokova, Marie Rambert and Ninette de Valois.

5 Some Chelsea residents in those years: Constant Lambert, Maurice Lambert, Cecil Gray, Philip Heseltine, the Sitwells, Eugene Goossens, Léon Goossens, M. D. Calvocoressi, Luigi Innes Meo, Augustus John, Jacob Epstein, Maresco Pearce, Oliver Bernard, Robin Legge, W. A. Darlington, Frank Dobson, Laura Knight, Margaret Morris, R. H. Wilenski, James Laver and Veronica Turleigh, Francis Toye, John Ireland, Bess Norriss, Percy Grainger, Francis Derwent Wood, Sybil Thorndike and Lewis Casson, Russell and Rosemary Thorndike, Henry Tonks and A. J. Munnings.

6 This little restaurant functioned throughout WWII.

7 Ronald Blythe, *The Age of Illusion, England in the Twenties and Thirties 1919–1940*, London, Hamish Hamilton, 1963; Phoenix Press edition, p. 57.

8 Wareing was joined by Graham Greene's brother Hugh Carleton Greene, later Director-General of the BBC.

9 This was a 60-page pamphlet by Ewald Banse, *Wehrwissenschaft, Einführung In Eine Neue Nationale Wissenschaft,* first published in 1932 with a second edition in 1933. I am indebted to Professor Sir Ian Kershaw for these details.

10 See Chapter 4, 'Ireland in London', p. 49.

11 Donal O'Sullivan, BBC Memorial Tribute to H. H., 9 October 1953.

Chapter 6   Strands

1 Marconi in conversation with Suzanne.

2 Maria Montessori (1870–1952) was the first woman doctor of medicine of the University of Rome. She studied philosophy and psychology and founded the Scuola Ortofrenica. She gave training courses in London from 1919.

3 Patrick Kavanagh, *The Green Fool*, Michael Joseph, 1938, Penguin Edition, p. 29.

4 This little shop was destroyed in the Blitz.

5 The Irish writer Colm Tóibín has shown a specifically Irish link (not found with Waugh or Greene) between writing and singing – with Samuel Beckett, John Banville, Sebastian Barry as examples. BBC Radio 3, 'Private Passions', 29 October 2006.

6 Eustace Wareing was the *Daily Telegraph*'s Berlin correspondent.

7 The script was by J. B. Priestley.

8 SHJ, 26 October 1937.

Chapter 7   Kaleidoscope

1 The French cellist Pierre Fournier called him 'a spoilt child on a grand scale'.

2 Katherine Goodson (1872–1958), English pianist, pupil of Leschetizky. Appeared in London with Beecham and the London Philharmonic Orchestra.

3 Harvey Sachs, *Toscanini,* London, Weidenfeld & Nicolson, 1978, pp. 208–10.

4 R. H. Legge to H. H., 'Thursday' undated (1931).

5 Elgar dedicated the *Nursery Suite* to the Duchess of York and the two young Princesses Elizabeth and Margaret Rose.

6 A. P. Herbert, Gerald Barry, Hugh Walpole, Rose Macaulay, the Gollanczes, the Lynds, Ivor Brown, A. J. Cronin, J. C. Squire, J. B. Morton ('Beachcomber'), Gerald Gould, Edmund Gwenn, Gertrude Lawrence, Gladys Cooper, Edith and Nora Heald and often the Ralph Richardsons.

7 Robeson's son speaking on a BBC World Service programme in the 1990s.

8 The lion-killer, Jack Webster, gave her a brooch made from the claw of his first lion, mounted on gold from a mine he had prospected. R. Findlater, *Lilian Baylis, The Lady of the Old Vic,* Allen Lane, 1975, p. 284.

9 R. Findlater, op. cit., p. 191. The composer Lawrance Collingwood (q.v.) was Musical Director.

10 After a three-day hearing in 1937 Natasha Brasova's claim was dismissed by the Polish judges. See below, Note 22.

11 Was this the impatience of two former infant prodigies? Adrienne cannot have been more than six years old.

12 Joachim himself had written sadly to a friend of this work, mentioning 'wearisome repetitions' and 'laboriousness'. Joachim to Andreas Moser, 5 August 1898, *Letters of Joseph Joachim,* Volume III, Berlin, Julius Barth, 1913.

13 BBC Sound Archives, Disc x13389, made 6 May 1949, British Composer series.

14 Lewis Foreman, *Bax, A Composer and His Times,* Aldershot, Scolar Press, 1983; Ashgate reprint, 1998, p. 13.

15 Beatrice Harrison, *The Cello and the Nightingales,* London, John Murray, 1985, p. 125.

16 Kilmacrenan Edition, arrangements for violin or cello and piano, Boosey & Co. from 1925.

17 *The Sackbut,* criticised by Ernest Newman for being gratuitously offensive, was praised by Hubert Foss for being 'often alarmingly right'. It carried non-musical material such as poems by the young Roy Campbell and drawings by Augustus John.

18 Ottoline Morrell found Heseltine/Warlock 'soft and degenerate' on only a brief acquaintance. The pianist Angus Morrison thought him sinister.

19 These contributions to the *Pomes Penyeach* settings in *The Joyce Book* are as follows: Bax: 'Watching the Needleboats at San Sabba'; E. J. Moeran: 'Tilly'; H. H.: 'She Weeps over Rahoon'.

20 H. H. to S. H., 3 August 1930.

21 Pauline Gray, *Cecil Gray, His Life and Notebooks,* London, Thames Publishing, 1989.

22 Natalie Brasova, née Cheremetevskaya, a commoner and divorcée (ex-Mamontov, ex-Wulfert) caused great scandal at the Russian court through her love affair with and eventual marriage to the Grand Duke Michael Aleksandrovich (1878–1918), the Tsar Nicholas II's only surviving brother. Michael was abducted and murdered in June 1918. Natalie Brasova died destitute in Paris in January 1952. She was buried with their son George who had died in 1935 as the result of a motorcycle accident.

23 Gray, op. cit., p. 36.

24 Gray, op. cit., pp. 115, 185.

25 I. Copley, *The Music of Peter Warlock*, London, 1979, cited in Barry Smith's *Peter Warlock, The Life of Philip Heseltine*, Oxford University Press, 1994.

26 G. Self, *The Music of E. J. Moeran*, London, Toccata Press, 1986, p. 102.

27 Andrew Motion, *The Lamberts*, London, Chatto & Windus, 1986, p. 155.

28 From Nichols's notes on his correspondence with Heseltine, British Library, Add. MS 57796. Cited in Smith, op. cit., p. 226.

29 H. H. was working on a biography of Chopin.

30 Felix Aprahamian in conversation with the author.

31 The Hart House Quartet was founded by Vincent Massey whose family had built Hart House, an arts centre attached to the University of Toronto. The original leader was Géza de Kresz, the Hungarian violinist who had plucked the brilliant refugee cellist Gregor Piatigorsky out of a Berlin café orchestra in the early twenties. In inviting him to join the Pozniak Trio, de Kresz initiated the Russian's second career.

32 Born in Budapest, Miklos Schwalb, a pupil of Dohnányi, appeared at fourteen with the Budapest Philharmonic. He had a successful career in the USA and later became Artist in Residence, Boston Northeastern University.

33 Fay Yeatman, Léon Goossens' first wife.

Chapter 8   Crossed Lines and Dislocations

1 Robert and Joy Newton were the lessees. The committee included Henry Ainley, Margaret Bannerman, Robert Boothby, Augustus John, Irene Ravensdale, Marjorie Newton and John McCormack. The theatre had opened a week earlier with short plays by Maupassant, O'Neill, Gertrude Jennings and Audrey Carten. 'We had a box for 5/-.' [SHJ, 14 January 1933] Joy Newton was married to Igor Vinogradoff, Ottoline Morrell's former son-in-law.

2 Pretentious character from the BBC Radio 4 soap *The Archers*.

3 Robin H. Legge had moved from *The Times* to the *Daily Telegraph* in 1906. He became Music Editor in 1908.

4 R. H. Legge to H. H., undated 'Monday' (*c*.1930).

5 H. H. to S. H., 3 August 1930.

6 Duff Hart-Davis, *The House the Berrys Built,* London, Hodder & Stoughton, 1990, p. 104.

7 This wariness could be explained by the taint of the IRA which for many people who remembered the Civil War still clung to de Valera. By this time, however, he had embraced constitutional politics; he had in short changed tack and become respectable.

8 Olga Lambert was married to the sculptor Maurice Lambert, Constant's brother.

9 F. R. Higgins (1896–1941), like his friend Austin Clarke, experimented with arresting musical effects drawn from Gaelic metre. The *Broadside Ballads* in which he collaborated with Yeats were published by the Cuala Press in 1935. Among his other work was a volume of poems *Arable Holdings* (Macmillan, 1933). He was a member of the Irish Academy of Letters.

10 The project, initially entitled *Nora O'Neale,* ended regrettably as *Irish Hearts*. Moreover the title had been used elsewhere in 1927.

11 On the night of 30 June–1 July 1934, the S. S. Blackshirts (the new élite guard) killed off the old stormtroopers, the S. A. Brownshirts, and eliminated Hitler's rivals Röhm, Strasser and von Schleicher.

12 The sons of Jimmy Field, H. H.'s old army friend. Laurie was working for the publisher Daniel Macmillan before joining the navy at the outbreak of war. His ship was to disappear in the Mediterranean with all hands.

13 Maria McKernan died peacefully in her sleep on 10 March 1935 and was buried at Stoke-by-Nayland. She was eighty-eight.

14 'A brilliant study of Berlioz (Oxford University Press) by Tom S. Wotton, who apparently knows his job from A to Z.' H. H. to S. H., 12 February 1935.

15 The sculptor Frederick Lessore (1879–1951).

16 Tracing this unsigned and undated watercolour took me a year. I knew only that I had seen it in a Mayfair gallery after the war and that it had ended up in the Antipodes, but exactly where I had no idea. It transpired that for ten years after H. H.'s letter it had remained unsold. The Felton Bequest then acquired it in 1945 from the estate for 40 guineas on behalf of the National Gallery of Victoria in Melbourne where it now hangs.

Chapter 9   The Light and the Dark

1 This trio was published by Augener in 1936.

2 E. J. Moeran to H. H., 11 February 1937.

3 John ('Jock') Murray to H. H., 3 April 1937.

4 *Guardian*, 9 February 1973.

Chapter 10   Palliatives

1 Lilian Baylis to S. H., 4 May 1937.

2 Barbara Watson, née Wake-Walker, had been a pupil of Tonks at the Slade where she had the nickname of Little Rosy Grey after a painterly hint from the master.

3 Florence Chuter, mother of Kit Lambert.

4 O'Sullivan was exaggerating. Filling in official forms in Irish was illegal in 1903 'and a handy way of infuriating the government at Dublin Castle' (Professor R. F. Foster).

Chapter 11   The Munich Waiting-Room

1 Gordon Meggie's Premier School ran correspondence courses in writing.

2 *The Green Table.* Ballet in 8 scenes by Kurt Jooss (b. Würtemburg, 1901, d. 1979). Music by Fritz Cohen. Costumes by Hein Heckroth. Première at Théâtre des Champs Elysées, Paris, 1932.

Chapter 12 The Green Table

1 *Pygmalion,* 1938, adapted from the G. B. Shaw play, directed by Anthony Asquith, with Leslie Howard and Wendy Hiller.
2 Herbert Howells chose Dorothea Aspinall to teach his daughter Ursula.

Biographical Notes

Allgood, Molly (1887–1952), stage name Máire O'Neill. Irish actress of the Abbey Theatre, muse and fiancée of the playwright J. M. Synge. Married 1st G. H. Mair (died 1926) and 2nd Arthur Sinclair (q.v.)

Allgood, Sarah (1883–1950), sister of the above. Worked in the same company. Married Gerald Henson and toured Australia and New Zealand, where both husband and daughter died of Spanish flu. Returned to Abbey Theatre, very successful in Synge's plays. Moved to America in 1940. Appeared in many Hollywood films.

d'Arányi, Jelly (1893–1966) Hungarian-born violinist, great-niece of Joseph Joachim (q.v.) and pupil of Hubay. Gave first British performance of Bartók's two sonatas dedicated to her, with composer at the piano. Premièred Holst's Double Concerto with her sister Adila Fachiri (q.v.); written for them. Twenty-year partnership with Myra Hess.

Arnaud, Yvonne (1892–1958) Paris-Conservatoire-trained pianist who became a successful actress.

Austin, Frederic (1872–1952) English baritone and composer. Initially organist and music teacher. Appeared at Covent Garden in 1908. Artistic Director of the British National Opera Company from 1924.

Backhaus, Wilhelm (1884–1969) German pianist born in Leipzig. Pupil of Reckendorf and d'Albert. First tour aged sixteen. Shone in the classical repertoire, especially with Beethoven. Heart attack during a concert prevented the completion of the cycle of 32 sonatas which he had undertaken at the age of eighty.

Barry, Gerald (1898–1968) Journalist and administrator. Director General of Festival of Britain, 1951.

Beaumont, William Comyns (1873–1956) Eccentric Scottish journalist, author and lecturer. On staff of *Daily Mail*, Italy correspondent of the *Daily Telegraph*. His writings earned him the label of 'cosmic heretic'. Uncle of English novelist Daphne du Maurier.

Bellezza, Vincenzo (1888–1964) Italian conductor. Guest conductor Covent Garden and NY Metropolitan. Later on staff of Rome Opera.

Bernard, Anthony (1891–1963) English composer, pianist and conductor. Studied with Bantock, John Ireland and Joseph Holbrooke. Began as organist, pianist and choir director. Appeared at festivals and all over Europe. Composed for radio, also chamber music and songs. Premièred Robert Simpson's Second Symphony (1956) of which he was dedicatee.

Bernard, Oliver (1881–1939) British architect and designer. Worked in the theatre (London, New York). Survived the sinking of the *Lusitania*. Served with distinction in WWI (MC). Famous for 1930 Lyons Corner Houses and spectacular art deco foyer of Strand Palace Hotel. Father of journalist Jeffrey Bernard and designer Bruce Bernard. Autobiography *Cock Sparrow*.

Bigger, Francis Joseph (1863–1926) Irish author, antiquary, solicitor and nationalist. Editor of *Ulster Journal of Archaeology*.

Birrell, Augustine (1850–1933) English barrister, politician and writer.

Blois, Lt Col Eustace Managing Director of the Royal Opera House Syndicate.

Bonavia, Ferruccio (1877–1950) Italian-born violinist, composer and critic. Successively on staff of *Manchester Guardian* and *Daily Telegraph*.

Bone, James (1872–1962) London correspondent of *Manchester Guardian*.

Brosa, Antonio (1894–1979) Spanish violinist, pupil of Crickboom. Majority of career in London. Duo partner of English pianist Kathleen Long.

Cairns, Hugh McCalmont, Earl (1819–1885) Born Belfast. Educated Trinity College Dublin. Bar, 1844. MP Belfast, 1852. Peerage, 1867. Lord Chancellor, 1868.

Calvocoressi, M. D. (1877–1944) Writer on music and Russian specialist. Born of Greek parents in Marseilles, studied at Paris Conservatoire. Settled in London, 1914. Died in Chelsea.

Capell, Richard (1885–1954) *Daily Telegraph* music critic.

Carroll, Sydney (1877–1958) Author and critic. Head of drama page *Daily Telegraph*, 1928–39. President Critics' Circle, 1931–2. Established Regent's Park Open Air Theatre, 1933.

Caruso, Enrico (1873–1921) World famous Neapolitan-born tenor. First sang in London, with Melba, in 1902.

Casement, Sir Roger (1864–1916) Born Co. Dublin. Entered British consular service. Joined Gaelic League, 1904. Produced highly-regarded reports on human-rights violations in Africa and South America. Knighted, 1911. Tried to enlist German support for the Irish struggle. Attempted to deter the Easter Rising 1916 but was captured and sentenced to death. The revealing of the 'Black Diaries' exposing his homosexuality prevented a reprieve and he was hanged in August 1916.

Catterall, Arthur (1883–1943) English violinist. Soloist and leader of Catterall Quartet. Many years professor at Royal Manchester College of Music.

Coates, Albert (1882–1953) English conductor and composer born in St Petersburg of Russian mother and English father. At Leipzig Conservatory studied cello with Klengel and conducting with Nikisch. Conducted operas first in German theatres and later in St Petersburg. Settled in London in 1919 having fled Revolution. Moved later to South Africa.

Codner, Maurice (1888–1958) English portrait painter in oil and water-colour. Lived in Dedham. His portrait of Kathleen Ferrier is in the National Portrait Gallery.

Cohen, Harriet (1895–1967). Born in London. Studied at Royal Academy of Music and with Tobias Matthay, making her début aged thirteen at the Queen's Hall, London. Promoted English music, especially that of Arnold Bax.

Collingwood, Lawrance (1887–1983) English composer and conductor. Studied at St Petersburg Conservatory. Assistant to Albert Coates (q.v.) at Mariinsky Theatre. Conductor at Old Vic, 1920. Principal Conductor when opera moved to Sadler's Wells. Musical Director, 1941–7.

Craig, Edward Gordon (1872–1966) Influential English set designer, writer and innovative man of the theatre. Son of Ellen Terry and architect E. W. Godwin.

Croker, John Wilson (1780–1857) Politician and author, born in Waterford. Educated Trinity College Dublin. Called to Bar; MP Downpatrick, 1807; wrote for *Quarterly Review* for 40 years; friend of Scott, Moore and Wellington. Secretary to Admiralty, 1809–30. Edited Boswell's *Johnson*.

Crowder, Henry (1890–1955) Black Amercian jazz pianist and composer.

Cunard, Nancy (1896–1965) Cunard shipping heiress and daughter of Maud 'Emerald' Cunard. Editor, publisher, writer and political activist known also for her scandals and her verbal war with her mother. Her wealth helped her support many new writers.

Dent, E. J. (1876–1957) English musicologist, teacher and critic, pupil of Charles Wood and Stanford. A founder of the International Society for Contemporary Music, and its president. Promoter of opera in England, especially by Mozart.

de Valera, Eamon (1882–1975) Pre-eminent leader in post-independence Ireland. Born in New York but educated in Limerick. Embraced Gaelic having joined Gaelic League. Joined Irish volunteers, last commander to surrender, 1916. Released, 1917. Sinn Féin MP from 1917 and its president until 1926. President of first Dáil Eireann, 1919. President of Irish Republic, 1921, but resigned on ratification of Anglo-Irish Treaty by the Dáil which led to the vicious civil war between pro- and anti-Treaty forces. In 1926 established Fianna Fáil party which came to power in 1932. President of the Irish Republic, 1959–73. In the forefront of Irish politics for more than half a century he nevertheless failed to obtain either the re-establishment of the Gaelic language or the re-unification of Ireland.

Dieren, Bernard van (1887–1936) Dutch composer and critic. Studied in Germany and the Netherlands. Wrote essays and a study of Epstein.

Dohnányi, Ernst von (1877–1960) Hungarian pianist, composer and conductor.

Douglas, Robert Langton (1864–1951) Art expert, author, lecturer. Lived in Italy, 1895–1900. Director National Gallery of Ireland, 1916–23. Staff captain in WWI. Father of Sholto Douglas, Marshal of the RAF in WWII.

Doyle, Jack (1913–78) Irish boxer, wrestler, singer and playboy. Double singing act with his 2nd wife Mexican starlet Movita who left him for Marlon Brando in 1945.

Dulanty, John Whelan (1883–1955) Civil servant in London. At Irish Free State request High Commissioner in London, 1930–50, later Ambassador for Republic of Ireland.

d'Erlanger, Baron Frédéric (1868–1943) Paris-born composer and opera director Covent Garden.

Ervine, St John Greer (1883–1971) Belfast-born dramatist, novelist, biographer and critic. Member of the Fabian Society. Controversial director of the Abbey Theatre. Joined Dublin Fusiliers in WWI and lost a leg in France. Retired to Devon where he wrote criticism and biography.

Evelyn, Clara (1882, 1884 or 1886–1980) English concert pianist and musical comedy singer. Infant prodigy pianist and double scholar at Royal College of Music. Studied piano with Marmaduke Barton and singing with controversial teacher Visetti. Joined George Edwardes' Gaiety Girls.

Fachiri, Adila (1886–1962) Hungarian violinist, sister of Jelly d'Arányi (q.v.) and great-niece of Joseph Joachim (q.v.), who gave her his Stradivarius violin. Married Greek lawyer Alexander Fachiri. Lived in Chelsea.

Fagan, James Bernard (1873–1933) Playwright and theatre director. Intended successively for Holy Orders, the Bar and the Indian Civil Service but turned to the theatre, working with F. R. Benson and Herbert Beerbohm Tree and writing plays. Produced many in London. Opened Oxford Playhouse, 1923. Director of Festival Theatre, Cambridge. Manager of Court Theatre, Chelsea (now Royal Court), 1918.

Farr, Florence (1860–1917) English actress and teacher. Mistress of G. B. Shaw who was captivated by her beautiful voice. Friend and collaborator of W. B. Yeats. Appeared in plays by Shaw, Ibsen and Yeats. Joined Theosophical Society and left to teach in Ceylon where she died.

Farrar, Gwen (1899–1944) Cellist, actress and vocalist. Gold medallist for music. Expert horsewoman. Lived in Chelsea.

Farcquarson, Robert (Robin) (1877–1966) Actor living in Chelsea. Played Vanya, Herod and Scrooge.

Firth, John B. (1859–1943) English journalist. Joined *Daily Telegraph* in 1889 as one of Matthew Arnold's 'young lions' and was the paper's parliamentary correspondent for 44 years.

Flaherty, Robert (1884–1951) Outstanding American documentary maker. *Man of Aran* was his third major film, filmed on the Aran Islands during 1931–3 and released in London in 1934. Best Foreign Film at Venice, 1934. Other films included *Elephant Boy* and *Nanook of the North*.

Flower, Robin (1881–1946) Poet, influential Gaelic scholar and translator. Educated Leeds and Oxford. Persuaded by Norwegian scholar Marstrander to study Gaelic on Great Blasket Island. Deputy Keeper of Manuscripts at the British Museum, 1929.

Forbes, Vivien (1891–1937) English painter. First solo exhibition Chicago, 1921, then several in London, 1924–36. His work is in the Tate Gallery, London Museum, etc. Memorial exhibition Redfern Gallery, 1938.

Foss, Hubert (1899–1953) Pianist, composer, editor and writer on music. Joined OUP in 1921 and organised its music department until 1941. Compositions include settings of Thomas Hardy's poems

Gaisberg, Fred (1873–1951) German-American pianist, recording engineer and talent scout, born in Washington DC, the first of the great classical-record producers. Artistic Director HMV (UK), 1921. Worked with Adelina Patti, Melba, Caruso, John McCormack and with Menuhin for Elgar's Violin Concerto, conducted by the composer, and with Casals in the Bach cello suites. Contributed in establishing 78 rpm as standard playing speed.

Ganz, Albert Barrister son of Adelina Patti's accompanist, Guildhall School professor Wilhelm Ganz (1853–1914). At one time holder of Berlioz letters.

Garcia, Gustave (1837–1925) Son of Manuel Garcia II (1805–1906), nephew of celebrated singers Malibran and Pauline Viardot. Taught singing at the Royal College of Music from 1883. H. H. accompanied his pupils, 1901–3.

Garvin, J. L. (1868–1947) Eminent editor of the *Observer*. Worked as clerk in Hull. Joined the *Daily Telegraph* in 1899. Lord Northcliffe detailed him to revive the *Observer* in 1908. Fierce critic of the Treaty of Versailles. Edited 14th edition of *Encyclopaedia Britannica* (1929). Disagreement with Lord Astor in 1942 led to his leaving the *Observer*. Wrote successively for the *Daily Express* and the *Daily Telegraph*.

Gedye, G. E. R. (Eric) (1890–1970) Journalist and author. Pre-WWII Central European correspondent of the *Daily Telegraph,* later of the *New York Times*. Worked in Vienna for the *Daily Herald*, the *Observer* and the *Manchester Guardian*. For his safety obliged to leave Austria, and later similarly Czechoslovakia. 'Special duties' in the Middle East, 1941. With his second wife Litzi engaged in special operations. MBE, 1945. Head of evaluation for Radio Free Europe, 1954 until retirement in 1961. Publications: *A Wayfarer in Austria*, 1928; *Heirs to the Habsburgs*, 1932: *Fallen Bastions* (his retort to the appeasers), 1939.

Gogarty, Oliver St John (1878–1957) Dublin-born, Trinity College Dublin-educated physician, poet, novelist and sportsman of waspish wit, model for Buck Mulligan in Joyce's *Ulysses*. Supporter of 1921 Anglo-Irish Treaty, IFS Senator in 1922. His autobiography *As I was Going Down Sackville Street* (1937) led to a libel case.

Goodson, Katherine (1872–1958) Distinguished English pianist, pupil of Leschetizky. Gave first Carnegie Hall performance of Schumann's *Kinderszenen* in 1908. Married Arthur Hinton (q.v.). Taught pianist Mark Hambourg's daughter Michal.

Gwynn, Stephen (1864–1950) Irish biographer, poet, author and critic. Secretary of Irish Literary Society, 1904. Nationalist MP for Galway, 1904–18. Served in WWI.

Hale, Lionel (1909–77) Drama critic and playwright. Joined OUDS while at Oxford and played Othello to Peter Fleming's Iago. Joined Oxford Rep. Assistant editor *News Chronicle*, 1933–7, and its drama critic, 1937–40. Worked for the government in WWII. Witty and successful broadcaster

Hambourg, Boris (1885–1954) Russian-born cellist, son of Mikhail Hambourg, pianist and teacher. Pupil of Becker in Frankfurt. With his father founded the Hambourg Conservatory in Toronto and the Hart House Quartet.

Hambourg, Jan (1882–1947) Violinist brother of Boris, pupil of Sevčík and Ysaÿe. Début Berlin, 1905. With his brothers Boris and Mark established the Hambourg Trio. Edited sonatas and partitas for solo violin by Bach, 1934. Died during a tour in France.

Hambourg, Mark (1879–1960) Pianist brother of Boris and Jan. Studied first with his father, then in Vienna with Leschetizky. Very successful concert pianist. Toured US in 1935 with his brothers before returning to England.

Hale, Philip (1854–1934) American music critic working in Boston.

Harrison, Beatrice (1892–1965) English cellist. Studied at Royal College of Music, then at Berlin Hochschule. Notable interpreter of Delius and Elgar.

Harrison, May (1891–1959) Violinist sister of Beatrice. Studied at Royal College of Music, then with Leopold Auer in St Petersburg. The sisters renowned for performances of Brahms's Double Concerto. Premièred Delius's Double Concerto. Dedicatee of his Third Sonata which she premièred in 1930 with Arnold Bax.

Heald, Edith Shackleton (1884–1976) English journalist with Irish connections. Special correspondent of *Evening Standard*, she covered WWI in Paris and after 1919 the Irish crisis. *Evening Standard* book critic.

Heald, Nora (1895?–1961), sister of Edith. Editor of *The Lady*.

Heger, Robert (1886–1978) Alsatian-born composer and conductor. Studied composition, then turned to opera conducting – Nuremberg, Vienna State Opera, Berlin State Opera, etc. Wrote operas, orchestra works, chamber music and songs.

Henry, Paul (1876–1958) Irish painter. Studied at Belfast School of Art, the Académie Julian, Paris, and with Whistler. Lived in London. Returned to Ireland, 1912. Founded Dublin Painters. Regular exhibitor at the Royal Academy. Married painter Grace Henry née Mitchell. Separated, 1929. Major exhibition at National Gallery of Ireland, 2004.

Heppenheimer, Brig. Gen. William (1860–1933) Lawyer. Member of New Jersey Assembly, 1887–91. Speaker, 1890. ADC to Governor General. President & Director NJ State Chamber of Commerce. Democrat. His daughter Gladys married Robert Vansittart (q.v.).

Heuvel, van den *see* **Vanden Heuvel**.

Heward, Leslie (1897–1943) English conductor and composer. Son of an organist, chorister at Manchester Cathedral. Studied with Stanford and Vaughan Williams at Royal College of Music while assistant master at Eton. Taught at Westminster School. Conductor of British National Opera Company on tours. Worked in South Africa. Succeeded Sir Adrian Boult at head of City of Birmingham Orchestra. Conductor première of Moeran's Symphony in G minor, Royal Philharmonic Orchestra, 1938.

Hinton, Arthur (1869–1941) English composer. Studied at Royal College of Music and Munich. Wrote orchestral works, a piano concerto premèred by his wife, Katherine Goodson, children's operettas and songs.

Hobson, Bulmer (1883–1969) Born Belfast. Joined the Irish Republican Brotherhood (IRB), 1904. Co-founder with Denis McCullough (q.v.) of the Dungannon Clubs (to promote Irish nationalism in the north) and the Ulster Literary Theatre, 1905. Organised the Howth gun-running in 1914. Later became a civil servant in the Irish Free State.

Hodges, Horace (1865–1951) English actor. Début Richmond Theatre, 1881. Worked with Fred Terry and Julia Nielson. Played Chauvelin in *The Scarlet Pimpernel*. Father of Katherine North.

Hurst, Brian Desmond (1892? 1895? 1900?–1986) Irish film director. Art student in Paris before moving to US to work as one of John Ford's assistants. Directed many films in Britain.

Jacobson, Maurice (1896–1970) English pianist, composer and publisher. Studied at Royal College of Music under Stanford and Holst. Successful career as pianist in 1920s. Director Curwen & Sons, 1933. Wrote cantatas *The Lady of Shalott* (1942) and *The Hound of Heaven* (1954). Adjudicating at Carlisle Festival in 1937 discovered Kathleen Ferrier.

Joachim, Joseph (1831–1907) German violinist of Hungarian extraction, peerless and influential teacher, master of the violin and friend of Brahms. Studied at Vienna Conservatory and Leipzig. Director Berlin Hochschule, 1868. Founded Joachim Quartet, 1869. One of principal conductors of Berlin Philharmonic, 1882–7. Frequent visitor to England. Great-uncle of Adila Fachiri and Jelly d'Arányi.

Jones, Jo (1894–1989) English painter. Daughter of the Bishop of Lewes. Studied at the Slade. Friend of Augustus John and Matthew Smith. Known especially for her paintings of the gypsies of Granada. Examples of these can be seen in the Gypsy Museum at Leeds University. Solo exhibition at Fieldbourne Gallery, Mayfair, 1981.

Jooss, Kurt (1901–79) German ballet-master and choreographer. Worked at Münster and Essen, left Germany when Nazis came to power. Established ballet at Dartington Hall. Barefoot style *à la* Isadora Duncan. *The Green Table*, Paris, 1932; London, 1933.

Keating, Seán (1889–1977) Irish painter. Studied at Metropolitan School of Art, Dublin, and under Orpen in London. Painted many years on Aran Islands.

Kennedy, Daisy (1893–1981) Australian violinist. Cousin of Lauri Kennedy, cellist (q.v.). Pupil of Sevčík in Prague. Gave many first performances in London. Married 1st the pianist Benno Moiseiwitsch and 2nd the poet John Drinkwater.

Kennedy, Hugh (1879–1936) Lawyer and first Chief Justice of the Irish Free State. President of the Society of Antiquaries of Ireland and Governor of the National Gallery of Ireland.

Kennedy, Lauri (1898–1985) Australian cellist, cousin of Daisy Kennedy and grandfather of Nigel, today's Kennedy. Studied in Vienna and London. Played in string quartet with Kreisler, Thomas Petre and William Primrose, recording in 1935–6. Leading cellist BBC Symphony Orchestra, 1929–35, London Philharmonic Orchestra, Covent Garden Orchestra and NBC Orchestra under Toscanini. Married pianist Dorothy MacBride.

Kerrigan, J. M. (1885–1964) Irish character actor of the Abbey Theatre, Dublin. Went to Hollywood in 1935 and did not return.

Kiernan, Dr T. J. ('Mac') (1897–1967) Diplomat and author. Secretary in High Commissioner's Office under J. W. Dulanty (q.v.), London, 1924. Director of Broadcasting, Dublin, 1935. Minister to the Holy See, 1941. Ambassador to W. Germany, Canada and USA. Retired 1964 and and remained in US to administer Irish-American Foundation established after JFK's 1963 visit to Ireland. Married popular ballad-singer Delia Murphy.

Kindler, Hans (1892–1949) Dutch-American cellist. Studied at Rotterdam Conservatory. Soloist, Berlin Philharmonic, 1910. Leading cellist, Philadelphia Symphony Orchestra, 1918–21. Founded National Symphony Orchestra, Washington DC in 1931 and conducted it until his resignation in 1948.

de Kresz, Géza (1882–1959) Hungarian-Canadian violinist. Pupil of Hubay in Budapest, Sevčík in Prague and Ysaÿe in Brussels. Solo début Vienna, 1906. Leader Berlin Philharmonic, 1917–21. Head of Stern Conservatory violin department. Settled in Toronto, 1923, where he was head of Hambourg Conservatory violin department until 1927, then leader of Hart House Quartet until 1935. (See under Hambourg, Boris.) Returned to Budapest to teach at Liszt Academy. Joined Toronto Conservatory, 1948. Frequently appeared with his wife, English pianist Norah Drewett. Nationalised Canadian, 1930. Rescued refugee Gregor Piatigorsky from Berlin café orchestra and invited him to join Pozniak Trio.

Kroll, William (1901–80) American violinist. Studied Berlin and New York. Leader Coolidge String Quartet in which he appeared at numerous festivals, US and Europe. Later led his own Kroll Quartet.

Kulenkampff, Georg (1898–1948) German violinist. Taught Berlin Hochschule, 1923. Left for Switzerland in 1943 and succeeded Carl Flesch at Lucerne. Duo partner of Wilhelm Kempff and Georg Solti, played under Furtwängler and Schuricht. Resuscitated Schumann Violin Concerto under Böhm in Berlin, 1937.

Lambert, Constant (1905–81) English composer, conductor and critic. Son of George Washington Lambert ARA. Studied at Royal College of Music. Ballet *Romeo and Juliet* commissioned by Diaghilev, 1926. Outstanding ballet conductor (Camargo Society and Sadler's Wells). Critic on *Sunday Referee*. In Anthony Powell's words 'moved with perfect ease in the three arts'. Author of celebrated iconoclastic book *Music Ho!* (1934).

Lambert, Maurice (1901–64) English sculptor, brother of Constant. Studied under Derwent Wood (q.v.). First one-man show at Claridge Gallery, 1927. Commissions for Cunard (*Queen Mary*, *Queen Elizabeth*). Master of sculpture RA Schools, 1950. RA, 1952. Worked with wood, marble, metal, stone, glass, concrete and cast iron.

Laver, James (1899–1975) English author and curator. Head of the Department of Costume at the V&A, London. Autobiography *Museum Piece* (1963). Married actress Veronica Turleigh.

Lavery, John (1856–1941) Painter born Belfast. Studied Glasgow Haldane Academy and Académie Julian, Paris. Influenced by Whistler in London. Appointed war artist but ill-health and a car crash prevented him taking up this work. Elected to Royal Academy in 1921 and knighted the same year.

Legge, Robin H. (1862–1933) English music critic and editor. Studied law at Cambridge, music in Leipzig. Assistant music critic *The Times*, 1891–1906, *Daily Telegraph*, 1906. Music Editor 1908–31. Of wide interests he developed music page to appeal to the general reader.

Legge, Walter (1906–79) Renowned English record producer. Joined HMV in 1927 working under Fred Gaisberg. As 'Gerald Young' wrote for The *Music Lover*. Critic on *Manchester Guardian*, 1933–8. Artistic Director at Covent Garden, 1938–9. Organised Hugo Wolf, Beethoven Sonata and Sibelius Societies. Founder Philharmonia Orchestra, 1945, subsequently of its Chorus. Recording Manager HMV, Angel Records and Columbia Records. Worked with Klemperer, Furtwängler, Karajan, Callas and other great artists. Married singer Elisabeth Schwarzkopf, 1953.

Leigh, Andrew (1887–1957) Actor and theatre producer. Member of the first Shakespeare Company at the Old Vic, 1914. Assistant producer, Old Vic, 1925–9. Responsible for 38 productions of Shakespeare and other plays.

Lennon, Michael (1891–1966) Irish judge. Called to the Bar in 1922, police magistrate and later District Judge (1937–57), eventually dismissed for his IRA sympathies.

Liddle, Samuel (1869–1951) English pianist, once called 'the Gerald Moore of his day'. Accompanied many singers, including Plunket Greene, Clara Butt, etc. Widely known for songs he wrote for ballad concerts.

Lynch, Charles (1906–84) Cork-born pianist of outstanding technique. Dedicatee of Arnold Bax's 4th sonata. Played Elizabeth Maconchy's Concerto in Dublin in 1938. The war interrupted his career but he continued to give recitals and master classes.

Lynd, Robert (1879–1949) Belfast-born essayist. On the staff from 1908 of the *Daily News*, later the *News Chronicle*, until his death. Under pseudonym 'YY' contributed to the *New Statesman and Nation*.

McCormack, John, Count (1884–1945) Italian-trained Irish tenor. Enjoyed a world reputation in opera and recitals but turned later to more popular music. The title was papal.

McCullough, Denis (1883–1968) Born Belfast. Co-founder with Bulmer Hobson (q.v.) of the Dungannon Clubs. Member of the Supreme Council of the Irish Republican Brotherhood, 1906. Supported the Easter Rising in 1916. Twice imprisoned.

McEvoy, Ambrose (1878–1927) English painter. Encouraged by Whistler, entered Slade aged fifteen. Became friend of Gwen and Augustus John. Worked with John and Sickert in Dieppe. Served in WWI. Began with genre painting but turned to portraits, mostly of society women. Elected ARA, 1924. Died of pneumonia, 1927. Married painter Mary Spencer Edwards, also Slade student (d.1941)

MacGreevy, Thomas (1893–1967) Irish art critic and author. Worked in Civil Service, served in WWI, entering Trinity College Dublin on return. Art critic Dublin and London. Lectured at Ecole Normale in Paris where he met James Joyce and Samuel Beckett. Director of National Gallery of Dublin, 1950. Studies of T. S. Eliot, Jack B. Yeats, Nicolas Poussin. Poems with foreword by Beckett, etc.

MacKenna, Stephen (1872–1934) Journalist and classicist of Irish extraction. Worked as journalist in London and Paris where he met Synge and Maud Gonne. Fought with Greeks against Turks, 1897. Europe correspondent *New York Post*. Covered Russo-Japanese War. Interviewed Tolstoy. Wrote for Dublin's *Freeman's Journal*, 1907. Supported Gaelic League with A. E. (George Russell) and James Stephens, to whom he taught Irish. Began life's work translating Plotinus, 1908. Wanted to join Easter Rising in 1916 but his chronic ill-health led him to be sent home from GPO by Padraic Pearse. His *The Eanneads* (1917–30) translation of Plotinus was judged matchless and was influenced W. B. Yeats.

Maconchy, Elizabeth (1907–94) English composer of Irish extraction. Studied piano with Arthur Alexander and composition with Vaughan Williams and Charles Wood at the Royal College of Music; later in Prague. Developed her own style and composed prolifically in all genres. Several of her works were performed at International Society for Contemporary Music festivals abroad. DBE, 1977.

Macnaghten, Anne (1908–2000) Violinist, child pupil of Jelly d'Arányi, of Davisson in Leipzig and later of André Mangeot and Antonio Brosa (q.v.). Teacher and promoter of composers, including Elizabeth Maconchy, Elizabeth Lutyens, Benjamin Britten, Alan Rawsthorne, etc. Founder of a quartet and with Iris Lemare and Elizabeth Lutyens of concerts of new music. A daughter of a High Court judge, she was fiercely anti-Fascist, in time abandoning the Communist Party in favour of Labour.

MacNeill, James (1869–1938) Irish civil servant and politician. Brother of nationalist Eoin MacNeill. Served under Michael Collins on committee drafting Irish Free State Constitution. High Commissioner in London, 1922. Governor-General of the IFS, 1927–32.

MacSweeney, Denis F. (?–1934) Irish-American friend and promoter of John McCormack. Joint promoter with Charles L. Wagner until 1924 when he became McCormack's sole manager until his death.

Mair, G. H. (1887–1926) Journalist and author. Asstant Director League of Nations Secretariat, 1919. Leader writer, literary editor, political correspondent on *Manchester Guardian*. Married Molly Allgood (q.v.), 1911.

Mangeot, André (1883–1970) French violinist. Studied at Paris Conservatoire, came early to London. Played in Queen's Hall Orchestra and at Covent Garden. Founder and leader of International String Quartet.

Collaborated with Peter Warlock on Purcell's String Fantasies. Chamber music coach to music clubs of Oxford and Cambridge. Lived in Chelsea.

Manson, J. B. (1879–1945) English painter. Studied Heatherley's and Lambeth Schools of Art, and at Académie Julian in Paris. Founder Camden Town Group, 1911, and London Group, 1914. Close friend of Lucien Pissarro. Joined Tate Gallery staff in 1917, becoming Director in 1930–8. Exhibited at Royal Academy from 1939.

Mencken, H. L. (1880–1954) American journalist, editor, critic and historian of language. Editor of *The Smart Set* and *American Mercury*. Championed many writers including Dreiser and Sherwood.

Meo, Luigi Innes (1886–1967) Landscape painter, watercolourist. Outstanding draughtsman admired by Augustus John. Studied at the Slade. Exhibited from 1910. Served WWI. Taken prisoner on the Somme when newly commissioned as war artist on Augustus John's recommendation. Taught at Bedales, 1925–41.

Milligan Fox, Charlotte (1864–1916) Folk music collector born Omagh, Co. Tyrone. Co-founded Irish Folk Song Society with Herbert Hughes. Published *Annals of the Irish Harpers* (1911) from the Bunting Papers. Sister of Alice Milligan, poet and dramatist.

Montessori, Maria (1870–1952) First woman doctor of medicine at the University of Rome. Studied philosophy and psychology. Founded the Scuola Ortofrenica to help deprived children. Her successful and influential child-centred method spread worldwide. She gave training courses in London from 1919. Author of many publications.

Morales Pedro (1879–1938) Spanish composer, conductor, poet and critic. Studied in Seville and at Royal College of Music in London where he settled. Wrote 20 songs and other works. Known as an all-round artist.

Morris, Margaret (1891–1970) Dance teacher and innovator, founder of Margaret Morris Movement. Child actress, working in Ben Greet's and Benson's Shakespeare Companies and many others. Studied dancing with Drury Lane ballet master D'Auban and developed her own style influenced by Greek movement and encouraged by Raymond Duncan, Isadora's brother. Married painter and designer J. D. Fergusson. Founded small Chelsea theatre before WWII. MM's Movement known worldwide. At nearly eighty she trained dancers for hit musical *Hair* in Glasgow.

Morrow, Edwin (1877–1952) Portrait and landscape painter and cartoonist born in Belfast. Won a scholarship to National Art Training School, South Kensington (now RCA), where he was one of the few to be trained in fresco. Exhibited at RA in 1903, 1905 and 1909. His illustrations for the *Bystander*, *London Opinion* and *Punch* well known. In 1943 painted reredos of Poling Church near Arundel.

Morrow, George (1869–1955) Prolific cartoonist and book illustrator, brother of Albert, Edwin, Harry, Jack and Norman. Studied in Paris. Best known for his weekly cartoons in *Punch* from 1906. He became its art editor in 1930. E. V. Knox, editor from 1932, said of him, 'Most things, especially things English, were absurd to George.'

Morrow, Harry (1866–1938) Brother of the above. Amateur actor. Founder in 1902 with Bulmer Hobson of the Ulster Literary Theatre and, under the pseudonym Gerald MacNamara, author of the play *Thompson in Tir na nÓg*.

Morrow, H. L. ('Larry') (1900–71). Son of Harry Morrow. Journalist and radio producer BBC and RTE.

Morrow, Norman (1879–1917) Topical cartoonist and landscape painter, one of the eight sons of George Morrow of Belfast, five of whom were artists. Norman designed sets, acted and managed the Ulster Literary Theatre founded by his brother Harry and contributed sketches and cartoons to the *Belfast Critic* before settling in London. Met Paul Henry and joined a literary club which included H. H. and Robert Lynd (q.v.) and met in Holborn. This led to the Dungannon Club No 4 which held its meetings in his King's Road studio. His portrait of H. H. appeared in the Belfast Museum and Art Gallery in 1927.

Morton, J. B. (1893–1979) English journalist and author, best-known as 'Beachcomber' of the *Daily Express*. Served in WWI. Replaced Wyndham Lewis as 'Beachcomber' and continued to produce stories, histories and a biography of Hilaire Belloc.

Murdoch, William (1888–1942) Australian-born pianist and author. Educated in Melbourne and at the Royal College of Music. Played chamber music with the violinist Albert Sammons. Wrote studies of Brahms (1933) and Chopin (1935) and made many arrangements of organ works of Bach.

Myers, Rollo H. (1892–1985) English critic. Studied at Oxford and Royal College of Music. Music correspondent of *The Times* and *Daily Telegraph* in Paris. On the staff of the BBC and the British Council. Author of studies of Debussy, Satie, Stravinsky. Composed songs.

Nevinson, C. R. W. (1889–1946) Painter, printmaker and author. Studied at St John's Wood School of Art, Slade and Académie Julian in Paris, and shared studio with Modigliani. With Marinetti issued manifesto of Futurist Art. Appointed war artist. Solo exhibitions 1916 and 1918 after being invalided out of the army. Wrote *Paint and Prejudice* (1937).

Newman, Ernest (1868–1959) English critic and writer on music. Educated in Liverpool. Music critic on successively *Manchester Guardian, Birmingham Post, Observer* and *Sunday Times*. Wrote books, especially on Wagner.

Newton, Ivor (1892–1981) English pianist and accompanist. Studied in London, Amsterdam and, for lieder, in Berlin. Accompanied many of the world's greatest artists.

Newton, Robert (1905–56) English actor. Début Birmingham Rep., 1920. Celebrated for film roles such as Long John Silver in *Treasure Island*, Pistol in *Henry V*, Javert in *Les Misérables* and Bill Sykes in *Oliver Twist*.

Nichols, Robert (1893–1944) One of the sixteen Great War poets commemorated in Westminster Abbey in 1985. Professor of English Literature at the University of Tokyo. Lived in Germany and France. Friend of Aldous Huxley.

Norriss Tait, Bess (1887–1939) Australian miniaturist and portrait painter in watercolour. Studied in Melbourne and at the Slade. Exhibited at the Royal Academy and other venues in London and Paris.

O'Flaherty, Liam (1897–1984) Irish writer. Wounded in WWI. Engaged in radical politics in Ireland before moving to London. Helped by Edward Garnett. Novels include *The Informer* (1926). Several volumes of autobiography.

Ogden, C. K. (1889–1957) Writer, linguist and translator. Originator of Basic English. Founder of *The Cambridge Magazine*, 1912. Collaborator with I. A. Richards on theory of language in *The Meaning of Meaning* (1923). Founded the Orthographical Institute. Study of Basic English encouraged by Churchill and Roosevelt.

Orage, A. R. (1873–1934) Journalist and author. Editor of *The New Age* which was a literary success but a financial failure. Heavily involved in mysticism and author of books on Nietzsche. Lectured in US, 1923–30. Launched *New English Weekly*, 1932.

O'Riordan, Conal (1874–1948) Irish actor, playwright, producer and novelist associated with Yeats, Drinkwater and Dowson. Played in first English production of Ibsen's *Ghosts* in 1894 and reviewed plays. Briefly theatre manager of Dublin's Abbey Theatre. Served in WWI. Wrote a twelve-novel series while living in London.

O'Sullivan, Dónal (1893–1973) Irish scholar, lawyer, author and lecturer. Clerk to Senate from 1925 until its abolition in 1936 by de Valera. O'Sullivan then retired to devote himself to research, principally on Irish folk music. Edited *The Bunting Collection of Irish Folk Music and Song 1927–1939* for the *Journal of the Irish Folk Song Society*.

Parratt, Walter (1841–1924) English organist, child prodigy. Studied with his father, at Oxford and at the Royal College of Music, where he became professor in 1883. Knighted, 1892. Master of the King's Music, 1893.

Pearce, Maresco (1874–1964) Architect and painter. Apprenticed to architect Sir Ernest George. Studied at Chelsea School of Art under William Orpen and Augustus John, in Paris under Jacques-Emile Blanche and in London with Sickert. First solo watercolour show, London, 1910. Elected to New English Arts Club, 1912. Painted architectural subjects. Married Anna, daughter of Halsey Ricardo, business partner of William De Morgan.

Philpot, Glyn (1884–1937) Painter and sculptor. Studied Lambeth School of Art and began exhibiting, 1904. Elected ARA, 1915. Invalided out of army, 1917. During war met painter Vivien Forbes (1891–1937), who became his lifelong partner, sharing house and studio at Lansdowne House, W11 (blue plaque). Converted RC ,he helped found Guild of Catholic Artists. Endured lifelong mental struggle between his religion and homosexuality. Forbes took fatal overdose after Philpot's funeral.

Poldowski, Irène, née Wieniawska (1879–1932) Polish-English composer, daughter of composer H. Wieniawski. Studied in Brussels with Gevaert. After marriage to Sir Aubrey Dean Paul studied in Paris under Gédalge and d'Indy at the Schola Cantorum. Wrote remarkable settings of French poetry, especially Verlaine. Her work has been deemed barely inferior to that of Debussy and Fauré.

Prunières, Henri (1886–1942) French musicologist, one of the founders of the International Society for Contemporary Music. Music correspondent in Paris for the *New York Times*. Editor of the *Revue musicale*.

Rosenthal, Moriz (1862–1946) Polish pianist. Entered Lwów Conservatory aged ten and studied under Karol Mikuli, a former pupil of Chopin. Studied in Vienna under Joseffy, and finished his studies with Liszt. First appearances in England, 1895.

Rosing, Vladimir ('Val') (1890–1963) Russian-American tenor, pupil of Jean de Reszke. Début at St Petersburg Art Opera in 1912. Sang on the Continent then settled in England. Directed opera season Covent Garden, 1915. Recitals in London, 1916–21. Director of opera department at Eastman School of Music. Founded opera company based from 1939 in Los Angeles.

Rummel, Walter (1887–1953) Pianist grandson of S. F. B. Morse, inventor of the telegraph. Born into distinguished German musical family. Pupil of Godowski in Berlin. Closely associated with Debussy in Paris. His first wife was pianist Thérèse Chaigneau with whom he gave recitals.

Rushbury, Henry (1889–1968) English painter and etcher. Studied at Birmingham College of Art. First one-man show at the Grosvenor Gallery, 1921. Specialised in architectural subjects. RA, 1936. Knighted, 1964. Lived in Dedham.

Russell, George ('A. E.') (1867–1935) Author, editor, poet, mystic and social reformer. His home a centre for discussions on art, literature, practical economics and politics and a haven for young writers. He died in England having become disillusioned with Irish cultural life.

Russell, Walter Westley (1867–1944) English painter. Studied Westminster School of Art. RA, 1926. Served in France in WWI, mentioned in dispatches. His works hang in the Tate Gallery. Lived in Chelsea. Knighted, 1935.

Schneider, Edwin ('Teddy') (1874–1954) Chicago-born pianist and composer of German extraction. Trained in Europe. Became John McCormack's accompanist, coach in German lieder, adviser and provider of moral support, 1912–37.

Schwalb, Miklos (1909–81) Budapest-born pianist. Studied with Dohnányi and appeared aged fourteen with Budapest Philharmonic Orchestra. Toured Europe. US début in 1942. Joined staff of New English Conservatory, Boston, 1946. Subsequently Artist in Residence, Boston Northeastern University.

Sharpe, Herbert (*c*.1862–1925) English pianist. Scholar at National Training School of Music, 1876, forerunner of Royal College of Music where he became professor in 1884, a post he retained for 40 years. Known as one of London's most successful pianoforte teachers. Member of the Associated Board of the Royal Schools of Music and one of its examiners. The Royal College of Music Fund was inaugurated in 1926 and the Herbert Sharpe Memorial Prize created as a memorial to him.

Sheridan, Margherita (Margaret Bourke Sheridan) (1889–1958) Irish soprano. Studied at Royal Academy of Music and in Italy. Sang at La Scala and made Covent Garden début in 1919. Also appeared with Chicago Opera.

Squire, Sir John (1884–1958) English poet, essayist, anthologist, reviewer. Editor of the *London Mercury*, later its chairman. Governor of the Old Vic, 1922–6. Knighted, 1933.

Starkie, Walter (1894–1976) Irish author and scholar, educated Shrewsbury and Trinity College, Dublin. Served in the Red Cross in WWI. Professor of Italian and Spanish, 1926–47. Travelled with the Romany gypsies in the Balkans and wrote successful books on the subject. Served on Abbey Theatre board, 1927–42. Spent WWII years at British Institute, Madrid, and taught at UCLA in the 1960s. Honoured by British and French governments.

Stephens, James (1882?–1950) Dublin-born poet, novelist, essayist, short-story writer and broadcaster whose works combine realism, fantasy and meditation. Registrar of National Gallery of Ireland under Langton Douglas (q.v.). Settled in London, 1925. Gave BBC talks, 1937–50.

Stratton, Hilary (1906–85) Sculptor in stone, clay, wood, ivory and metal. Pupil of Eric Gill, 1919–22, and at RCA, 1933–6. FRBS.

Symons, Arthur (1865–1945) Poet, author and critic. Translator of D'Annunzio and Baudelaire. Wrote Epilogue of *The Joyce Book* (1932–3).

Tabouis, Geneviève (1892–1985) Unsinkable French writer, journalist and diplomat. A pre-WWII Cassandra much quoted in the English press who predicted Hitler's intentions and, having escaped to the USA, was punished by Vichy with the confiscation of her assets and loss of French citizenship. Returned to Europe and was very active after the war.

Terry, Sir Richard (1865–1938) English composer, organist and music-ologist. Organist and choirmaster at Downside Abbey and later at Westminster Cathedral (1901–24), where he revived Catholic church music of the early English masters to the highest standards (Byrd, Tallis, Morley, etc.). Wrote and edited much church music. Knighted, 1922.

Thomas, Alan (1896–1969) Barrister and author. Overseas Secretary to League of Nations Union. Four times wounded in WWI. Neighbour of Lynds in Keats Grove.

Tonks, Henry (1862–1937) Gave up medicine and the teaching of anatomy to devote himself to the teaching of drawing and painting. Slade Professor of Fine Art at London University, 1917–30. Emeritus Professor, 1936. Influenced Augustus John, Stanley Spencer, Wyndham Lewis, Mark Gertler. Deplored Post-Impressionists.

Turner, W. J. (1889–1946) English poet, novelist and music critic, for many years on *The New Statesman and Nation*.

Tynan, Katharine (1861–1931) Prolific poet and novelist born in Dublin. Lifelong friend of W. B. Yeats. Married barrister H. A. Hinkson.

Vanden Heuvel, Count Frederick (1885–1963) Diplomat and company director. Served in WWI. Attaché at British Legation in Berne, 1940–5, and at British Embassy in Rome, 1947. Married Kay, sister of Mrs J. B. Morton.

Vansittart, Robert (1881–1957) Diplomat and author. Secretary to Lord Curzon. Secretary of State for Foreign Affairs, 1920–4. Permanent Under-Secretary of State for Foreign Affairs, 1930–8. Famous Germanophobe. 1st Baron Vansittart, 1941.

Waddell, Samuel (1878–1967) Irish author and playwright, pseudonym 'Rutherford Mayne'. Born in Japan, brother of scholar Helen Waddell. Educated Belfast. Worked as engineer. Acted and wrote for the Ulster Literary Theatre. Married Josephine, sister of poet Joseph Campbell.

Wareing, Eustace (1890–1958) Journalist, author and translator. *The Times* correspondent in Munich, 1912–14. Intelligence work in France, 1915–18. Secretary General of Inter-Allied Rhineland High Commission, 1918. *Daily Telegraph* correspondent in Rome, Vatican, Berlin (1933–8), Paris (1938–40) and Algiers (1943). Translator of diverse learned works.

Watson, A. E. (1880–1969) Editor of the *Daily Telegraph*. Fierce opponent of the Nazis during the 1930s, deploring Munich Agreement and incurring Lord Halifax's complaints to the proprietor. The war brought his support for Chamberlain, which was doubled with the arrival of Churchill.

Wetzler, Hermann Hans (1870–1943) German-American composer and conductor. Born in Frankfurt but childhood spent in USA. Studied in Frankfurt with Humperdinck, Clara Schumann and others. For 4 years organist in New York church. Returned to Germany. Retired in 1930 to Ascona but in 1940 settled in USA. Wrote opera, chamber music and songs.

Wilenski, R. H. ('Reggie') (1887–1975) Artist, author and art critic. Served in War Office Intelligence, 1914–18.

Wood, Charles (1866–1926) Armagh-born composer. Scholar at Royal College of Music, 1883. Studied under Stanford, later at Cambridge. Organist at Caius. Succeeded Stanford as Professor of Music at Cambridge, 1924. At Royal College of Music where he conducted orchestral and opera classes, taught H. H., and later Michael Tippett. Knighted, 1901.

Wood, Francis Derwent (1871–1926) English sculptor. Trained Karlsruhe and National Art Training School, South Kensington (now RCA). Assitant to Legros at Slade. During WWI in charge of masks for plastic surgery at Wandsworth Hospital. Succeeded his teacher Lantéri at RCA, 1918–23. Maurice Lambert (the composer Constant's brother) was for a time his assistant.

Wortham, H. E. ('Hugo') (1884–1959) Journalist, critic and author. Foreign correspondent *Daily Telegraph*. Later on music staff before taking over 'Peterborough' of the 'London Day by Day' column.

Bibliography

Arnold, Bruce, *Orpen, Mirror to an Age,* London, Jonathan Cape, 1981

Barbirolli, Evelyn, *Life with Glorious John*, London, Robson Books, 2002

Bax, Arnold, *Farewell My Youth*, London, Longmans Green, 1943

Bax, Clifford, *Some I Knew Well*, London, Phoenix House, 1951

Beaumont, Cyril, *The Complete Book of Ballets*, London, Putnam, 1937

Blunt, Reginald, 'Those were the Days', unpublished typescript, 1943

Blythe, Ronald, *The Age of Illusion, England in the Twenties and Thirties, 1919–1940*, London, Hamish Hamilton, 1963

Brendon, Piers, *The Dark Valley, A Panorama of the 1930s*, London, Jonathan Cape, 2000

Cardus, Neville, *Talking of Music*, London, Collins, 1957

Carter, Miranda, *Anthony Blunt, His Lives*, London, Macmillan, 2001

Catleugh, Jon, *William De Morgan Tiles*, Shepton Beaumont, Richard Dennis, 1991

Chambers, Anne, *La Sheridan, Adorable Diva*, Dublin, Wolfhound Press, 1989

Clements, Keith, *Henry Lamb, The Artist and His Friends*, Bristol, Redcliffe Press, 1985

Cohen, Harriet, *A Bundle of Time*, London, Faber, 1969

Colum, Mary, *Life and the Dream*, Dublin, Dolmen Press, 1966

Colum, Padraic and Mary, *Our Friend James Joyce*, London, Gollancz, 1958

Cook, Judith, *Priestley*, London, Bloomsbury, 1997

Coote, Stephen, *W. B. Yeats, A Life*, London, Hodder & Stoughton, 1997

Corrigan, D. Felicitas, *Helen Waddell, A Biography*, London, Gollancz, 1986

Craig, Edward, *Gordon Craig, The Story of His Life*, London, Gollancz, 1968

Crawford, R. and D., *Michael and Natasha, The Life and Love of the Last Tsar of Russia*, London, Weidenfeld & Nicolson, 1997

Cumberland, Gerald, *Set Down in Malice*, London, Grant Richards, 1919

Davies, Norman, *Europe, A History*, Oxford University Press, 1996

De Courcy, Anne, *1939, The Last Season*, London, Thames & Hudson, 1989

Deghy, Guy and Waterhouse, Keith, *Café Royal, Ninety Years of Bohemia*, London, Hutchinson, 1955

Denny, Barbara, *Chelsea Past*, London, Historical Publications, 1996

Dibble, Jeremy, *Charles Villiers Stanford*, Oxford University Press, 2002

Fay, Gerard, *The Abbey Theatre, Cradle of Genius*, London, Hollis & Carter, 1958

Fielding, Daphne, *Emerald and Nancy, Lady Cunard and Her Daughter*, London, Eyre & Spottiswoode, 1968

Findlater, Richard, *Lilian Baylis, The Lady of the Old Vic*, London, Allen Lane, 1975

Foreman, Lewis, *Bax, A Composer and His Times*, Aldershot, Scolar Press, 1983

Foster, R. F., *Modern Ireland, 1600–1972*, London, Allen Lane, 1988

—— *W. B. Yeats, A Life*. 2 volumes, Oxford University Press, 1997, 2003

Gaunt, William and Clayton-Stamm, M. D .E., *William De Morgan*, London, Studio Vista, 1971

Gedye, G. E. R., *Fallen Bastions, The Central European Tragedy*, London, Victor Gollancz, 1939

Goodman, Jean, *The Life of Alfred Munnings*, London, Collins, 1988

Goossens, Eugene, *Overture and Beginners, A Musical Biography*, London, Methuen, 1951

Gorman, Herbert, *James Joyce*, London, John Lane, The Bodley Head, 1941

Gray, Cecil, *Musical Chairs*, London, Home & Van Thal, 1949

—— *Peter Warlock, A Memoir of Philip Heseltine*, London, Jonathan Cape, 1934

Gray, Pauline, *Cecil Gray, His Life and Notebooks*, London, Thames Publishing, 1989

—— *The Grand Duke's Woman*, London, Macdonald & Jane, 1976

Gregory, Lady, *Sir Hugh Lane, His Life and Legacy*, Gerrards Cross, Colin Smythe, 1973

Guthrie, Tyrone, *A Life in the Theatre*, London, Hamish Hamilton, 1960

Gwynn, Stephen, *Experiences of a Literary Man*, London, Thornton Butterworth, 1926

Hamann, Brigitte, *Winifred Wagner, A Life at the Heart of Hitler's Bayreuth*, translated by Alan Bance, London, Granta Books, 2005

Hamilton, Mark, *Rare Spirit, A Life of William De Morgan 1839–1917*, London, Constable, 1997

Harding, James, *Gerald du Maurier*, London, Hodder & Stoughton, 1989

Harkness, D. W., *The Restless Dominion, The Irish Free State and the British Commonwealth of Nations 1921–1931*, London, Macmillan 1969

Harrison, Beatrice, *The Cello and the Nightingales*, London, John Murray, 1985

Hart-Davis, Duff, *The House the Berrys Built*, London, Hodder & Stoughton, 1990

Hart-Davis, Rupert, *Hugh Walpole*, London, Macmillan, 1952

Hartwell, Lord, *William Camrose, Giant of Fleet Street*, London, Weidenfeld & Nicolson, 1992

Hill, Lionel, *Lonely Waters, The Diary of a Friendship with E. J. Moeran*, London, Thames Publishing, 1985

Holroyd, Michael, *Augustus John, A Biography*, 2 volumes, London, Heinemann, 1974, 1975

Hone, Joseph, *The Life of Henry Tonks*, London, Heinemann, 1939

— *The Life of George Moore*, London, Victor Gollancz, 1936

Hughes, Spike, *Opening Bars*, London, Pilot Press, 1946

— *Second Movement*, London, Museum Press, 1951

Hunt, Hugh, *The Abbey, Ireland's National Theatre 1904–1978*, Dublin, Gill & Macmillan, 1979

Kennedy, Michael, *Barbirolli, Conductor Laureate*, London, MacGibbon & Kee, 1971

Lambert, Constant, *Music Ho! A Study of Music in Decline*, London, Faber, 1934

Lavery, John, *The Life of a Painter*, London, Cassell, 1940

Ledbetter, Gordon T., *The Great Irish Tenor*, London, Duckworth, 1977

Loeb Shloss, Carol, *Lucia Joyce, To Dance in the Wake*, London, Bloomsbury, 2004

Longmire, John, *John Ireland, Portrait of a Friend*, London, John Baker, 1969

Lynd, Robert, *Searchlights and Nightingales*, London, Dent 1939

Lyons, F. S. L., *Culture and Anarchy in Ireland 1890–1939*, Oxford University Press, 1979

McCoole, Sinead, *Hazel, A Life of Lady Lavery*, Dublin, Lilliput Press, 1996

McKibbin, Ross, *Classes and Cultures, England 1918–1951*, Oxford University Press, 1998

McCormack, W. J., *Fool of the Family, A Life of J. M. Synge*, London, Weidenfeld & Nicolson, 2000

McMahon, Deirdre, *Republicans and Imperialists, Anglo-Irish Relations in the 1930s*, New Haven and London, Yale University Press, 1984

Mazower, Mark, *Dark Continent, Europe's Twentieth Century*, London, Allen Lane, 1998

Morgan, Charles, *The House of Macmillan*, London, Macmillan, 1943

Motion, Andrew, *The Lamberts*, London, Chatto & Windus, 1986

Mowat, C. L., *Britain Between the Wars 1918–1940*, London, Methuen, 1955

Nesbitt, Cathleen, *A Little Love and Good Company*, London, Faber, 1975

O'Casey, Eileen, *Seán*, London, Macmillan, 1971

Palmer, Christopher, *Herbert Howells, A Centenary Celebration*, London, Thames Publishing, 1992

Plunket Greene, Harry, *Charles Villiers Stanford*, London, Edward Arnold, 1935

Pyle, Hilary, *Jack B. Yeats*, London, André Deutsch, 1989

Sachs, Harvey, *Toscanini*, London, Weidenfeld & Nicolson, 1978

Saunders, Norah and Kelly, A. A., *Joseph Campbell, Poet and Nationalist 1879–1944*, Dublin, The Wolfhound Press, 1988

Searle, Muriel, *John Ireland, The Man and His Music*, Tunbridge Wells, Midas Books, 1979

Self, Geoffrey, *The Music of E. J. Moeran*, London, Toccata Press, 1986

Seymour, Miranda, *Ottoline Morrell, Life on the Grand Scale*, London, Hodder & Stoughton, 1992

Smith, Barry, *Peter Warlock, The Life of Philip Heseltine*, Oxford University Press, 1994

Spicer, Paul, *Herbert Howells*, Bridgend, Poetry Wales Press, 1998

Stirling, A. M.W., *William De Morgan and His Wife*, London, Thornton Butterworth, 1922

Summerfield, Henry, *That Myriad-Minded Man, A Biography of George William Russell 'AE', 1867–1935*, Gerrards Cross, Colin Smythe, 1975

Symons, Julian, *The Thirties, A Dream Revolved*, London, The Cresset Press, 1960

Tuohy, Frank, *Yeats*, London, Macmillan, 1976

The Designs of William De Morgan, catalogued by Martin Greenwood, Shepton Beaumont, Richard Dennis, 1989

The Victoria History of the Counties of England, History of the County of Middlesex, Vol. XII, Chelsea, edited by Patricia E. C. Croot, University of London Institute of Historical Research, Woodbridge, Boydell & Brewer, 2004

Acknowledgements

I would like to thank Roy Foster, Carroll Professor of Irish History at Oxford, for finding the time to read the Irish chapters and ensure my safe passage through Irish complexities. Dr Michael Kennedy read a lengthy musical section at short notice, and Sir Ian Kershaw found me a Nazi source. Stephen James Joyce gave me permission to quote from his grandfather's works and the present John Murray allowed me to reproduce a letter to my father from his father, John ('Jock') Murray. To all I offer my warmest thanks.

I am indebted to Anthea Morton-Saner and to Sara Maitland for their expertise. Mavis Gallant and Isabel Quigly were constant sources of encouragement. The Authors' Foundation awarded me a grant towards the research: the panel's names are inscribed in my head. My daughter Natalie brought me, as always, her lucidity and discernment. My children and grandchildren, the dedicatees, both put me up and put up with me and my work. They deserve great credit for that.

My gratitude also goes to the following, all of whom gave me information or advice: Martin Anderson, the late Felix Aprahamian, the late Lady Barbirolli, Matthew Boyle, Christopher Bordet, Colin Buckenham, John Catleugh, Hazel Cook, Rowan Cope, Oliver Davies, the late Lord Deedes, Máiréad Delaney, Colin Dunn, Alexandra Erskine, Baron Eduard von Falz Fein, Kate Farquhar-Thomson, Marie Farrelly, Brigid Ferguson, Alexander Fijis-Walker, Lewis Foreman, Prince Yuri Galitzin, the late Mrs Alice Gedye, Robin Gedye, Pauline Gray, Mary Hallett, Dr Peter Horton, Niel Immelman, Kathleen Judy, Jo Kendall, Uri Liebrecht, Linde Lunny, Ann Meo, Colin Merton, Paul Mitchell, Hedy Morrow, Sheevaun Nelson, George Newkey-Burden, Neil Parkinson, Naomi Pearce, Pauline Sowry, Jonathan Summers, Pam Thompson, Gillian Vaughan Hudson, and at the National Gallery of Victoria, Melbourne, Michael Watson and Irena Zdanowicz.

A. C. H.

Index